PRAISE FOR
POSITIVE DISCIPLINE: A TEACHER'S A–Z GUIDE

"Bravo! This book not only goes straight to the heart of the matter—dealing with self-esteem and a positive attitude—but it does so without a wasted word. It will be a great help to parents, teachers, and mentors!"

—Ken Johnson, coordinator of Children First, Corpus Christi, Texas

"*Positive Discipline: A Teacher's A–Z Guide* is an easy-to-read book with a wealth of wisdom that has the potential to change society. This book should be placed right next to William Bennett's *Book of Virtues.*"

—Alice Arnerich, mother of six children, director of
Extended Daycare program, Santa Rosa, California

"This book addresses . . . new ideas that I had never heard before regarding how to equip children with problem solving skills. Teachers too often try to solve the problems for their students instead of giving them the tools to do it themselves."

—Patti Wick, kindergarten teacher, Sheppard Accelerated
Elementary School, Santa Rosa, California

"*Positive Discipline: A Teacher's A–Z Guide* is a winner. The book is firmly anchored on principles, values, and attitudes rather than on quick fixes and short-term techniques."

—Michael L. Brock, principal, Mary Immaculate School,
Farmers Branch, Texas

"An inspiring account for both teachers and parents. [It shows how] students can take ownership of their responsibilities while keeping their dignity intact."

—Donna Presti, fourth-grade teacher,
Flowery Elementary School, Sonoma, California

"*Positive Discipline: A Teacher's A–Z Guide* is outstanding and should become an essential handbook for every educator."

—Suzanne Smitha, school psychologist,
Sharon School, Charlotte, North Carolina

"Our school continues to reap the rewards generated by our positive discipline policy. *Positive Discipline: A Teacher's A–Z Guide* will provide a wonderful supplement to further secure the success of our students!"

—J. Michael Fike, school counselor, Morgantown, West Virginia

"The book gives a logical set of steps to follow in implementing a very complete discipline plan. The plan emphasizes an inner locus of control, the child's self concept, and cooperation whether applied in the home or at school."

**—Ligia Cardenas, Ed.D., principal of
Reynaldo Garza Elementary, Brownsville, Texas**

"Since our school adopted the positive discipline philosophy, we've noticed an incredible difference. Behavior problems are disappearing, children are solving their own problems, and teachers have more time to teach. This easy-to-use book is a must in our quest to raise a future generation of confident, responsible, and respectful adults."

**—Kris Richards, school counselor,
Lakewood Elementary School, Lakewood, Washington**

"*Positive Discipline: A Teacher's A–Z Guide* is an encouragement to parents, teachers, and others who work with children: its content recalls the reader to constantly consider that children deserve, demand even, to be treated with dignity and respect. The format uses a teaching method of repetition from many perspectives making clear to the reader the process of encouragement and cooperation required by both the child and the adult involved in problem-solving."

**—Mary Schau, principal, Immaculate Conception School,
Mt. Vernon, Washington**

"I really liked the format of the book. It was easy to follow and provided good ideas for implementing in the short and long run. I especially enjoyed the examples from real classes and class meetings."

**—Sue Reese, kindergarten teacher,
Sheppard Elementary School, Santa Rosa, California**

"A heartwarming book . . . never have I read a how-to-help volume that left me alternately in smiles and in tears . . . and all the while feeling positive about the challenges of children."

**—Robert C. Hauck, M.D., FAAP, pediatrician and
parent of six, Shoreline, Washington**

Jane Nelsen, Ed.D., Linda Escobar, M.A., M.F.T., Kate Ortolano,
Roslyn Duffy, and Deborah Owen-Sohocki, M.S.

Positive Discipline: A Teacher's A–Z Guide

REVISED 2ND EDITION

Hundreds of Solutions
for Almost Every
Classroom Behavior Problem!

 THREE RIVERS PRESS • NEW YORK

Published by Three Rivers Press, New York, New York.
Member of the Crown Publishing Group, a division of Random House, Inc.
www.crownpublishing.com

THREE RIVERS PRESS and the Tugboat design are trademarks of Random House, Inc.

Originally published by Prima Publishing, Roseville, California, in 2001.

The case studies are based on actual events, but names have been omitted or changed to protect the privacy of people involved.

All products mentioned are trademarks of their respective companies.

Illustrations by Paula Gray

Printed in the United States of America

Library of Congress Cataloging-in-Publication Data
Positive discipline: a teacher's A–Z guide : hundreds of solutions for almost every classroom behavior problem! / Jane Nelsen [et al.]. — Rev. 2nd ed.
    p.   cm.
  Includes index.
   1. School discipline—United States. 2. Classroom management—United States.
3. Problem children—Education—United States. 4. Behavior modification—
United States. I. Nelsen, Jane. II. Series
LB3012.2.P67   2001
371.5'0973—dc21   2001032858

ISBN 0-7615-2245-X

10 9 8 7
Second Edition

*We thank Alfred Adler, Rudolf Dreikurs,
and the many others whose work precedes ours.*

*We dedicate this book to all the teachers, principals, school
counselors, and psychologists who have practiced these principles
with students, found them effective, and then shared their stories.
We share with you a dream of classrooms where people treat one
another with respect and learn life skills for now and the future.*

CONTENTS

Introduction · xiii

PART 2 Positive Discipline Solutions · 63

INTRODUCTION

Children in Alaska chew gum in class, children in Montana tattle on each other during math lessons, and children in Zurich squabble over seats on the school bus. Wherever children gather into classes, teachers struggle with common concerns. In researching this book, we listened to the problems of teachers around the globe. These are your difficulties, stories, and successes—from A to Z.

Yet this book is about much more than solving the problems experienced by teachers and students everywhere. It's about understanding children and the beliefs that motivate their misbehavior. It's about treating both children and teachers with dignity, respect, and faith in their abilities. *Positive Discipline: A Teacher's A–Z Guide* explains how to create an environment in which students and teachers can learn important skills that will serve them in every area of their lives—jobs, friendships, family relationships. Problems can be the catalyst for learning. Teachers will come to see each problem as a gift.

We have divided this book into two parts. In Part 1 we present the subjects that are fundamental to understanding the basic philosophy, tools, and concepts that constitute positive discipline. These are as follows:

Encouragement—the cornerstone of Positive Discipline and the key to empowering students and changing behavior

Mistaken Goals (Hat Messages)— break the code of misbehavior by using visual aids

Self-Esteem—how to build a foundation that helps stabilize its ups and downs

Control—have control instead of being controlling

Rewards and Punishment—learn nonpunitive ways to encourage children's development of effective life skills

Firmness and Kindness—a basic adult attitude that is necessary for implementing all the ideas in this book

Limits—help students develop the skill of working within a system

Follow-Through—how to use firmness and kindness to help students understand limits and that you say what you mean and mean what you say

Social Interest—help students see themselves as contributing members of society

Jobs for Everyone in the Classroom—teach social interest and create a sense of belonging and significance

Take Time for Training—a process that will clarify expectations and provide steps for success

Mistakes—opportunities to learn rather than to lose the courage to take risks

Problem Solving—skills that encourage students and teachers to see problems as learning opportunities

Positive Time-Out—a method of dealing with misbehavior that doesn't shame children but allows them to calm themselves

Special Time—an opportunity to help students develop a sense of belonging and significance that is then reflected in their behavior

Class Meetings—a process that teaches important life skills and helps students fulfill the most important need of all: to belong and feel significant

Conferences—expand the concept of conferences to include parent, teacher, and student so all can work together on common goals

After reading these basic concepts, you will be ready to explore any or all of the problems presented in "true" alphabetical order in Part 2. You will be ready to see every problem as an opportunity for you and your students to master important life skills.

Follow the suggestions that best suit your personality and that of your class. You might use the ideas you find here to generate discussion with your students during your own class meetings, allowing them to make suggestions that might work even better for them.

We believe you will benefit by reading every subject, even those that aren't among your current concerns. All suggestions are based on a philosophy of treating children with dignity and respect, and teaching them social interest and life skills. Each section invites your own creative exploration of other solutions that would fit within this framework and address your unique situations and concerns. Success grows from the process itself.

We'd Like to Hear from You

Please share your own inspirational stories or class meeting solutions with us. Send an email to us at JaneNelsen@aol.com on any subject we have discussed, or suggest others you would like to see addressed. We anticipate periodic updates of this book and will use your name, grade level, school, city, and state with published stories.

PART 1

Positive Discipline Fundamentals

Encouragement

Discussion

People do better when they feel better. A theme of Positive Discipline (and Adlerian psychology) is that a misbehaving child is a discouraged child. The most powerful motivation for change is encouragement. If a child—or adult—misbehaves out of discouragement, it follows that the motive for misbehavior is removed when he or she feels encouraged.

In the Positive Discipline alphabet, *E* comes first because encouragement is the foundation of Positive Discipline in the classroom. The following story by Dr. Daniel Eckstein, from his book *The Encouragement Process in Life-Span Development*, captures the essence of encouragement:

It was the spring of 1962. I was in the seventh grade at Johnnycake Junior High School in Baltimore, Maryland, section "7B" to be precise. In earlier years, the distinction between classes had been the "redbirds" and the "bluebirds," in a vain attempt to avoid labeling one class the smart one and the other class (mine) the "dummy" group. But we all knew who was who relative to the hierarchy of redbirds and bluebirds. So in seventh grade the pretense was dropped in favor of "7A" and "7B."

All my neighborhood friends were in the coveted "A" class; as for me, I was majoring in playground. I was also an "honor" student . . . as in "yes, your honor; no, your honor, I won't do that anymore, your honor."

I was a classic left-handed, dyslexic, hyperactive boy who consistently received "unsatisfactory" conduct scores. Classes were much too long, the desks far too small, and the outdoor activities way too short.

The teacher for both "7A" and "7B" was like a great redwood tree to me, a colossal giant who, at 6 feet 2 inches tall, seemed twice as awesome from my diminished vantage point. "Mr. King" was the well-named title of our teacher. He was kind, knowledgeable, and much revered by both sections "A" and "B," a rare feat in and of itself for any teacher.

One day quite unexpectedly, Mr. King approached my "7A" friends and observed that . . . "There is someone in '7B' who is just as smart as any of you; trouble is, he just doesn't know it yet. I won't tell you his name, but I'll give you a hint . . . he's the kid who out-runs all of you and knocks that ball over the right field fence."

Word of Mr. King's declaration reached me that afternoon as we boarded the school bus. I remember a dazed, numb, shocked feeling of disbelief. "Yeah sure, you've got to be kidding," I nonchalantly replied to my friends; but on a deeper, more subtle level, I remember the warm glow that came from the tiny flicker of a candle that had been ignited within my soul.

Two weeks later, it was time for the dreaded book reports in front of the class. It was bad enough to turn in papers that only Mr. King read and graded. Alas, there was no place to hide when it came to oral book reports!

When my turn came, I solemnly stood before my classmates. I began slowly and

awkwardly to speak about James Fenimore Cooper's epic book The Pathfinder. As I spoke, the images of canoes on the western frontier of 18th century America collided with lush descriptions of the forest and Native Americans who glided noiselessly over lakes and streams. No Fourth of July fireworks have ever surpassed the explosion that took place inside my head that day; it was electrifying.

Excitedly, I began trying to share my experience with my classmates. But just as I began a sentence to tell about the canoes, another scene of the land collided with the Native Americans. I was only midway through one sentence before I jumped to another. I was becoming "hyper" in my joy, and my incomplete sentences made no sense at all. The laughter of my classmates at my "craziness" quickly shattered my inner fireworks. I felt embarrassed and humiliated. I wanted so *badly to either beat up my tormentors or run home and cry in my mother's arms . . . but long ago I had learned how to mask those feelings . . . so, trying my best to become invisible and disappear, I started to return to my desk.*

The laughter ceased at the sound of Mr. King's deep, compassionate voice. . . . "You know, Danny," he reigned forth . . . "you have a unique gift: that of having the ability to speak outwardly and to think inwardly at the same time. But sometimes your mind is filled with so much joy that your words just can't keep up with it. Your excitement is contagious; it's a wonderful gift that I hope you can put to good use someday." There was a pause that seemed to linger forever as I stood stunned by Mr. King's words once more . . . and then it began . . . clapping and congratulatory cheers from my classmates as a miracle of transformation occurred within me on that 7th grade day.

Thirty years later, I take my turn to say "thank you" to all the nameless Mr. and Ms. Kings who are the teachers of our young people. I now have fancy sounding names like "encouragement" or "turning a perceived minus into a plus" to describe how Mr. King helped me to reframe my life forever. Though often underpaid and faced with far too many students and too little resources, I salute all our teachers by acknowledging that in many subtle ways they DO make a difference![1]

You may be interested in knowing that Dr. Eckstein is now a college professor, a workshop leader, and the author of seven books.

When a person feels encouraged, he or she can leap tall buildings in a single bound—metaphorically speaking, of course. It isn't the obstacles, mistakes, or deficiencies people experience that will ultimately define them. It's the way in which they respond to these challenges, and the most necessary ingredients are the attitudes and skills they have learned through encouragement.

Encouragement comes in many forms. Each of the many principles of Positive Discipline is designed to help children feel better (encouraged), so they are motivated to do better.

The root word of *encouragement* is, of course, *courage*. When we strive to encourage others and ourselves, we are actually helping develop courage to face life's challenges and difficulties.

In these times so many teachers are discouraged, believing there is nothing they can do. They lament, "If only the parents would do their job, if only the students would be respectful and care about what they are learning, if only the administration would back us up, if only I could teach instead of spending all my time disciplining, if only. . . ."

---

1. Daniel Eckstein, *The Encouragement Process in Life-Span Development* (Dubuque, IA: Kendall-Hunt, 1995).

These teachers believe they have no response or ability (notice these words together equal *responsibility*) left because they are caught up in all their problems. This also saps their energy. They need to feel encouraged about what they can do, what is still within their realm of influence. It's hard to lack courage and energy when you focus on what you can do. Each teacher has influence within the four walls of his or her classroom. Whether you are a preschool, elementary school, or high school teacher, you have a certain number of minutes per day to influence the students who come your way. Once you close your door, your classroom becomes a system where you can make a difference, even in a forty-five-minute period.

Much of what takes place in homes and classrooms, though intended to encourage, does not foster courage. Adults attempt to motivate change through punishment and reward. Positive results are temporary and usually involve a heavy dose of discouragement. Children may do better to avoid the punishment or to gain the reward, but the price they pay is the loss of an inner locus of control, the loss of self-confidence, and the loss of opportunities to learn life skills.

Cooperation encourages everyone. The students in a classroom that uses the class meeting process learn to help one another and seek solutions together. It's a win–win environment. Competition has win–lose or lose–lose results.

Praise and encouragement are different. Praise is accorded to those who achieve or succeed. Encouragement is unconditional because it accepts and supports a person whatever the outcome of her efforts.

Teachers can learn to respond encouragingly to any kind of effort. It's usually easy to encourage the efforts that led to an accomplishment: "This report card shows how diligently you've worked this quarter. You must feel a real sense of satisfaction to bring home such high marks." When the effort is the focus, there is real encouragement. A praising comment such as, "This report card is great. You are simply wonderful," implies that if your grades changed for the worse, you might no longer be wonderful. Praise places conditions on what it takes to be an acceptable person.

It's also possible to respond encouragingly when an effort has produced less-than-stellar results. Involve the student in assessment and problem solving by asking open-ended questions: "What do you think about your science project? Want to talk about what it was like to do this project? What did you learn even though it didn't turn out the way you hoped?" Questions such as these can turn discouragement into encouragement, even if the results of the effort remain unchanged.

You may want to acknowledge the student's disappointment: "I can understand if you feel discouraged, and I have confidence that you can figure out what you need to do." This statement shows empathy, which means the teacher understands how the student feels, rather than sympathy, which can be condescending. Furthermore, an expression of faith in the student's ability to cope promotes the inner strength that leads to overcoming obstacles.

Suggestions

1. Teach and model the many facets of Positive Discipline: cooperation; mutual respect; kindness and firmness; offering choices and involving students in the decision-making process; valuing people as they are while helping them develop the skills and attitudes that facilitate improvement.

2. Nonverbal communication can be wonderfully encouraging. A wink or thumbs-up sign from across the room sends a beam of warmth and connection from one person to another. It says, "I have confidence in you. I know you can do it!"

3. Find what individual students do well and acknowledge it. Encouragement is specific. A comment on a report might say, "Sally, the poem you included in this report on Harriet Tubman moved me very much. May I share it with a friend of mine?" Consider how you would feel when reading such a comment if you were the student. Contrast that to a smiling-face stamp on the report that says, "Great job." Real encouragement comes from specific, honest feedback.

4. Use encouragement to let a student know that you recognized his effort to practice a new behavior: "I noticed that you got up and moved your chair to a different place when Eddie kept poking you this morning. I appreciate the self-control and initiative you showed by handling that situation so calmly." This statement is specific and thoughtful, and it focuses on the student's effort.

5. Rather than thinking that we are encouraging a student by saying, "Try harder," plan on spending some special time with the student. (See "Special Time.") Take this opportunity to let the student participate in brainstorming ideas about what "Try harder" may look like for him. Agree on a first step, helping the student be very clear about what that first step looks like. Let him know that you will check back with him at a specific time.

6. Follow-through is an encouragement to students because it demonstrates to them

that we have faith in their ability to work and show respect within a system. (Refer to "Follow-Through.")

7. Taking time for training is also considered encouragement because it allows the student to see the parts of the whole. For some students, it will increase their perception of their capabilities, thereby giving them courage to proceed. (Refer to "Take Time for Training.")

Planning Ahead to Prevent Future Problems

1. Put up a classroom banner that says, "People do better when they feel better." Discuss how encouragement relates to this motto. Invite students to talk about times in their lives when they felt good about themselves and how they acted when feeling that way.

2. Change your grading system. Instead of marking the incorrect answers, mark the correct answers. Focus on how many items a student answers correctly rather than how many mistakes he makes.

3. Eliminate punishments and rewards from your classroom. (Refer to "Rewards and Punishment.")

4. Create a win–win environment in your classroom through the use of class meetings, in which students learn to give and receive compliments, to help one another solve problems, and to plan fun events together.

5. Develop an atmosphere of encouragement. Point out to your students that saying helpful things to one another is appropriate anytime, not just during class meetings.

6. Remember to decode the goals of misbehavior by understanding the belief behind it; use encouragement to motivate improved behavior. (Refer to "Mistaken Goals [Hat Messages].")

Inspirational Stories

Messages from the Heart

The children graduating from the eighth grade at St. Matthew's School in Seattle, Washington, voted to invite their fourth-grade teacher, Margaret Stephens, to give the commencement address. During the course of this speech, as Margaret related a story or incident about each of the graduating students by name, it became clear why she was their choice. Her simple stories illustrated the fine qualities of individual students.

She spoke of one boy who throughout his seventh-grade year had gone into the first-grade teacher's classroom and emptied her trash: "No one asked you to or told you to; you just did it. That's the kind of person you are. You make the world good."

Another child, Margaret explained, would always greet her with an enthusiastic "Hi!" The teacher said, "I don't believe anything can make me feel better than hearing a joyfully said 'Hi, how's it going?' I'll miss that marvelous 'Hi!' a lot next year."

When she came to the girl who had graduated with honors, Margaret didn't mention academic achievement. Instead, she said, "You love your dad so much and are always ready to show him that love. Many, many times I have seen you with the biggest smile of all time when your dad came to pick you up. Your face shows the marvelous love that is all around us." (Just imagine the encouragement both this girl and her father felt at hearing these words.)

Child by child, Margaret Stephens offered the graduates glimpses of themselves, both from their pasts and into their futures. She showed them how their small actions revealed the value within them. Joyful tears and smiles filled the room. Her speech was a benediction of encouragement.

The Power of Words

A story from Delores Alexander, fifth-grade teacher, Waterloo, Ontario, Canada

I keep thinking my little world within the walls of my classroom may make the difference between success or failure for some of these kids. One parent came in and said, "I don't know what you're doing, but my son thinks he'll be prime minister one day." I promptly replied, "I hope you told him it was possible. He's a great kid."

At this point she cried and said he hated school until this year. What are you doing? I invited her to come for a class meeting or visit the classroom at any time and watch him in action. He's one in a million. I also told her if she wanted to come, to let me know because I'd need permission from the class to have a visitor. She smiled and left. Every once in a while someone releases a rope, and we hang on knowing for sure there's a rescue ship not far behind.

Mistaken Goals (Hat Messages to Break the Code of Misbehavior)

Discussion

There is a belief behind every behavior. Too often teachers deal only with a student's behavior, which is futile when they don't also try to understand the motivating belief. The psychiatrist Rudolf Dreikurs taught that a misbehaving child is a discouraged child. No matter what form the discouragement takes, it's always based on the child's belief that she lacks belonging and significance. It doesn't matter if the child does belong and adults think she is significant. What matters is what the child believes, because that is the basis for her behavior.

As Dreikurs studied children's behavior, he discovered four inappropriate or mistaken goals that children adopt as rationales for misbehaving. They are called "mistaken goals" because they are based on mistaken beliefs about how to achieve belonging and significance. Dreikurs identified the four mistaken goals of behavior as undue attention, misguided power, revenge, and assumed inadequacy (or giving up). As a teacher, you have three clues to help you understand a student's goal: (1) your feelings, (2) your reactive actions, and (3) the student's response to your reactive actions. (See the Mistaken Goal Chart on pages 12–13 for examples.) Once you understand the goal, you can encourage the student in various ways that modify the belief as well as the behavior. Punishment isn't effective because it intensifies the discouragement and thus sustains the misbehavior.

In Positive Discipline workshops, we use hats to help parents and teachers remember that there is a coded message behind misbehavior. (The general coded message behind all misbehavior is "I am a student, and I just want to belong"; the secondary coded messages are described later.) By the end of the training, a teacher who sees a student behaving in a certain way can picture one of the four hats on that student's head. This helps the teacher respond with appropriate encouragement.

The suggestions listed here after the Hat Messages are just a few examples of possible corrective measures that can be used to encourage students. See the last column of the Mistaken Goal Chart for additional encouragements.

Undue Attention

The hat that represents undue attention is a large straw hat decorated with flowers and bells and a sign that says, "Notice me! Involve me usefully." When you respond to this message, you will find many positive ways to encourage the student whose mistaken goal is undue attention.

The discouraging belief that motivates a student seeking undue attention is "I belong only if you pay constant attention to me." Everyone wants attention, but there is a difference between wanting attention and needing attention to prove your worth. Moreover, there are ways to gain attention that are useful and constructive and ways that are useless and annoying.

A teacher may respond to a student's behavior by feeling annoyed, irritated, worried, or guilty. (This is the first clue that the student's goal is attention.) The teacher tends to react by reminding, coaxing, or doing things for the student that he could do for himself. (This is the second clue.) The student's response to the teacher's reaction is usually to stop seeking undue attention temporarily, but he will soon start up his misbehavior again. (This is the third clue.)

Suggestions for Dealing with the Goal of Undue Attention

1. One way to encourage students who seek undue attention is to help them receive attention through constructive activities. Give them jobs, let them teach lessons, or invite them to tutor others.

2. Make time for students to share their feelings, thoughts, and ideas. Ignore misbehavior at the time it occurs, but flash the student a wink or put your hand on his shoulder. This way you ignore the behavior but not the student.

3. Kindness and firmness are an effective combination. The kindness says, "I care about you and will give you respectful attention." The firmness says, "I don't buy into your belief that you need undue attention."

Misguided Power

The hat for misguided power is a hard hat with a sign that says, "Let me help! Give me choices." When you respond to this message, you will find many ways to encourage the student who uses power to disrupt or harm.

Everyone wants power, and students can learn to use power constructively. Unfortunately, when teachers react to the behavior of the power-hungry student instead of understanding her motivating belief, they feel angry, challenged, threatened, or defeated (clue 1). They react by fighting, giving in, insisting that they are right, or trying to control the student (clue 2). The student's response is to intensify her defiant behavior or become passive-aggressive (clue 3).

Suggestions for Dealing with the Goal of Misguided Power

1. One way to encourage students who seek power is to ask for their help. Don't underestimate how inviting this can be to the student seeking power.

2. Admit to the student that you have been trying to control him, declare that you don't want to do this anymore, and tell him that to stop this pattern you need his help.

3. Offer choices to students who want power. Invite them to join the rest of the class in setting up rules, limits, and routines.

4. Encourage students to put their concerns on the class meeting agenda or, if they are upset or angry, to take a positive time-out to cool off. (See "Positive Time-Out.")

5. Many of the suggestions for helping students who are seeking undue attention are also effective for helping power-hungry students use their power constructively. They can tutor other students, teach lessons, and undertake useful classroom jobs.

6. Combine kindness with firmness. The kindness says, "I care about you and appreciate respectful power." The firmness says, "I won't let you use power to dominate others." (Many teachers have to learn not to use power this way themselves before they can teach students that domination isn't an acceptable use of power.)

7. Class meetings can help everyone use power constructively through the process of finding nonpunitive solutions.

Revenge

The hat representing revenge is a baseball cap turned backward with a sign that says, "I'm hurting. Validate my feelings." When you respond to this message, you will find many ways to ease the student's painful feelings and redirect the energy he is expending on revenge.

The belief that motivates a student seeking revenge is "I don't belong and that hurts, but at least I can get even." When

human beings feel hurt, their gut reaction seems to be a desire to hurt back. The tricky part here is that students sometimes feel hurt by occurrences or actions that weren't intended to hurt them. For example, children often feel hurt when a new baby is born. Students have even felt hurt because their teacher took time off to go to a workshop. Sometimes reasons are more obvious. Many foster children feel abandoned by their parents and take revenge for their pain by trying to hurt their foster parents or teachers.

When teachers fail to understand the belief behind the hurtful behavior, they feel hurt, disappointed, disbelieving, or disgusted (the first clue). Their reaction is often to retaliate, either by punishing the student or trying to make her feel guilty through a "How could you do such a thing?" lecture (the second clue). The student's response is to escalate the war by hurting you again, hurting others, or damaging property (the third clue).

*Suggestions for Dealing with
the Goal of Revenge*

1. Break the revenge cycle by not retaliating. Students who engage in hurtful behaviors may be used to being treated disrespectfully and have learned to expect retaliation in any form. By not retaliating, we can begin to change a pattern, teaching that hurt doesn't need to lead to more hurt.

2. One way to encourage students who are seeking revenge is to deal with their hurt feelings. Sometimes you have to guess as to the source of their pain. You might say, "I feel hurt by what happened, so I'm guessing you must feel hurt. Would you be willing to tell me what hurt you?" It's important not to dwell on your own hurt; just take it as a clue that the student feels hurt. Use reflective listening (listen carefully, state the student's feelings and explanations back to him, and ask him whether you've understood correctly), make amends if you caused or contributed to the hurt, and show you care. Share times when you have felt hurt by others.

3. Respond with kindness and firmness. The kindness says, "I don't want to hurt you or for others to hurt you." The firmness says, "I don't want to let you hurt me or anyone else."

4. This student will benefit from hearing compliments during class meetings (as do all students). A student who is engaging in hurtful behavior could be assigned a secret pal who will look for positive things about this student to use as compliments.

5. If a student has been engaging in hurtful behaviors with other students, they may benefit from some coaching in friendship skills. Consulting with a school counselor for assistance may be indicated.

Assumed Inadequacy

When a student's goal is assumed inadequacy, she seeks to show teachers that she isn't capable of behaving as other students do or of accomplishing what teachers and parents expect of her. This belief may present itself in different ways. Some students may use sidetracking, some students sit quietly and try not to draw attention to themselves, and some may act like the class clown to cover up their feelings of inadequacy in academics. The hat for assumed inadequacy (giving up) is a ski hat pulled down over the eyes with a sign that says, "Don't give up on me. Show me a small step." When you respond to this message,

Mistaken Goal Chart

The student's goal is:	If the teacher/parent feels:	And tends to reach by:
Undue attention (to keep others busy with him/her, or to get special service)	Annoyed Irritated Worried Guilty	Reminding Coaxing Doing things for the student he/she could do for him/herself
Misguided Power (to be the boss)	Provoked Challenged Threatened Defeated	Fighting Giving in Thinking, "You can't get away with it" or "I'll make you behave" Wanting to be right
Revenge (to get even)	Hurt Disappointed Disbelieving Disgusted	Retaliating Getting even Thinking, "How could you do this to me?"
Assumed inadequacy (to give up and be left alone)	Despair Hopeless Helpless Inadequate	Giving up Doing the student's tasks Overhelping Showing discouragement

And if the student's response is to:	The belief behind the student's behavior is:	What the student needs (hat messages) and what adults can offer for encouragement:
Stop temporarily, but later resume the same or another disturbing behavior	I belong only when I'm being noticed or getting special service. I'm important only when I'm keeping you busy with me.	**Notice me—involve me.** Redirect by involving student in a useful task. "I care about you, and I will spend time with you later." Avoid special service. Say it only once, then act. Plan special time. Set up routines. Take time for training. Use class/family meetings. Touch without words. Set up nonverbal signals.
Intensify behavior Comply defiantly Feel he/she's won when teacher/parent is upset Exercise passive power	I belong only when I'm in control. I need to prove that no one can boss me. "You can't make me."	**Let me help—give me choices.** Acknowledge that you can't make him/her, and ask for his/her help. Offer a limited choice. Withdraw from conflict and calm down. Be firm and kind. Act, don't talk. Decide what you will do. Let routines be the boss. Get help from student to set a few reasonable limits. Follow through on agreement. Redirect to positive power. Use class/family meetings.
Retaliate Hurt others Damage property Get even Escalate the behavior or choose another weapon	I don't think I belong so I'll make others hurt like I do. I can't be liked or loved.	**I'm hurting—validate my feelings.** Deal with the hurt feelings: "Your behavior tells me you must feel hurt. Can we talk about it?" Use reflective listening. Don't take behavior personally. Share your feelings. Apologize. Avoid punishment and retaliation. Show you care. Encourage strengths. Use class/family meetings.
Retreat further Be passive No improvement No response	I don't believe I can belong, so I'll convince others not to expect anything of me. I am helpless and incapable; it's no use trying because I won't do it right.	**Don't give up on me—show me a small step.** Take time for training. Take small steps. Make the task easier until the child experiences success. Show faith. Encourage any positive attempt, no matter how small. Don't give up. Enjoy the child. Build on his/her interests. Encourage, encourage, encourage. Use family/class meetings.

you will find many ways to encourage the student who assumes she is inadequate and wants to stop trying.

The discouraging belief that motivates a student who wants to stop trying is "I can't belong. My only choice is to give up and be left alone." (Sometimes students seeking undue attention behave as though they were inadequate, but the difference is that they don't want you to leave them alone.)

When teachers don't understand the despairing student's motivating belief, they feel despondent, hopeless, helpless, and inadequate (clue 1). They tend to react either by giving up, just like the student, or by trying to rescue or overhelp the student (clue 2). The student will then retreat further, be passive, and avoid responding (clue 3).

Suggestions for Dealing with
the Goal of Assumed Inadequacy

1. One way to encourage students who want to stop trying is to take small steps to reteach them. Break the task down into smaller steps. Don't give up. Be persistent. A student with this goal may do something just to get you to leave her alone. If she experiences some success in the process, however, she will feel encouraged. (Refer to "Take Time for Training.")

2. Stop all criticism, avoid pity, and focus on assets.

3. Invite the student to choose a peer tutor.

4. Build on the student's interests. Incorporate them into lesson plans to motivate her.

5. Combining kindness with firmness is very effective. The kindness says, "I understand your discouragement." The firmness says, "I refuse to feel sorry for you or do your work for you because I know you can do it yourself. I will help you until you experience success in small steps."

6. When dealing with a student who brings out feelings of hopelessness and helplessness, we often end up feeling inadequate ourselves. This is a time to consult with others for suggestions and support.

Inspirational Story

Workshop participants were asked to role-play the reactive feelings and actions of teachers when faced with a student's misbehavior and then to role-play effective actions teachers can take when they understand the student's goal and respond to the message on the imaginary hat.

During the first part of a role play, a student continually interrupted a teacher as she was working with another student. The teacher reacted to each interruption by asking the student to wait at his seat. She felt irritated as the role play continued. During the second part of the role play, the teacher responded to the message on the hat for attention, "Notice me. Involve me usefully." The teacher responded by handing the student a timer so she could let the teacher know when the ten minutes were up. The student took the timer back to her desk and set it for ten minutes. She quietly did her seat work while periodically looking at the timer and glancing at the teacher. When the teacher came to her desk before the timer went off, the student said, "You still have two more minutes." The teacher said, "Thank you. I'll be back in two minutes."

Another role play was about misguided power. In the first part a student kept kicking the seat of the student in front of him. When the teacher lectured and threatened him with punishment, the kicking intensified. During the second part, as soon as the student started kicking, the teacher said, "Stu, I need your help. Will you please come up and write these questions on the board for me?" Stu was distracted from his destructive use of power and used his power to help.

The role play about revenge involved a teacher overhearing a student make a degrading comment about her to another student. During the first role play, the teacher stormed over to the student and said, "How dare you say such a thing about me!" Her overall demeanor was threatening and humiliating. In the second role play, the teacher responded to the Hat Message "I'm hurting. Validate my feelings." She stifled her desire to attack and instead said, "I can tell your feelings have been hurt. If you would like, I would be happy to talk with you after class." The student looked surprised and relieved. She dropped her defiant demeanor and dropped her head as though trying to control her tears. The teacher left her alone to deal with her feelings and met with her after class where they discussed what had happened in a kind and respectful manner.

The final role play focused on the goal of assumed inadequacy. This time the teacher felt hopeless and helpless, wanting to give up and let someone else deal with the student. The role play involved a teacher trying to convince a student that she could indeed attempt cursive writing, but ultimately ended with the teacher walking away. During the second part, the teacher assured the student that he had faith in her ability. He then noticed what it was that the student could do, pointed that out, and then worked on the next small step with her.

Self-Esteem

Discussion

For many people, self-esteem is a state of mind that changes moment to moment, depending on their current circumstances or their beliefs about their current circumstances. Think about a day when you were feeling pretty good about yourself but then you made a mistake, received someone's criticism, or listened to your inner critic telling you that you didn't do a task well enough. What happened to your self-esteem then?

Some methods of developing children's self-esteem can be counterproductive. When children are told that they are special (and even sing songs about being special), they are learning to depend on outside validation or superficial words to feel good about themselves. What then happens when someone tells them they aren't special? And what happens when they don't believe another person's reassurance that they're special because they are paying more attention to their inner critics?

A foundation for healthy self-esteem is built through the kind of encouragement that helps children see mistakes as opportunities to learn, learn skills that help them deal with life's ups and downs, experience their own capabilities, and develop social interest. Children have a more stable, wholesome self-concept when they have developed strength in the three perceptions and four skills that make up the Significant Seven:[2]

1. Perception of personal capabilities ("I am capable.")

2. Perception of significance in primary relationships ("I contribute in meaningful ways, and I am genuinely needed.")

3. Perception of personal power or influence over life ("I can influence what happens to me or decide how I will respond to circumstances.")

4. Intrapersonal skills: the ability to understand one's own emotions and to use this understanding to develop self-discipline and self-control

5. Interpersonal skills: the ability to work with others and develop friendships through communicating, cooperating, negotiating, sharing, empathizing, and listening

6. Systemic skills: the ability to respond to the limits and consequences of everyday life with responsibility, accountability, flexibility, and integrity

7. Judgment skills: the ability to use wisdom and to evaluate situations according to appropriate values

Lectures do not teach the Significant Seven. Students can develop these skills and powers of perception only through practical experience. Given opportunities to exercise their judgment, to feel significant, to work with others, and so forth,

2. How to help children develop strength in the Significant Seven is one of the main themes of *Raising Self-Reliant Children in a Self-Indulgent World* by H. Stephen Glenn and Jane Nelsen (Roseville, CA: Prima Publishing, 2000).

children build a healthy sense of self-esteem that will make it less likely that temporary setbacks will evoke self-doubt or despair. Class meetings are a teacher's most powerful tool for helping students absorb the attitudes and learn the skills that stabilize the ups and downs of self-esteem.

All suggestions for developing students' self-esteem require planning ahead.

Planning Ahead to Prevent Future Problems

1. Encourage a student in ways that help her develop an ability to evaluate and trust her own perceptions, which is often referred to as an *inner locus of control.* (Refer to "Encouragement.")

2. Actively teach the concept that mistakes are wonderful opportunities to learn, and help students experience this by treating mistakes as resources instead of catastrophes. (Refer to "Mistakes.") See the following "Inspirational Story" for one way to help students learn from mistakes.

3. Ask "what," "how," and "why" questions with an attitude of genuine interest in what the student thinks and feels and in her ideas about what she's learning and how she can solve problems. (For an explanation of "what" and "how" questions, refer to "Problem Solving.")

4. Help students understand that it's important to work for improvement and not perfection.

5. Have regular class meetings, so students can gain experience in the life skills they need to solve problems, develop empathy, and communicate well. (Refer to "Class Meetings.")

6. Spend special time with students. (Refer to "Special Time.")

7. Opportunities for students to develop social interest should be built into the classroom culture. Examples are programs for peer counseling and peer tutoring as well as class meetings, in which students learn to help one another. (Refer to "Social Interest.")

Inspirational Story[3]

Jason, a new student in Mr. Bradshaw's fifth-grade class, had been labeled by many adults as having low self-esteem. He had difficulty in getting along with other students, looked sullen, failed to complete, or even attempt, many assignments and often mismanaged his anger. Almost immediately on joining Mr. Bradshaw's class, Jason lost his temper on a regular basis. Mr. Bradshaw tried several forms of punishment, but they only seemed to intensify Jason's outbursts. The teacher tried sending

---

3. This story is taken from the newly revised edition of *Positive Discipline,* by Jane Nelsen (New York: Ballantine, 1996), chapter 6.

him to the principal's office. He tried having Jason stay after school to write five hundred sentences about controlling his temper. He tried demanding that Jason leave the classroom to sit on a bench outside and think about what he had just done. Jason would slam the door on his way out. Sometimes he would pop up and down in front of the window making faces. When he returned to the room, his demeanor was belligerent, and he would soon have another blowup.

Finally, Mr. Bradshaw decided to try encouragement. He began by asking Jason to stay after class, so they could talk alone. At the start of this discussion, Mr. Bradshaw owned his part of the problem by sharing how much it upset him when angry outbursts disrupted the class. He also admitted that he had been using punishment in his attempts to motivate Jason to improve his behavior.

"I made a mistake," Mr. Bradshaw said. "I don't want to use punishment anymore, and I need your help." He asked Jason whether they could work on a solution together. Jason wasn't yet willing to cooperate and claimed he couldn't help the fact that the other kids made him so mad. Mr. Bradshaw said he could understand that feeling, because sometimes other people made him very angry, too. Jason looked up, surprise and relief showing in his eyes. Mr. Bradshaw went on to say that he was aware of certain things happening in his body when he got angry, such as a knot forming in his stomach and his shoulders

stiffening. He asked Jason whether he was aware of things happening in his body when he got angry. Jason couldn't think of any. Mr. Bradshaw then asked Jason whether he was willing to try an experiment: would he pay attention to what happened in his body the next time he lost his temper? Jason said he would. They agreed to get together after school the next time it happened, so that Jason could share what he discovered.

Five days passed before Jason had another angry outburst in class. This was a long time for Jason to go without a blowup. He had felt a sense of belonging and significance just because Mr. Bradshaw had taken some special time to work with him in a friendly, respectful manner. For a while after this, Jason didn't feel the need to seek belonging through misbehavior. However, it didn't last forever.

The next time Jason had a temper tantrum, Mr. Bradshaw intervened by asking, "Jason, did you notice what happened to your body?" That question interrupted

Jason's tantrum by inviting him to think. Mr. Bradshaw sounded interested and excited as he added, "Come see me after school and let me know."

Talking to Mr. Bradshaw after his next explosion, Jason said he had noticed that he clenched his fists and felt like hitting someone when he was getting angry. Mr. Bradshaw asked Jason whether he would be willing to catch himself the next time he started to get angry and take responsibility for himself by stepping outside the door until he had cooled off. Mr. Bradshaw added that there would be no need to ask permission, because he would know what was going on and because he had faith in Jason to handle it all by himself. Mr. Bradshaw then asked Jason what he could do while standing outside the door to help himself feel better. Jason said he couldn't think of anything. The teacher said, "How about counting to ten or a hundred, or thinking happy thoughts, or simply appreciating the beautiful day?" Jason agreed to try.

Again, it was five or six days before Jason had another tantrum. Once more, he was encouraged when his teacher discussed the problem respectfully with him. However, the effects of the encouragement didn't last forever. The next week Jason stepped outside the door three times, remaining outside for three to five minutes each time before coming back into the classroom, noticeably calmer. Mr. Bradshaw would give him a thumbs-up and a wink to acknowledge his responsible behavior. Mr. Bradshaw wasn't sure what his student did to calm himself down, but he was grateful that Jason wasn't making faces through the window. In the following weeks, Jason continued to assume this responsibility, leaving the classroom four or five times a week.

Three weeks went by before he lost his temper and shouted at a classmate, forgetting to step outside. Mr. Bradshaw talked with Jason during recess and remarked on how well he had been doing. The teacher added that everyone makes mistakes while learning and asked whether Jason would keep working for improvement. Jason said he would.

For the rest of the year Jason would occasionally step outside the door but had very few outbursts. Every time he reentered the room after cooling off, Mr. Bradshaw winked at him and smiled. Jason's behavior didn't become perfect, but it improved significantly. "Jason used to lose his temper several times a day," Mr. Bradshaw noted. "Now he loses control once or twice a month. I'll take it." The teacher was also pleased because Jason's self-esteem improved significantly as he developed responsibility for his actions and self-control.

Control
Discussion

There is a difference between being in control and being controlling. When people lack effective skills, they feel inadequate and powerless, and they attempt to cover this up by trying to control everything and everyone around them. The more out of control a person feels, the more controlling his behavior becomes—even though controlling behavior doesn't work. It's a vicious cycle.

The sport of skiing provides an excellent analogy. Beginners snowplow most of the time because they haven't developed other skills and feel out of control. Expert skiers are in complete control without trying to be because of their well-honed skills.

When teachers feel out of control, they may grasp at regaining control through the use of punishment—inflicting some form of blame, shame, or emotional pain. They don't like to do this, and it doesn't work. They just don't know what else to do.

At a workshop on Positive Discipline in the classroom, a school faculty discussed the various reasons teachers use punishment with students. They talked about the good intentions as well as the not-so-good. This is their list:

What we were taught
Control
Power
To vent
To teach a lesson
Don't know what else to do
The teacher is expected to do something
Need to be consistent
To model the way the world is
To get back at them
To stamp out the behavior

To set an example for other students
To scare them into doing better
It works! (at least short term)

These teachers participated in several activities that convinced them that even though punishment may work in the short term, it isn't effective over time. Through role playing and experiential activities, they learned what students are thinking and feeling as well as what they are deciding to do in the future when they are punished or controlled by teacher-imposed rules.

Many teachers are reluctant to give up controlling behavior and punishment because they think the only alternative is anarchy. A primary purpose of this book is to teach skills that help teachers be in control without acting in a controlling manner.

Suggestions

1. Have faith in students. They are able and willing to cooperate when treated with dignity and respect, and they can learn problem-solving skills that encourage self-control.

2. Forgive yourself when you get "hooked" by a student's behavior. Take some time out to cool off, make amends and apologize, and then deal with the problem from a position of kindness, firmness, dignity, and respect for yourself and the student.

3. Turn the problem over to the class. Ask for their help immediately, or put the

problem on the class meeting agenda for future consideration.

4. Ask for help from fellow teachers. Know that it's normal to be great at solving other people's problems while struggling with your own.

Planning Ahead to Prevent Future Problems

1. Develop an understanding of the long-range results of controlling behavior. Participate in role-playing situations in which someone tries to control you. Get in touch with how this makes you feel and decisions you make about thwarting people who try to control you in the future.

2. Learn how to implement effective class meetings.

3. Trust the process of effective class meetings to help students learn self-control, cooperation, accountability, responsibility, problem-solving skills, and social interest.

4. Don't underestimate the importance of taking care of yourself. When people feel overwhelmed, they often resort to short-term solutions. It's easier to be in control of a situation when we feel in control of ourselves and our environment.

Inspirational Stories

The Marine Turned Teacher

During a workshop on Positive Discipline, teachers who had been using class meetings were invited to share their experiences. One man shared that this method had saved his teaching career. He explained that he was a former marine and had thought his military training would work in the classroom. Instead, he was inciting rebellion and defiance. He was ready to reenlist when someone told him about class meetings. He now enjoys being a teacher, and his students appreciate the opportunity to have a voice in creating a cooperative classroom.

Mrs. Bittle and Gilbert

Mrs. Bittle was having trouble with one of her ninth-grade students, Gilbert. She found herself trying to control his inattentive and mildly disruptive behavior with blame and shame. She welcomed opportunities when she could refer him to in-school suspension because then she didn't have to face her inability to control him in class.

Meanwhile, Gilbert quickly moved from seeking undue attention to power struggles to revenge. He was quick to blame Mrs. Bittle for his many trips to in-school suspension and his lack of progress in her algebra class.

The other students in Mrs. Bittle's second period algebra class took sides. The situation went from bad to worse, and Mrs. Bittle seriously considered giving up teaching. Then a colleague talked to her about Positive Discipline in the classroom. Learning about the class meeting process and the four mistaken goals of misbehavior gave Mrs. Bittle a whole new way of looking at her students, especially Gilbert. She realized she had been taking his behavior as a personal affront instead of looking at it in terms of its context and purpose.

Mrs. Bittle held a class meeting in which she apologized to her students for trying to control them through blame, shame, and punishment. She shared her concerns for their academic future if they didn't learn the material and explained that the ongoing misbehavior was making it difficult for her to teach. Then she asked the students whether they were willing to work with her to create a classroom where everyone worked toward solutions without placing blame and offered input on how the material was covered.

The high school students were blown away by her apology and suggestion. They unanimously voted to work with Mrs. Bittle on creating a new kind of classroom. They agreed to give this new classroom a try for two months and then evaluate how it was going.

After receiving the class's cooperation, Mrs. Bittle set up a private conference with Gilbert. She apologized for her part in their relationship difficulties and shared her feelings regarding his behavior. This opened the door for Gilbert to tell Mrs. Bittle that he had always thought she was picking on him because he was Hispanic and that he had felt left out. In frustration, he had begun planning ways to make her life miserable.

This was the beginning of Gilbert becoming a staunch ally of Mrs. Bittle and the movement to create a new classroom.

In fact, when the two-month evaluation period was up and the class voted to continue holding class meetings, Gilbert's one suggestion to improve the process was significant. He felt that the class needed to do compliments and appreciations more than just once a week. Mrs. Bittle and the rest of the students heartily agreed.

The Positive Discipline class meeting process forged such a dramatic change in this class that the following year Mrs. Bittle introduced it to all her classes and the rest of her colleagues.

Rewards and Punishment

Discussion

Workshops on Positive Discipline in the classroom start with participants brainstorming to produce a list of characteristics and life skills that they believe students need to be successful in life—that is, to be happy, contributing members of society. The lists from different workshops are always very similar to one another; they tend to include courage, confidence, self-discipline, responsibility, accountability, the ability to cooperate, problem-solving skills, respect for self and others, healthy self-esteem, motivation to learn, empathy, relationship skills, communication skills, and a sense of humor.

The next questions posed to workshop participants are (1) Is the development of these abilities and inner strengths just as important as academics? and (2) How do we help students develop them? The answer to the first question is yes when teachers are given an opportunity to think about it. (In fact, most feel the development of the characteristics and life skills are more important.) The answer to the second question is certainly not rewards and punishment.

Think about any program or method that involves rewards and punishment. Who is responsible? It's invariably an adult's job to catch students being "good" and give them rewards as well as to catch students being "bad" and mete out punishment. What happens when the adult is no longer around? Considerable research has demonstrated that children who experience an external locus of control don't develop the previously mentioned skills and characteristics. In fact, a heavy-handed approach to teaching children how to behave is not only less effective but also more likely to be associated with disruptive and aggressive behavior patterns when the child is away from home.[4]

Many teachers are now asking, "If not rewards and punishment, then what?"

Suggestions and Planning Ahead

As you deal with the situations and problems highlighted in this book, you will be presented with ideas and strategies that are alternatives to rewards and punishment. You may notice that practicing these alternatives may require a shift in thinking and behavior. The major shift is moving from *short*-term solutions to *long*-term teaching. Keep in mind that practicing Positive Discipline today helps students develop the inner strength and life skills that will help them become successful adults.

Inspirational References

For many years the authors of this book have advocated the elimination of rewards and punishment. Positive Discipline books and workshops are devoted to helping parents and teachers learn nonpunitive ways to encourage children's development of effective life skills and valuable personal qualities.

The volumes of research presented in Alfie Kohn's book *Punished by Rewards* support the Positive Discipline premise. This book is recommended highly to anyone who wants to investigate the ineffective and often damaging method of managing children's behavior through rewards and punishment. The following excerpts are from *Punished by Rewards*.

Alfie Kohn on Rewards

The unsettling news is that rewards and punishments are worthless at best, and destructive

---

4. Alfie Kohn, *Punished by Rewards* (New York: Houghton Mifflin, 1993), 230. Kohn cites many studies on the effects of rewards and punishment at home and at school.

at worst, for helping children develop such values and skills. What rewards and punishments do produce is temporary compliance. They buy us obedience. If that's what we mean when we say they "work," then yes, they work wonders.

But if we are ultimately concerned with the kind of people our children will become, there are no shortcuts. Good values have to be grown from the inside out. Praise, privileges and punishment can change behavior (for a while), but they cannot change the person who engages in the behavior, at least not in the way we want. No behavioral manipulation ever helped a child develop a commitment to becoming a caring and responsible person. No reward for doing something we approve of ever gave a child a reason for continuing to act that way when there was no longer any reward to be gained for doing so.[5]

Alfie Kohn on Punishment

We convince ourselves that we are not just imposing our will, but teaching the child what happens when he misbehaves, and that this will prevent future misbehavior. Moreover, we see ourselves as administering an elemental sort of justice: having broken a rule, the child must now be punished.

In chapter 9, I argued that the first rationale is fatally flawed; punishment teaches about the use of power, not about how or why

to behave properly . . . The commitment to punishing children typically reflects a fear that the failure to respond this way will mean that they "got away with something."

If we dig still further, we find that this perception upsets us for two reasons. First, it implies that the child has "won." Our authority has been challenged, and the more we construe a relationship as a battle for power, the more wildly we will lash out to preserve that power. Second, we are concerned the child will come away thinking he can repeat whatever it was he did. This concern, in turn, betrays a particular assumption about children's motives, namely that a child is inclined to do what he can get away with and will keep doing it until forcibly restrained. Ultimately, our need to punish (or dread of not punishing) is predicated on a tacit theory of human nature . . .

In my view, there are two fundamentally different ways one can respond to a child who does something wrong. One is to impose a punitive consequence. Another is to see the situation as a "teachable moment," an opportunity to educate or to solve a problem together. The response here is not, "You've misbehaved; now here's what I'm going to do to you," but "Something has gone wrong; what can we do about it?" . . . But does this work in the real world? Actually, the more apt question is, Does punishment work in the real world? Experi-

---

5. Ibid., 161.

ence and research teach us that troublesome behavior increases when children are punished, that underlying problems aren't solved, that dubious values are modeled.[6]

. . . [Constance] Kamii, drawing from [Jean] Piaget's work, argued that punishment leads to three possible outcomes: "calculation of risks" (which means children spend their time figuring out whether they can get away with something), "blind conformity" (which fails to teach responsible decision-making), or "revolt." . . . Piaget put this point more succinctly: "punishment . . . renders autonomy of conscience impossible." (Constance Kamii, "Obedience Is Not Enough," Young Children [May 1984]: 11–14.) (Jean Piaget, The Moral Judgment of the Child. *Translated by Marjorie Gabain. [New York: Free Press, 1965]: 339.)*[7]

Inspirational Story

Mrs. Owen taught first-grade Chapter One summer school in a town in south Texas. At teacher orientation, she was given a large number of certificates, colorful pencils, and scratch-and-sniff stickers. She and the other teachers were encouraged to come up with all kinds of incentive programs to keep the students motivated about showing up for summer school,

since attendance was not mandatory, though necessary to keep the teachers employed. Mrs. Owen believed in the intrinsic motivation of lifelong learning. She quietly put the stickers, certificates, and pencils in her desk drawer. She did not hang up an attendance chart, as the other teachers did, with the inducement of ice cream or popcorn for those who had perfect attendance at the end of the week.

On the second day, Mrs. Owen asked her students to complete an assignment. Her first graders chorused, "What are you going to give us?"

Mrs. Owen replied, "Guess what? I'm not going to give you anything! But you are going to give yourselves something, because when you finish this assignment you will have money in your brain. And you know what? It's the kind of money that no one can steal from you. Right now a thief could run into our room and steal my purse, and I would lose the money inside it. But no one can steal the kind of money that you get in your brain when you learn something. And not only do you get money in your brain, but when you share what you know—when you share that money in your brain—you get more money, but this time in your heart."

Then Mrs. Owen asked, "How many of you believe you could be my teacher?"

---

6. Ibid., 230–232.
7. Ibid., 168

Her students shook their heads, some of them saying, "You've been to college. We couldn't teach you anything."

"How many of you know Spanish?" queried Mrs. Owen. All the children's hands went up. As natives of south Texas, their second language—if not their first—was Spanish. Mrs. Owen was born in Ohio and had never learned to speak Spanish. She said, "I'll bet each of you could teach me a hard word in Spanish. Now make sure you give me a hard one. I know all the easy ones."

The children thought up the hardest Spanish words they knew. First Mrs. Owen tried to pronounce a word. The children had great fun helping her get the pronunciation right. Then they told her the word's meaning.

"Now," said Mrs. Owen, "I have money in my brain that I didn't have before, thanks to all my Spanish teachers here! And now you have money in your hearts because you shared your brain money with me. If one of you knows something that another one doesn't know, you can be that person's teacher, whether you have been to college or not and no matter how young you are."

Throughout the summer Mrs. Owen continued to encourage the students to get money in their brains from learning and then to share the money with others. Using class meetings and cooperative learning, she and the children created a classroom family. These first graders became teachers to one another, to others in the school, and to Mrs. Owen. Furthermore, Mrs. Owen never had to resort to bribes to keep her students attending school.

Firmness and Kindness

Discussion

The formula that develops capable young people is a balance of firmness with kindness. *Firmness* means using appropriate principles with confidence. *Kindness* means maintaining dignity and respect for yourself and your students while using those principles.

Being kind is easy for some teachers, but they have difficulty being firm. The formula usually leads to excessive permissiveness. Other teachers find it easy to be firm and forget about kindness. This formula usually results in excessive strictness. Neither formula is healthy for students. Kindness without firmness invites students to manipulate and avoid responsibilities. Firmness without kindness invites students to defy and rebel. Firmness *with* kindness guides students to cooperate and to develop the life skills they need to be happy, contributing, and capable.

Suggestions

1. Check your facial expressions, your tone of voice, and your body language. They should communicate respect.

2. Avoid piggybacking. *Piggybacking* is adding something that is unnecessary and hurtful, such as "Maybe this will teach you." "You can just sit there and think about what you did." Piggybacking punishes for the past instead of solving for the future. It is based on the belief that we have to make our students feel worse in order to make them do better.

3. Avoid using humiliation, blame, and shame as discipline strategies.

4. Don't fall in the trap of feeling sorry for your student. Realize that making excuses with the student buys into the belief that she is not capable. It may be obvious that using humiliation and shame are disrespectful to the student. It may not be as obvious that rescuing and excusing can be equally disrespectful

5. All of the Positive Discipline tools rely on firmness and kindness as a foundation. In the absence of firmness or kindness, we miss the opportunity to help students develop life skills.

Planning Ahead to Prevent Future Problems

1. Be aware of your tendency to use a permissive style of teaching (kindness without firmness) or an authoritarian style (firmness without kindness). This awareness helps you see areas in which you can begin to make changes. Focus on taking a step toward a more balanced approach.

2. Balancing firmness and kindness is a skill. In developing any skill, one needs encouragement. Practicing the ideas and suggestions in this book will give you courage to continue working toward this balance.

Inspirational Stories

Maintaining Balance

Mr. Klein, a student teacher, was a person who liked to be in control. Without being aware of how he spoke, he was using sarcasm and name-calling to control the behavior of his students. One morning his adviser was observing Mr. Klein's class. She noticed how he handled a student who often interrupted him or fellow students. After the third interruption, Mr. Klein told the student to move, with her work, to the back of the class. As she got up to move, he rudely commented that she was turning into "quite a mouth."

During the next break, Mr. Klein's adviser asked to speak privately to him with regard to this incident. "I noticed that when you disciplined Sarah, you got half of it right. You do need to maintain order in your class. But it is possible to do that without resorting to humiliation. In my experience, when a teacher uses the technique of being both firm and kind, the student's focus is on his or her own behavior—not on the teacher's behavior. I encourage you to notice when you are using only firmness *or* only kindness, and what you can do to keep yourself more in balance."

The next morning, Mr. Klein had another opportunity to deal with Sarah. She was teasing one of her classmates and making loud comments to other students. Mr. Klein noticed that his first instinct was to say something to put Sarah in her place. Remembering what his adviser had said, he chose his words carefully. "What you are saying is hurtful and disrespectful. Please take your seat and begin the assignment." He stopped. He resisted the temptation to piggyback on his comment to discipline Sarah further. He was pleased that he was able to maintain order without using a dose of humiliation. As the weeks went by, he was surprised at how many opportunities he had to practice being both firm and kind—and how much the students followed his model and became more respectful to him and each other.

An Exemplary Attitude Adjustment

A story from Stephanie Corvese, second-grade teacher, St. Catherine of Sienna, Woodbridge (Toronto), Ontario, Canada

I'll never forget my first year of teaching. What a nightmare! I had a split grade 1/2 class and several behavior problems. I wanted to have the best year of my life, but somehow it turned out to be the worst. I wanted to be a kind and respectful teacher, but I just didn't know what to do when kids would tell me off or interrupt my lesson, so instead I yelled at them all year. In fact, I had so many problem kids that year and lack of experience, I dreaded waking up each morning. I cried every day after school, because I felt so exhausted from the day and I felt so helpless and didn't know what to do to get them to listen to me. I tried stickers and treats, but it never really worked in the long run. So, I'd get angry and yell at them.

The following year, I changed schools, was given a second-grade class of twenty-eight students and made the decision to create the most positive environment ever. I knew that I had to make this year different. Let's just say, by the end of the first week, it was clear that there were a lot of behavioral kids and it was going to be difficult, but I knew I couldn't repeat the previous year. I didn't want to feel angry all year. I wanted to wake up each morning and feel excited to go to work.

I began with class meetings immediately. Whenever there were problems in the school yard or in class, the kids would put the problem on our class agenda, and we would solve it at the end of the day. I shared personal stories with them, laughed with them, smiled at them, and in a short time I began to love those kids, and the awesome thing was that I knew they loved me. Sure, there were really tough days when a child would interrupt me constantly or another would swear, but no matter what, I tried to always remind myself that they are kids, not little adults, and it's my job to be the change I want to see. If I want them to be respectful toward others, then I made sure I was respectful toward them.

Now that I'm teaching grade 2 again and using the Positive Discipline principles, I know I could never go back to my old ways. The most interesting thing, too, was that whenever I was absent from work, supply/substitute teachers would leave me notes about how "bad" they were. Even other teachers at my school would come up to me and say, "Wow, how do you handle them? They're crazy." The thing is, I cared about these children, I listened to their problems, I respected them, and in turn, they did their best for me. I think kids want to behave when they know their teacher likes them.

Limits

Discussion

Anyone involved in establishing limits must consider their long-range purpose: to help children learn skills and attitudes that will allow them to become happy, contributing members of society. Established limits can improve the quality of life for both children and adults. Knowing the boundaries of appropriate behavior provides comfort and a feeling of safety. While this may be obvious to most adults, many students may interpret limits as existing only to control them. The challenge is to help students see their response to established limits as an opportunity to learn important life skills, such as self-discipline,

responsibility, cooperation, social interest, and how to solve problems.

Additional benefits accrue when students are actively involved in the creation of limits. Students are likely to be enthusiastic and motivated about following limits that they helped establish. Moreover, when students participate in setting limits, they are developing skills that will serve them throughout their lives.

Suggestions

1. The attitude behind what you do is more important than what you do. Maintain the dignity of all concerned when working with students on setting limits. Your attitude should be respectful and not authoritarian.

2. Be clear in establishing your limits. For example, when students are working in small groups, state that they can continue working while the noise level remains such that you can easily carry on a conversation with individual students. If the noise exceeds that comfort level, tell your students, "I see that this isn't working. We need to change to working individually on this project." Issuing multiple warnings teaches students that they can go beyond the set limit.

3. Sometimes teachers must quietly, kindly, and firmly lead young students away from what they shouldn't be doing or toward what they should be doing. Do this with a

friendly attitude instead of a scolding, controlling one. Sometimes it's most effective to eliminate words. Use a friendly smile or a knowing wink instead.

4. Decide what you will do instead of what you will try to make students do. A teacher might sit quietly until her students are quiet (having decided that she won't teach until her students are ready). Teachers who have created an atmosphere of mutual respect in their classrooms will find this very effective. Let your students know in advance what you are going to do under certain circumstances, and then follow through with what you have declared—calmly and without lectures.

5. Don't see students as defiant when they go beyond set limits. This is not the time for punishment or permissiveness. Whenever they're having trouble abiding by a limit or routine, discuss the problem during a class meeting and engage them in problem solving. Let them figure out why the limit or routine isn't working. Students are good at brainstorming and solving problems when they have been taught these skills and then set free to carry out the process.

6. Get older students involved in setting classroom limits. Class meetings are a great time to involve students and to discuss with them which limits they find useful and why. Teachers who involve their students in setting the class rules find that they are usually responsible about staying within these boundaries.

Planning Ahead to Prevent Future Problems

1. It would be worth the time to have a discussion with students about the purpose of limits, not only ones they experience in the school setting but all those that exist in society.

2. When we take time for training, we give students and ourselves an opportunity to rehearse what the limit looks like. Practice not only the ideal but also areas where difficulties might arise. (Refer to "Take Time for Training.")

3. Take some time for self-evaluation. With a colleague or as a staff, ask about how you have traditionally handled setting limits. Do I give multiple warnings, do I feel like the *bad* guy when I follow through, am I consistent?

Class Meeting Solution

A story from Barbara Evangelista, kindergarten paraprofessional, Rocky Mount Elementary School, Marietta, Georgia

The kindergartners decided they needed a silent signal to help remind fellow classmates of the "we decided" rules. The students chose from seven suggestions to find their solution: They would tap the top of their heads with one finger. This would mean "Stop and think and make a respectful choice." The signal has been very successful. No adult directions, corrections, or shushing are needed—just a tap on the head and a smile.

Inspirational Story

Mrs. Noonan's fourth-grade class was an enthusiastic group of students. They were a high-energy group and usually a joy to teach. However, when they were working in cooperative groups, she often found herself reminding her students many times and in many different ways that they needed to stay on task and to keep the noise level within reasonable limits. When she felt they had exceeded the limit, Mrs. Noonan would resort to several different techniques that had been helpful to her in the past. She would turn the classroom lights off and wait for their attention. Then five minutes later, she would need to do this again. She tried thanking the groups who were on task, but the others didn't seem to notice. By the end of these lessons, Mrs. Noonan felt exhausted, irritated, and disappointed in her ineffectiveness.

One day at her lunch break, Mrs. Noonan shared her frustration with another teacher. After their discussion, she realized that although she was always very clear in the limit that she set, she was actually teaching her students to ignore that limit by neglecting to follow through.

That afternoon, during her math lesson, Mrs. Noonan took the time to explain that the class would be working in groups as long as they were able to remain on task and the noise level allowed her to talk easily with individual students. She reiterated to her students that if they were not able to stay within that limit, they would continue the lesson working individually. They got into their groups quietly, but it only took a few minutes for the noise level to rise. Mrs. Noonan noticed that she was uncomfortable with the level of the noise and she started to give them just one warning. She found herself thinking that giving them just *one* chance would be a helpful reminder. But, rather than reverting to her old pattern, she quietly stood up. In a calm voice, she told the class to move back into their seats and continue the lesson working by themselves. They were surprised and promised that they would work quietly, if she would just give them one more chance. She maintained a friendly attitude and responded by telling them that they would work in groups again tomorrow. Mrs. Noonan was pleased to notice that she felt confident and calm. She also noticed that she didn't have any of the resentment and frustration that she usually had after group activities. She was actually looking forward to their next cooperative group session.

The next day, when the students were working in cooperative groups, she noticed one group starting to get too noisy. She was about to follow through when she heard someone in the group say, "We need to get more quiet, or we won't be able to work together." The noise diminished considerably. Mrs. Noonan couldn't help the smile on her face as she realized how much easier it was to use kind and firm follow-through to teach her students that she meant what she said—and that they could trust her to follow through regarding the limits that were established.

Follow-Through

Discussion

Follow-through helps teachers be proactive instead of reactive. It is an excellent alternative to authoritarian methods or permissiveness. Follow-through means teachers decide what they are going to do and then follow through with kind and firm action instead of lectures and punishment. By using this tool, teachers find it is possible to meet the needs of the situation while maintaining dignity and respect for all concerned.

What are students learning when you follow through? That what they do has a logical consequence; that you mean what you say and will follow through with firm and kind action. Students are learning about responsibility, accountability, and mutual respect. They are learning the life skills they need to feel good about themselves and to be contributing members of society.

Part of effective follow-through involves the adult being proactive. This means that the adult must be aware of the long-range goal, so that he can clearly plan the steps needed to reach that goal with dignity and respect. For that reason, we will present the ideas for "Planning Ahead" before we present "Suggestions."

Planning Ahead to Prevent Future Problems

1. Make sure that students have a clear understanding of deadlines, times, and consequences. Allow time for questions and clarification, and possible role plays of specific situations.

2. Be aware that students have different priorities. At the same time, be aware of the importance of sticking to issues and following through. It can be easy to get sidetracked by the student's priorities and lose sight of the needs of the situation. We then may feel sorry for the student and accept excuses or we may feel disappointed and decide to retaliate.

3. Find agreements when possible. During class meetings or when conferencing with a student, involve them in possible solutions. Pick one that both you and the student or students can live with and make sure that everyone is clear on the new agreement. It can be beneficial to write down the agreement as a point of reference.

4. Teach **Opportunity = Responsibility = Consequence**. Help your students understand that for every opportunity they have, there is a related responsibility. The obvious consequence for not accepting the responsibility is to lose the opportunity. A student who has the opportunity to participate in recess has the responsibility to respect equipment and people. If the student's behavior is disrespectful to a person or property, they lose the opportunity to participate in recess. This formula is effective only if the consequence is enforced respectfully and students can regain the opportunity as soon as they show they are ready for the responsibility.

5. Follow-through is an opportunity to model and practice mutual respect. Using some of the tools listed here as suggestions helps us maintain dignity and respect for our students and for ourselves.

Suggestions

1. When it is time to follow through, keep your comments simple and concise. Keep the message short—ten words or fewer—and stick to the issue. In fact, using only one word can be more effective than a lecture.

2. Give a limited choice. "It's time to clean up. Do you want to do it by yourself, or do you want to pick someone to work with you?"

3. Say what you mean and mean what you say. Rather than use threats, demonstrate to your students that you will follow through with firm and kind action. (Refer to "Limits.")

4. When a student objects or seems to have forgotten about a rule or an agreement, ask, "What was our agreement?" or "What are the rules about behavior in the lunchroom?"

5. In some situations, using nonverbal communication is effective. Pointing to the clock or stopping the lesson gives students the opportunity to get themselves back on track.

6. Stick to the issue. Part of sticking to the issue is ignoring other concerns that arise. These concerns can be addressed at a later time either with an individual student or placed on the agenda for a class meeting.

7. Use firmness and kindness as the basic ingredients of follow-through. (Refer to "Firmness and Kindness").

Inspirational Story

At Margaret Allen Elementary School, the school yard space was limited. With this in mind, past students and teachers together developed guidelines for the use of the yard and the equipment. Students could play kickball, dodgeball, four-square, and basketball on the blacktop. Playing unstructured, wild games with the balls was not permitted.

Miss Fontaine used her first class meeting of the school year to present these guidelines to her students. They had the opportunity to get clarification and to role-play situations that might arise. They began to understand that safety and respect for others were the reasons that these rules were developed. Part of Miss Fontaine's challenge was to teach the relationship between *opportunity* and *responsibility*. She made it clear that the consequence for not accepting the responsibility of following the guidelines was that they would lose the opportunity to use the area and the equipment for a short time.

The following afternoon, Miss Fontaine observed three of her students ignoring the rule about unstructured ball games and kicking a ball from one end of the blacktop to the other. She approached them and asked them what the rule was about playing ball on the blacktop. The students admitted they knew the rule, but the upper grade students had been doing the same thing earlier that morning. She was tempted to accept their excuses and ignore the behavior. However, she realized the importance of following through with firmness and kindness. Miss Fontaine proceeded by appreciating them for remembering the guidelines and asked for them to hand her the ball. The students were disappointed. They begged her to let them have the ball and promised they would never do it again. She maintained a friendly attitude and assured them that they could play with the ball again the next day.

Social Interest

Discussion

The authors of this book believe that the development of social interest in all people would solve most of the problems in the world. Alfred Adler called this enlightened regard for all humans, creatures, and places *gemeinschaftsgefühl,* a word he coined in German that doesn't translate well into English. Some of the phrases that partially capture the meaning of gemeinschaftsgefühl are concern and caring for our fellow human beings, a feeling of community, a desire to make a contribution, and active interest in the environment (local and global). Perhaps social interest is love in its purest form.

If all children and adults had a strong sense of social interest, there would be no violence or vandalism. People wouldn't litter or pollute the environment. They wouldn't steal. Politicians would truly work for the people instead of for personal power and profit. Individuals would get together and find solutions to unemployment and starvation. Gangs would engage in productive activities instead of destruction.

The world will never be perfect because people are imperfect. But a faulty world creates countless opportunities for individuals to keep learning and growing. And people with a strong sense of social interest will work together to solve problems out of real concern for each other, the community, and the environment.

Suggestions

1. Understand the importance of developing students' social interest. Social interest is as important as academic subjects (if not more important).

2. See problems as opportunities for personal growth for you and for your students. Use role plays and discussions to foster social interest. These methods, in particular, help students develop empathy, which Alfred Adler eloquently defined as "the ability to see with the eyes of another, to hear with the ears of another, and to feel with the heart of another."

3. Notice that most of the suggestions in this book are designed to help develop social interest.

Planning Ahead to Prevent Future Problems

1. Use class meetings to teach students decision-making skills, problem-solving skills, and social interest.

2. Use class meetings to involve students in discussions of class problems, community problems, and government problems.

Help students see that they have the power and responsibility to address world problems, human rights concerns, and environmental issues. Encourage them to plan and carry out projects and activities that can make a difference.

3. Model empathy through your own compassionate responses to others; model social interest through your own concern for all people and for the natural world. Students who have empathy and social interest are less likely to hurt their classmates. They are aware that the world doesn't revolve around their needs and therefore are more likely to look for solutions to difficulties that satisfy everyone's needs.

Inspirational Story

Bronia Grunwald, coauthor with Rudolf Dreikurs and Floy Pepper of Maintaining Sanity in the Classroom (2d ed.; Washington, D.C.: Accelerated Development, 1998), used class meetings for more than twenty-five years. Bronia had such faith in the class meeting process that she asked to have all the problem kids. Her philosophy was, The more problems, the more opportunities to teach problem-solving skills. In the process, her students were endowed with a strong sense of social interest.

Bronia had classes of more than forty students. During an interview she said, "That many students made more work correcting papers and having conferences with parents, but I also had more students to help solve the problems." Even though Bronia taught mostly problem students, their misbehavior always disappeared by midyear because they had learned mutual respect, cooperation, and how to solve problems.

However, Bronia didn't simply coast through the rest of the year. Whenever she noticed that a colleague was having trouble with a student, she would ask her students during a class meeting, "How would you feel about inviting Janey from Mrs. Smith's class to join our class? She's having problems. How many of you think we could help her?" Every time her class would enthusiastically agree to invite the problem student into their class so they could use their skills to help.

Jobs for Everyone in the Classroom

Discussion

In the community of the school classroom, a sense of belonging is crucial. One excellent way to create this is to include each student in the myriad tasks necessary for the smooth flow of daily activities. Classroom jobs give students a chance to contribute, and hence they feel needed and they practice social interest.

Suggestions

1. Brainstorm to create a list of classroom jobs that must be done on a regular basis.

The list may include such positions as paper passer, pencil monitor, hamster helper, and trash monitor. Brainstorm until all students have jobs, whether they are working individually or are sharing a responsibility.

2. Create a system for job assignment and rotation. One of the many possibilities is to use a list of students' names and print a new job next to each name every week (writing a task beside each name can be one of the jobs). Another possibility is to list the jobs on separate slips of paper and put them in a box; each student then draws from the box to discover his or her job of the week. Use your creativity as well as that of your students to come up with ideas about how to display your class job chart.

3. For younger students, pictures of the tasks are helpful. Have the students draw the pictures or cut them out of magazines. Keep the pictures in place and move the students' names around. Or you may want to create a "helping hands" chart, which has cutout tracings of each child's hand inscribed with his or her name. The hand at-

taches beside the picture or description of the task. Another idea is to staple small paper pockets, with the tasks written on them, to the bulletin board. Each student has a name card that is placed in a pocket, and these are rotated weekly.

4. Set special times each day for certain jobs to be done. This makes jobs a cooperative group activity and forestalls complaints.

5. Think in terms of schoolwide jobs. Older students see doing these jobs as a privilege and younger students look forward to them.

Planning Ahead to Prevent Future Problems

1. Involve students in all aspects of jobs. Students can designate tasks, decide on rotation times, make charts and tags, and announce job times.

2. Remember to take time for training. This is an opportunity to teach skills and for students to feel capable. (Refer to "Take Time for Training.")

3. Build a rover or substitute job person into the system. The student in this position fills in for anyone who's absent. This job should rotate, too.

4. Learn to let go and entrust students with more responsibility. They can do so much and will feel great about themselves in the bargain.

5. If a problem surfaces, invite a student to put it on the class meeting agenda (or do so yourself), so the students can find a solution together.

Class Meeting Solution

A story from Trilby Cohen, second-grade teacher, Syre Elementary School, Shoreline, Washington

I have found that jobs themselves can be a means of solving problems. My students were bothered by the classroom coat closet being messy. After discussing the problem at a class meeting, they voted to add a new position to their job list. They designated a closet helper, and the issue was resolved.

The same type of solution worked for my class when students lining up at recess were being noisy. The quiet-keeper job was created, and peace returned.

Inspirational Story

A story from Loretta Sedran, French teacher for grades 1 through 8, Holy Jubilee Catholic School, Toronto, Ontario, Canada

Being on rotary can be a very difficult task. Last year I was fortunate to have my own classroom where the students came to me. I decided I would have a "Job Wall." I had six classes, and each class had its own chart of jobs. I found that library pockets on a bristol board worked the best for me. Each class brainstormed the jobs that they particularly needed as well as keeping in mind the time of day they had French. For example, my eighth-grade students decided that two students should come in early and take down all the chairs. This worked for them, but none of the other classes, as the chairs were already down. Washing boards was another job that only two classes could have: the class before lunch and the one before home time.

This year things were much more difficult. I moved to a school where I did not have my own room. I had to travel from class to class. It was much more difficult to brainstorm jobs because you have to keep in mind that you are in someone else's classroom. The first thing I made sure I did was to ask the classroom teacher for some space where I could keep a chart posted. The bristol board format still worked, but I had to make sure it was somewhere highly visible.

Another tip that I found works is having graphics or pictures on the job pocket for the primary grades. The older students were okay with having it written, and we incorporated some French by giving the jobs French names. Most of the jobs the fourth through sixth grades came up with were standard, but some were unique. Therefore, my sixth-grade class came up with the idea of having a "Job Description Book." It is a duotang that has the title of the job and what is required. Students brainstormed in groups of four and then asked the rest of the class what they wanted to add or delete. Once it was completed, all jobs had a description.

I have found that if a teacher on rotary can maintain a job chart for six to seven classes (which translates to 200 to 230 students), a classroom teacher should have no problem for one class of thirty to forty students.

Take Time for Training

Discussion

The importance of taking time for training may seem obvious to those in the teaching profession. What may not be obvious is that taking time for training is considered a fundamental part of Positive Discipline. The reason it is included as a tool is that it helps students develop academic, social, and life skills and encourages their abilities to succeed. Taking time for training shows a respect for the needs of the situation and the needs of the student.

Many of the "Suggestions" and the ideas for "Planning Ahead" listed here are useful not only when dealing with students but also when preparing adults who will be involved with your class.

Suggestions

1. When approaching any new task, be sure to break it into workable steps. Recognizing the importance of small steps is a key element in the success of any training.

2. Take each step and demonstrate or ask for clarity from your students about what that step may look like. Take the time to

help your students understand how each step builds toward the goal.

3. In some situations, it is helpful to invite students to work alongside you. For example, in learning to do research in the library, students may need to sit next to an adult as they access information.

4. Provide occasional hints and help along with lots of encouragement. Celebrate as students accomplish tasks.

5. Taking time for training helps reduce the anxiety that many students may have when making transitions. This applies to transitions made within the school day as well as those when a student advances to a different grade.

6. Don't move ahead until most students have an understanding about what they have just done. You may need to give additional support around a particular task for some students.

7. Use visual aids such as charts and schedules. Charts help students see the parts and the goal. A schedule keeps them focused and moving toward the goal.

8. Once students have an understanding and appear to be competent, pull back and let them know that you are available if they need you.

Planning Ahead to Prevent Future Problems

1. Remember to keep your expectations and standards realistic. Pay special atten-

tion to what your students may be telling you through their actions. Check with your colleagues for guidance.

2. Help minimize misunderstandings by making sure everyone knows the parts of the whole and what is required within each of the parts.

3. Avoid making assumptions about students' academic or social abilities. Appreciate the uniqueness of the individuals or the group. Have the wisdom and the courage to start over with the basics and proceed from there. Your students will set the pace.

4. Focus on progress, not perfection. Let your students know that making mistakes is part of any learning process.

Inspirational Story

Mr. Tohlmann had experimented with assigning jobs to students in his classroom in previous years. He was always disappointed with the results. He would find himself frustrated at the end of the day when he noticed

that most of the jobs were incomplete or not done to his standards. He abandoned the idea of sharing jobs with students but noticed that he was then overwhelmed with the amount of extra work in the classroom.

He did some thinking and realized that a missing piece in previous years was that he had neglected to take the time to train students for their jobs. He decided that this year would be different. After listing all the jobs with his students, he explained that he would create a written job description for each one. The first step for a student would be to read over the description and take notes on any questions they may have. They would then make an appointment with Mr. Tohlmann and review all the components and actually practice the *how to's*.

As the semester went on, Mr. Tohlmann evaluated this process. Although it had taken more time and training than in previous years, he was pleased with the results. He also realized that there was an additional benefit in taking time for training that he had not foreseen. He was able to spend special time with each student and to learn a little more about each of them. This whole process contributed to the feeling of belonging and cooperation within his class.

Mistakes

Discussion

Most of us received discouraging messages about mistakes when we were growing up.

When students are taught that mistakes mean they are failures, stupid, or inadequate in any way, they lose the courage to take risks—or they get very creative at hiding their mistakes. Because schools by their very nature are performance related, it's crucial to teach students that mistakes are important and necessary parts of the learning process. When this is the message we communicate, students can see mistakes as wonderful opportunities to learn.

Suggestions

1. When a student feels bad about making a mistake, say, "Isn't that wonderful! You made a mistake. Let's pretend we're detectives and see what we can learn from this." (Of course, your language may differ, depending on the age of your students.)

2. When a student makes mistakes on his papers, point to the things that he did well. Then ask him whether he can see areas that need improvement. Ask him whether he needs help (from you or a peer tutor) or can work alone on improving in these areas.

3. When a student makes a mistake that involves her fellow students, invite her to put it on the class meeting agenda or use the problem-solving steps.

4. When you make a mistake, model an effective response by admitting it to your students as soon as possible. In some situations, you may want to put it on the agenda so you can receive the class's help. Another

option is to use the Three R's of Recovery (described in the fourth item under "Planning Ahead to Prevent Future Problems").

Planning Ahead to Prevent Future Problems

1. Lead your students in a discussion of mistakes. Ask them what messages about mistakes they have received from adults. Ask the students what these messages led them to decide about themselves and about what they should do in the future when they make mistakes.

2. Ask your students how many of them would like to learn to see mistakes as wonderful opportunities to learn. Invite them to discuss why and how this is true.

3. Point out that class meetings offer an opportunity for students to have a whole roomful of consultants (worth thousands of dollars) who can brainstorm to find solutions for mistakes. Ask, "How many of you would feel like admitting you made a mistake if you knew you would receive blame, shame, and punishment?" Then ask, "How many of you would be willing to take responsibility for your mistakes if you knew you would have a whole roomful of consultants who want to help you?"

4. Teach students about the Three R's of Recovery from mistakes: (1) *Recognize* your mistake. (2) *Reconcile* by saying you're sorry. (3) *Resolve* the problem with the others involved. Explain that it's not effective for a person to work on number three until he has done the first two. A hostile atmosphere changes to an atmosphere of forgiveness and cooperation after the person takes responsibility for his mistake and apologizes. It can be effective to personalize this process by sharing an experience from your own life.

Inspirational Stories

Learning to Say "I'm Sorry"

A second grader named Mickey kicked another little boy. The teacher, Mrs. Heaton, was very upset with Mickey and wanted to teach him not to hurt other people. She took him outside the classroom door to admonish him. She said, "How would you like it if other people kicked you?"

In her attempt to teach him how it felt, she raised her voice more than she meant to. Mrs. Heaton felt terrible that she had reacted with so much anger. She believed in the principles of Positive Discipline and had been trying to implement them in her classrooms for years. She called an author of this book to ask, "What went wrong? How could I have done such a thing? What else could I do?"

First, Mrs. Heaton was assured that she is normal. Is there a parent or teacher on this planet who has never lost control and reacted in anger?

Second, Mrs. Heaton was commended for being aware that she had made a mistake. She was encouraged to pat herself on the back instead of beating herself up. Too many parents and teachers wouldn't have realized that they had made a mistake.

Third, her desire to improve her approach to this type of situation was applauded. She was encouraged to see this as a gift (or a wake-up call), motivating her to seek better methods of responding.

All teachers need to realize that it's human to get hooked into reacting instead of acting. Most adults truly mean well—they simply want to teach children to be more respectful. But when teachers react, they use disrespectful behavior in their attempts to teach respect. While reacting, they focus on making a child pay for what she has done. They aren't thinking about the long-range effects on the child.

Fortunately, no matter how many times a teacher reacts to misbehavior and forgets to use the principles of Positive Discipline, she can return to the principles and clean up the messes she made. Every time she makes a mistake, she can use it as a wonderful opportunity to learn.

When adults realize their mistakes with children and use the Three R's of Recovery, they will find that the kids are very forgiving. It took Mrs. Heaton more than a week to recover from her embarrassment and self-flagellation. Then she took Mickey aside and apologized. She said, "Mickey, I'm so sorry I yelled at you. I was so mad at you for kicking Joey, but I was just as disrespectful to you. That wasn't very smart of me, was it?"

Though Mickey just looked at her sheepishly, she had his attention. She continued, "It wasn't very nice of me either, was it?"

Mickey stuck out his lower lip and shook his head.

Mrs. Heaton asked, "Does it make you feel any better to hear me say I'm sorry?"

Mickey nodded.

Mrs. Heaton asked, "How do you think it would make Joey feel if you told him you were sorry?"

"Better," Mickey muttered.

"How would you feel about apologizing to Joey, and then the three of us could get together and work on ways to handle the problem you were having with Joey?" Mrs. Heaton suggested. "Or we could put it on the class meeting agenda and get the whole class to help. Which would you prefer?"

Mickey said, "Just us."

Mrs. Heaton asked, "How much time do you need to apologize to Joey and to ask him whether he would join us for a problem-solving session?"

Brightening, Mickey said, "I can do it today."

"Great," Mrs. Heaton said, "You let me know when you and Joey are ready, and we'll set a time."

Mrs. Heaton, Mickey, and Joey got together the next day and discussed each boy's perception of what had happened and what had caused it to happen. They discussed how they felt about it, what they had learned from the experience, and their ideas on solving the problem. Together they picked a solution to try for a week. The boys walked away from the meeting feeling very pleased with themselves and satisfied with the agreement they had made.

This is an excellent example of how a mistake provides numerous opportunities for learning. Mrs. Heaton was able to take responsibility for her mistake and apologize, providing a good role model for the students. She then helped Mickey feel good about apologizing for his mistake. Next she helped the boys practice listening to one another's perceptions of the experience. Finally, the boys practiced the important life skill of brainstorming for solutions and agreeing on one they would both like to try.

Patience Pays

A story from Therese Durston, second-grade teacher, St. Olivier School, Saskatchewan, Canada

It was the first week of school after Christmas. Things were going great. At 1:00 we went to the gym. When we got to the gym, I noticed that Alisha was not with us. I sent a student to find her and bring her to the gym. When we returned to the classroom, a student exclaimed that four of her lip glosses were missing. I realized that Alisha had the time to "borrow" them, so I looked in her bookbag and found them. I talked to her about them, and she insisted that someone put them in her bookbag. I let her go.

I desperately looked for my *Positive Discipline: A Teacher's A–Z Guide* book and realized I had left it at home. I gave it some time. (I remembered the importance of a cooling of time so we could both think more rationally.) Then I brought her to another room. We re-created the crime scene. We talked about people making mistakes. We also talked about good decisions and bad decisions. (We were studying that in the Lion's Quest unit.) I also told her that sometimes it's hard to tell and it's easier to show. I told her to show me exactly what happened. She went to the lip glosses on the desk and paused for a couple of minutes, and then she put them in her bookbag. I asked her what she was thinking when she paused. She said, "I was thinking if it was a good decision or a bad decision." We discussed what kind of decision she made. I asked her how she was feeling. She said, "Bad." We talked about making mistakes.

Then we replayed the scene. We discussed her feelings again. I asked her whether there was anything else to talk about. She said, "No, everything was fine." I told her that I loved her and that I was there if she needed to talk. We hugged and then returned to class.

The next day, there had been a few things broken in the class (sort of accidentally), and in a class meeting we discussed how people feel when their belongings are broken, borrowed without asking, or taken. The students shared their feelings. I noticed a pencil in Alisha's desk pocket that didn't belong to her. I just ignored it for the time. About thirty minutes later she gave me the pencil and told me that it didn't belong to her. I thanked her for it, and then I went to another room where I jumped for joy and celebrated Positive Discipline.

Problem Solving

(see also "Class Meetings")

Discussion

"You can't play with us," taunt A-Yueh and Mary Ann to their second-grade classmate Irene. Irene sticks out her tongue at A-Yueh and Mary Ann's retreating backs.

Mrs. Fernandez is giving her ninth graders a history lesson. Gilbert, Juan, and Diego are making annoying sounds at the back of the classroom, and the rest of the students laugh.

Mrs. Lavronne's high school English class is planning a field trip during a class meeting. The students are having difficulty coming up with a location that fits all the curriculum requirements and is also interesting to the students.

Life is full of problems that need solutions. Every day in schools across the country, opportunities abound for teaching students the art and skills of solving problems. Unfortunately, instead of using these wonderful opportunities, teachers and administrators usually step in to attempt to settle problems that students could solve

for themselves if they had the tools. (Refer to "Class Meetings" to learn about the importance of developing students' problem-solving skills and emotional intelligence so that they can become happy, self-reliant, successful adults.)

When teachers take the time to train students in problem solving and give them opportunities to exercise the skills, they become effective problem solvers. These students can then be actively involved in everything from helping classmates with special needs to preventing violence on school grounds. Furthermore, they will be well equipped for the future because they will know how to empathize, how to seek solutions that satisfy all parties, and how to treat people, places, and property with respect.

Suggestions

1. Embrace problems as opportunities to practice problem-solving skills.

2. Stop telling and start asking. Too often teachers tell students what happened, what caused it to happen, how they should feel about it, and what they should do about it. Students learn problem-solving skills when teachers ask such questions as, "What happened?" "What do you think caused that to happen?" "What were you trying to accomplish?" "How do you feel about what happened?" "What did you learn from this?" "How can you use what you learned in the future?" "What ideas do you have to solve the problem now?" The word *educa-*

tion comes from the Latin word *educare*, which means to draw forth. Asking draws forth. Telling stuffs in.

3. Have faith in students to be the wonderful problem solvers they can be when they have sufficient training and are allowed the opportunity to use their skills.

4. When students come to you with a problem, refer them to the Problem-Solving Wheel of Choice (see "Planning Ahead," item 8).

Planning Ahead to Prevent Future Problems

1. Promote the development of self-control. A major step in learning to solve problems is learning to control impulses (or learning to extend the time between having a feeling and taking action). The first tool to give your students for controlling impulsive reactions is positive time-out. This involves leaving the scene of the problem for a short period to regain emotional calm.

2. The second tool to give your students for controlling impulsive reactions is a set of self-calming techniques. These techniques can be selected to suit the student: When a classmate grabs the ball from ten-year-old Andy, he takes a deep breath and envisions a stop sign rather than snatching the ball back. Sixteen-year-old Xavier visualizes a cold waterfall splashing over his red-hot anger when Joe calls Xavier's mother names. Both boys experience the power of having an inner locus of control.

3. The third tool to give your students for controlling impulsive reactions is knowledge of how to use the four problem-solving suggestions. The first three, once learned, require no teacher involvement. Some teachers provide a problem-solving area in the classroom, with a chart displaying the suggestions. Other teachers have the suggestions written on four-by-five cards, so the students with the problem can take a card and find a quiet place where they can work together. The problem-solving suggestions are as follows:

A. Ignore it. It takes more courage to walk away than to stay and fight. Students can ignore the problem by doing something else (finding another game or activity) or by going somewhere else to cool down.

B. Talk it over respectfully. Each student tells the others how he feels and listens to how the others feel. Then each shares what he thinks he did to contribute to the problem and tells the others what he is willing to do differently himself.

C. Agree together on a solution. Students can work out a plan for sharing or taking turns and/or offer apologies.

D. Ask for help. If students can't work the problem out among themselves, they can put it on the class meeting agenda, so the whole class can help. Or they can talk it over with a parent, teacher, or friend.

4. The fourth tool to give your students for controlling impulsive reactions is the class meeting. Use of the class meeting agenda provides a built-in cooling-off period. Committing the problem to paper gives the student a chance to do something constructive with her anger or distress. Teachers are amazed to observe extremely upset students relax and return calmly to work after writing their problems on the agenda. This is the result of trusting the process of class meetings as well as the student's knowledge that she will be heard. In addition, use of the class meeting agenda shows the student that problems are best solved when tempers have cooled. It also teaches that what was a tremendous problem yesterday, or the day before, loses importance as emotions ebb.

5. Use role playing to facilitate one student's understanding of another student's perspective. A role play allows the students involved in a dispute to walk in one another's shoes and helps them develop empathy.

6. Teach alternatives to violent responses. When a class discusses what Amy might do if another student hits her, a typical suggestion is "She can hit him back." The teacher asks, "If Amy hits the other child back, what is likely to happen?" A student answers, "She might get hit again." This is the process by which students learn to examine their ideas critically.

7. Periodic problem-solving sessions serve as prevention. If you regularly use class

meetings to solve small problems, they will be less likely to snowball into major crises.

8. The Problem-Solving Wheel of Choice (on the following page) is a tool that many teachers have found to be useful. This chart includes many of the ideas stated already. Some teachers post it in their classrooms, and some schools have painted it on the playground surface for easy referral. It is important to spend time teaching the parts of the wheel to your students. This can be done through role play and discussion.

Class Meeting Solutions

A story from Cheryl Eliason, fifth-grade teacher, Mary Immaculate, Farmers Branch, Texas

Each year principal Mike Brock and I hold a Positive Discipline workshop at our school. Mike presents the theory and framework of class meetings, and I talk about the practical application. A special feature of the workshop is a real, live, unrehearsed class meeting by my fifth-grade homeroom. I also like to tell the workshop participants some of my favorite class meeting stories.

One of these involves a complaint from my students that I wasn't allowing them enough time at the lockers to gather all the books and supplies they needed. After the problem was read from the agenda by that day's student secretary, I asked the class, "How many of you are experiencing this difficulty?" Some three-

PROBLEM-SOLVING WHEEL OF CHOICE

Try at least two of these ideas
when you have a problem.

After you have tried at least two solutions
(or in an emergency), ask an adult to help.

Adapted from Susan Varin's Problem-Solving Wheel

fourths of the students raised their hands. I hadn't had any idea that this was a problem for them.

I thanked the class for their response and then opened the subject up for discussion. After reminding the students that their challenge was to come up with a reasonable, respectful solution, I initiated a brainstorming session. The students generated some helpful ideas, which were then held up for a vote.

The solution was to set a certain amount of time for students to collect their materials, using a stopwatch to make sure they stayed within this limit. After discussing how long they needed, the students chose two minutes. This solution respected both my need to ensure that minimal time was spent at the lockers and the students' need to gather all of their materials without undue time pressure.

Inspirational Story

Mrs. Clutter's first-grade class was mostly made up of the students who had exhibited behavior problems in last year's kindergarten classes. From the beginning of the school year, Mrs. Clutter had been teaching them problem-solving skills. The students were learning to help each other and to take advantage of the class meeting agenda when they had problems. They even began to use the language of class meetings as they talked about finding "win–win solutions."

In time behavior problems all but disappeared in Mrs. Clutter's classroom. Even her most challenging little boy, who struggled with an explosive temper, was improving, thanks to his classmates' help. However, Mrs. Clutter was wondering whether the students' problem-solving skills would transfer to areas outside her classroom walls.

She soon had her answer in the form of an experience the school counselor, Mrs. Pekulda, shared with her. Mrs. Pekulda was monitoring the cafeteria at lunchtime when she noticed a group of Mrs. Clutter's first-grade boys flicking kernels of corn across the table at each other. Because Mrs. Pekulda knew the language of the class meeting process, she said to the boys, "It looks like we have a problem here, because food fights are not allowed in the cafeteria. What are your suggestions for solving this problem?" The boys huddled together and conferred for about three minutes. They then told the counselor that their solution was to put all the corn trays at the end of the table where no one was sitting, so no one would be tempted to cause this problem again.

Positive Time-Out

Discussion

As adults, when we're upset, we often lose our perspective, our objectivity, and our better judgment. We sometimes say and do things we later regret. In other words, we usually misbehave, just as children do.

What causes adults to get upset? Just like children, adults can become discouraged. They may be hurt or feel disappointed. They generally get upset when they're criticized harshly or insulted. They may become angry about some perceived injustice or wrongdoing, or they may simply feel hopeless and powerless about a certain situation.

Whatever the reason, adults don't need more discouragement. Punishment or lectures will make them feel even worse. Adults need time to cool off; only then can they start to feel better (encouraged) again.

Some people take a time-out by walking around the block, taking a nap, reading a book, or meditating. Some just go about their business until the upset feeling passes. And some feed their inner turmoil by dwelling on the problem and filling themselves with anger and hatred. (These people would do well to remember an anonymous adage: "Anger does more damage to the vessel in which it is stored than to the object on which it is poured.")

Are students any different from adults in how they deal with strong emotions? When a student is upset, he doesn't need punishment, but he may well need a positive time-out to cool off. The concept of positive time-out doesn't include blame, shame, pain, or any form of punishment. Its purpose is to help students do better, not to make them feel worse.

A cooling-off period may be all that a student needs. But more often it's helpful to follow up with some kind of problem-solving process. Involve your students in creating a positive time-out plan that addresses the purpose of time-outs, how and where they may spend this time, and ways they may wish to resolve the issues that lead students to need time-outs.

The format is reversed for this subject, because planning ahead is essential to establishing the positive time-out process in your classroom.

Planning Ahead to Prevent Future Problems

1. Teach students about what happens when people get upset. Explain that all human beings get upset from time to time. Share times when you have taken a positive time-out or when you may in the future.

2. Have a general discussion. Present this thought to your students: "Where did we ever get the crazy idea that to make children do better, first we have to make them feel worse?" Ask the students how they feel after being punished. Does it make them feel better? Does it make them want to do better? If so, what is the cost to their self-esteem and self-confidence?

3. Creating a positive time-out area can be a fun activity that teaches students how to brainstorm. Have students get into groups of six, and give each group butcher paper

and a marking pen. Allow them five minutes to brainstorm about the ideal time-out area. Let them know that no idea is too outrageous (or too practical) during brainstorming and that they should write down every idea that's mentioned without analyzing or criticizing it. (Explain that the reason for giving them only five minutes is to elicit enthusiasm.) Afterward, have each group read its suggestions, and analyze the ideas to form a plan. Ask each group to come up with a design for a positive time-out area that would be practical, respectful to everyone in the classroom, and helpful to those who need it. Feel free to offer your ideas. Many time-out areas include books, stuffed animals (even for high school students), and a small portable cassette player for listening to soothing music.

4. After students have learned about listening skills, they can make a listening buddy part of the positive time-out plan. This means a student can choose a friend who will go to the time-out place with her and listen while she talks about what's upsetting her. Sharing a problem while someone just listens can be very healing.

5. Ask students to include guidelines for the use of the cooling-off area in their positive time-out plan. Ask them to consider such common objections of teachers as, "What if students misbehave just so they can go listen to music?" or "What if students stay in time-out for hours because they would rather play with toys or sleep in the beanbag chair than do assignments or attend to lessons?" Proposed guidelines should address these concerns. Students need to see positive time-out as a means for them to regain composure, not as a substitute for participating in classwork.

6. Being outdoors can be a place for everyone to calm themselves. If your whole class is in need of a positive time-out, consider taking them for a quiet walk around the campus. After only five minutes, you and your students may be ready to focus yourselves again.

Suggestions

1. Don't use time-out as a form of punishment; there should be no blame, shame, or pain attached to taking a time-out. Don't admonish students to think about what they did or ask them to write out a hundred "I will not" vows.

2. When a student is upset or misbehaving, ask in a friendly voice, "Do you think a time-out would help you right now?" When students understand that the purpose of positive time-out is to help them feel better, they usually find it worth-

while. The attitude of the adult affects whether the student sees it as hurtful or helpful. "You go to time-out right now!" is a thinly veiled punishment to anyone's ears. Remind the student that you have faith that he will do better as soon as he feels better.

3. Don't worry about positive time-out becoming a reward for misbehavior. When students understand that the purpose of this method is to encourage them so they can improve their behavior, they rarely misuse it. If they do, try the next suggestion.

4. If students don't want to use time-out, or if they misuse it, put the problem on the class meeting agenda and invite them to discuss what isn't working and why. Let them look for solutions to the problem. Both students and teachers may need some time to get used to the idea that a method of dealing with misbehavior or strong emotions can be helpful instead of punitive. Discussing problems and finding solutions enhances the process.

5. Don't think of time-out as your only tool when a student is upset or misbehaving. This book is loaded with possibilities. Positive time-out is just one method of encouraging a student and is most effective when he's asked, "Do you think a positive time-out would be helpful for you?" Sometimes you may want to offer a limited choice in which time-out is one option. Ask the student, "Which do you think would be most helpful to you: to take some time to cool off or to put this problem on the class meeting agenda?"

6. Use the positive time-out yourself when you need it. At times you may want to tell students, "I'm too upset to deal with this problem right now. I need a positive time-out to cool off."

Inspirational Story

A story from one of the authors

During an in-service workshop, a teacher presented a concern about a student who wouldn't take a time-out even after she had set it up to be an encouraging experience. I had what I thought was a wonderful, original idea. I said, "Why don't you see whether it would help if he took a buddy into time-out with him?" Another teacher said, "I've been doing that for years, and it's very effective." (So much for my original idea.) This teacher went on to share the story of a boy in her class. Jeff had a difficult time with self-control, she explained, and she had thought time-out would help him calm down and learn to govern his impulses.

She said, "He used to refuse to go to time-out until I told him he could choose a buddy to go with him. All the kids in the classroom raised their hands, hoping to be chosen. He chose one of them, and they went into time-out for about five minutes and talked quietly. Then they both went back to their schoolwork.

"Jeff used to be friendless, but he made friends by choosing kids to go to time-out with him. Now they are nicer to Jeff all day. Jeff makes his face twitch in a certain way when he's about to lose control. The kids watch for him to show signs of losing control and start raising their hands to be chosen even before I invite him to try time-out for a while."

Special Time

Discussion

When teachers hear that they need to spend special time with their students, they may feel overwhelmed and discouraged. They think it's impossible to spend special time every day with each of thirty individuals. But these moments of sharing don't have to last a certain number of minutes to be "special," and they can be incorporated into the daily routine.

Spending special time with a student is often more effective in changing misbehavior than dealing directly with the behavior because it can help a child feel a sense of belonging and significance and thus remove the need to misbehave.

Suggestions

1. Take a look at your definition of special time. You may be discouraging yourself with an unrealistic idea of how much time you have to spend or how intense the interaction must be.

2. Special time can be as simple as addressing each student by name when you say hello in the morning or good-bye at the end of the day. Some teachers take the time to shake the hand of each student as he or she comes through the door.

3. You might take a few minutes with a student to inquire about his interests, activities, and family. This attention and concern makes a student feel that he belongs and is special. It is also effective to share some special interests or activities that you enjoy.

4. During silent reading time, on a rotating basis, invite a student to sit with you at your desk. This would be a good time for a quiet chat in which you ask questions about the student's interests, activities, and family.

5. Invite students to share their personal news on a bulletin board. At a certain time each day, read the items from that board to the class.

6. A teacher's taking the time to attend extracurricular activities can have a dramatic effect on students.

Planning Ahead to Prevent Future Problems

1. At a teacher in-service program, share ideas about special time and brainstorm to find other ways of encouraging students.

2. When a student feels hurt because of a misunderstanding or difficulty with you, focus on rebuilding your relationship with her rather than attending only to her behavior. You may need to schedule special times for friendly discussions or simply shooting hoops.

3. Think of the class meeting as a period when you are devoting special time to all of the students in your class—and as a period when they are giving special time to each other.

Inspirational Story

A story from Robert Rasmussen, eleventh- and twelfth-grade teacher, Cottonwood High School, Salt Lake City, Utah

I decided to try the special time concept with my students. To see whether it made any difference, I planned to use it in two classes, not use it in two classes, and give special time to only half of the students in a fifth class.

Because I have so many students, it took half the semester to meet with each

student in two and a half classes. I accomplished this by having students sit next to me, one at a time, during seat work time. I spent only two or three minutes with each student, asking him or her to share with me special interests, goals, and needs for special help he or she might have.

I noticed a distinct difference between the classes in which students received special time and the classes in which students did not. There was an atmosphere of respect and cooperation in classes where students had spent time talking with me individually. An interesting thing happened in the class where I did individual interviews with only half of the students: Every student who hadn't received special time asked me, "When do I get my interview?" This was enough to convince me of the value of spending time with every one of my students, even if it takes all semester.

Carl and Mrs. VanDermick

Carl was a new member of Mrs. Van-Dermick's algebra class. Since starting at this school, he had acquired a reputation for being belligerent and rude. He would saunter down the hallways, come to class late, and interrupt others repeatedly. He believed that all his teachers disliked him, and he was determined to show that he didn't care.

Mrs. VanDermick tried several methods of encouragement to increase Carl's sense of belonging in the classroom. She addressed him directly by name, showed interest in his family, and asked him how things were going with his basketball team. Carl rebuffed all her attempts at making contact.

Mrs. VanDermick was determined to connect with Carl and to show him that she considered him likable. She was an avid fan of all the school's organized sports and liked to attend games and competitions to show support for her students. She realized that because of her busy schedule, she hadn't attended any of the basketball games this season. She decided to make a special effort to get to the next few games.

Carl was aware that Mrs. VanDermick was at his next game, but he shrugged her off when she tried to talk about it the following day. After another game, Mrs. VanDermick congratulated Carl on a particular defensive move he had made. Carl was surprised at how he felt when she mentioned this, and he automatically said, "Thanks."

Mrs. VanDermick smiled inside as she felt this shift in her relationship with Carl. She had confidence that this was the first step of many toward Carl seeing himself as an important person who could contribute in positive ways to the school.

Class Meetings

(see also "Class Meetings, Disruptions," and "Class Meetings, Refusal to Participate")

Discussion

Many teachers have found one of the most efficient and effective ways of making a difference is through the use of Positive Discipline class meetings. This process gives students the tools they need to develop to their fullest potential and to apply the academic knowledge they gain in school. As you are about to see, the skills honed in class meetings are vital to surviving and thriving in the adult world.

In June 1991, the U.S. Department of Labor issued a federal report that had been commissioned by President George H. Bush. It was called the *Secretary's Commission on Achieving Necessary Skills* [SCANS for short] *Report for America 2000*. The report was based on discussions and meetings with business owners, public employers, union members and leaders, and workers and supervisors in plants and stores.

The SCANS report listed the following competencies, skills, and personal qualities as vital to our children's future and as things to be taught and encouraged in America's classrooms.[8] An asterisk appears by each one that is accomplished or enhanced through the Positive Discipline class meeting process.

Five Competencies

- *Resources: identifies, organizes, plans, and allocates resources
- *Interpersonal: works with others
- *Information: acquires and uses information
- *Systems: understands complex inter-relationships
- Technology: works with a variety of technologies

Three-Part Foundation of Skills and Personal Qualities

- *Basic skills: *reads, *writes, *performs arithmetic and mathematical operations (such as budgeting when planning a project, party, or field trip in a class meeting), *listens, and *speaks coherently
- *Thinking skills: *thinks creatively, *makes decisions, *solves problems, *visualizes, *knows how to learn, and *reasons
- *Personal qualities: *displays responsibility, *self-esteem, *sociability (social interest), *self-management, *integrity, and *honesty

In addition to the implications of the SCANS report, Dr. Daniel Goleman of the New York Times News Service reported in September 1995 on what is being labeled emotional intelligence, or EQ.[9] *EQ* is defined as skills in empathy, cooperation, persuasion, consensus building, reading one's own feelings, controlling one's own impulses and anger, calming oneself down, and maintaining resolve and hope in the face of setbacks. Research has discovered EQ to be vastly important to success in life.

Goleman's story says that "emotional intelligence appears to be in startling decline among American children. . . . This across-the-board drop in children's emotional intelligence is in many ways a more troubling social trend than a dip in the Scholastic Aptitude Test taken for college admission. Deficits in emotional intelligence are linked with a range of social perils," such as dropping out of school, fighting, delinquency, drug use, teen pregnancy, and eating disorders. Goleman also reports that "the rate of decline [in EQ] was the same for all, privileged and impoverished alike."

Goleman goes on to state, "Children in the courses [addressing EQ skills] show marked improvements in the ability to control their impulses, show empathy,

---

8. U.S. Department of Labor, *Secretary's Commission on Achieving Necessary Skills Report for America 2000* (Washington, D.C.: U.S. Government Printing Office, 1991).

9. *Corpus Christi Caller Times*, September 11, 1995.

cooperate with others, manage anger and anxiety, focus on a task, pursue goals, and resolve conflicts. Delinquency, fights and drug use drop. And there is an added bonus: achievement test scores rise too."

Positive Discipline class meetings address all of the emotional intelligence skills mentioned earlier. Teachers who use class meetings to teach the SCANS requirements and EQ skills report fewer discipline problems and reduced referrals to the principal's office. They have more energy and time for the actual work of teaching. However, their greatest reward is knowing they have helped equip their students with the skills and attitudes they need for success in life.

Suggestions

1. As it would be impossible to explain the entire process of class meetings in this space, the reader may want to refer to four sources for more information: chapter 7 of *Positive Discipline*,[10] *Positive Discipline in the Classroom*,[11] and the training and activity manual for *Positive Discipline in the Classroom Facilitator's Guide*.[12]

2. Understand that life skills are as important as academic skills and that the two must go hand in hand if the student is

going to be effective as an adult in the working world.

3. Hold daily class meetings (fifteen to thirty minutes in length), so students can learn and retain the skills involved. (Junior high and high school students can retain the process when class meetings are held weekly, although they will benefit more if meetings are held more often.)

4. Don't allow students to use any form of punishment or blame or to inflict shame or pain on one another. If this happens, stop the class meeting and reteach the relevant skills. Another possible course is to ask redirecting questions, such as "How many of you think we are finding solutions that help and encourage others?" "How many of you think we are making suggestions that are hurtful and discouraging?" "Are we here to help or to hurt each other?" Often these questions are all it takes to redirect students' and sometimes the teacher's thinking from trying to place blame to trying to find solutions.

5. Be familiar with six reasons why class meetings fail:

    A. Not sitting in a circle

    B. Not holding them regularly (three to five times a week for elementary school

---

10. Jane Nelsen, *Positive Discipline* (New York: Ballantine, 1998).

11. Jane Nelsen, Lynn Lott, and H. Stephen Glenn, *Positive Discipline in the Classroom,* third edition (Roseville, CA: Prima Publishing, 2000).

12. Available from Empowering People Books, Tapes, and Videos, (800) 456-7770.

and once a week or once every two weeks in middle and high school)

    C. Not trusting the process and consequently not allowing time for students to learn skills for effective meetings

    D. Not understanding that even so-called tattletale problems provide opportunities to practice the class meeting process or not understanding that solving similar problems over and over provides opportunities for practice

    E. Not having faith in students' abilities; talking down to them (patronizing)

    F. Not going around the circle and allowing every student a chance to speak or pass

Planning Ahead to Prevent Future Problems

1. Take time to teach the perceptions and skills necessary for effective class meetings. The Eight Building Blocks for effective class meetings, from *Positive Discipline in the Classroom,* are (1) forming a circle, (2) giving compliments and appreciations, (3) creating an agenda, (4) developing communication skills, (5) learning about separate realities, (6) role playing and brainstorming, (7) recognizing the four reasons people do what they do, and (8) finding nonpunitive solutions. Teachers all over the country have confirmed that when they take the time to teach the skills, their students experience fewer difficulties in learning the process of class meetings.

2. Many parents have questions and even fears about class meetings. At the beginning of the school year, send a letter to your students' parents explaining the new program, "Positive Discipline in the Classroom, featuring Class Meetings," that you will be implementing in your classroom or throughout the school. List the lifelong and academic benefits of the program. (Better yet, obtain a summary of the SCANS report by going to the Web site http://wdr.doleta.gov/SCANS, and send the summary home with your letter stating that this program will be following the SCANS guidelines. For more information on the importance of emotional intelligence, contact Yale University's Collaborative for the Advancement of Social and Emotional Learning.) You may also want to invite parents to visit your classroom to observe a meeting or the activities that teach the social skills. Your enthusiasm about class meetings will be contagious to parents, students, and colleagues.

3. At a PTA meeting, have the students demonstrate either the activities that teach class meeting skills or an actual class meeting.

Inspirational Stories about the Power of Class Meetings

Better Late Than Never

Dixie Binford teaches middle school. Her students are from a barrio in south Texas.

Some students regularly bring knives and guns to school, and teen pregnancy rates are high. Before using class meetings, Ms. Binford had tried many techniques. She sometimes wanted to quit teaching because nothing she did worked. When she heard about class meetings, she was already tired and discouraged, and she decided that she had nothing to lose by trying out this latest idea. It was late January, the year partly over, when Ms. Binford began class meetings with her seventh graders. Within a few months, fights no longer took place in her classroom, more time was spent teaching content instead of putting out fires, and her relationship with her students had improved (she realized that she was no longer afraid of them). By the end of the year, Ms. Binford was bubbling with energy and looked forward to starting regular meetings when the next school year began.

Behavior Turnaround

A story from Kim Clutter, first-grade teacher, John C. French Elementary School, Cuero, Texas

During October one year, I was trained in the use of Positive Discipline in the classroom. Though excited, I was also a little nervous about getting started. One little girl in my room had spent the majority of her previous (kindergarten) year in the principal's office. She was extremely disruptive and displayed behaviors more typical of a three-year-old. I had been concerned upon learning she would be in my class but,

being a good disciplinarian, I had felt certain I could handle her. This child had very low self-esteem and hated school and herself—and just about everything and everyone. Although she believed that she was stupid, she was quite intelligent. She had been diagnosed with ADHD and put on medication but still had many problems.

I began using class meetings seriously in January of that year. It was the only way I could have made it through the year with this particular child. First of all, during the training, I role-played a problem with this little girl, playing her part. That gave me a whole new perspective for working with her.

Next, I talked to my class about being helpers. I explained to them that many things were especially difficult for this person and she needed help from all of us. They truly became teachers. They were so supportive and patient. We put her in the middle of the circle during one of our early class meetings and gave encouragements. She beamed for the rest of the year about that. The students enjoyed the class meetings and really learned to help this child, as well as each other, through the meetings.

At the end of every year, I have my students fill out a form that they leave in their desks for the next year's students. The form tells the next group what my class is like, what they enjoyed about it, and what they didn't enjoy. I didn't read these until the beginning of the next year. When I got to this little girl's form, I cried. She said that she liked my class because the people cared about her. That was the one thing I had wanted her to get during first grade.

The CD Solution

A story from Loretta Sedran, French teacher for grades 1 through 8, Holy Jubilee Catholic School, Toronto, Ontario, Canada

My seventh-grade class was a challenging bunch, from academic difficulties to behavior issues. The students informed me of a problem they were having in their regular classroom. Each classroom was given a CD player at the beginning of the year. During the first five weeks, the CD player was broken during a lunch hour. The teacher was angry, and the principal was twice as angry. No one owned up to having broken the CD player, and things were quiet—until there was to be a dance. At this time the principal decided that this class would not be allowed to go to the dance because of the CD player.

When the students brought this up with me, I suggested we hold a class meeting and brainstorm some solutions to the problem. As we went around the circle, we recorded all the suggestions and then voted on the one the class wanted to try. They decided that they would put in $5 for the dance, $3 of which would go toward the dance ticket and $2 to the CD fund. At first those students that had nothing to do with it thought, "Why do I have to pay for something I wasn't involved in?" We talked about this, and the majority voted for this option. They figured that it was worth

being able to go to the dance even if they had to pay the extra $2.

The next thing they did is that they wanted the student who came up with the idea to inform the principal and the teacher of their decision. We invited them to the meeting, and the student explained the solution. All was fine with everyone. A new CD player was purchased, and the students went to the dance. What was also interesting was that when the class got the new CD player, they decided that it would not be used unless a teacher was present in the room.

A Cool Concept

A story from Stephanie Corvese, second-grade teacher, St. Catherine of Sienna, Woodbridge (Toronto), Ontario, Canada

Just the other day, a student of mine from last year walked by my classroom and started talking to me. He popped into my classroom and commented on how I'd changed some things around in the class. I asked him what the best thing about being in my class was, and he said with the biggest smile, "Class meetings. Yeah—they were cool."

Kudos for Compliments

A story from Leanne Stallone, second-grade teacher, St. Catherine of Sienna, Woodbridge (Toronto), Ontario, Canada

Compliments worked very well in our class meetings. The children loved them, and they loved to time themselves to see how long the group would take. At the beginning compliments took them seven to ten minutes. Near the end of the year it was two to three minutes. One little boy liked compliments so much that one day he jumped in the middle of the circle and told the kids and me that we had to give him compliments today. So that day every student gave that little boy a compliment. He had a smile on his face for a very long time, and it boosted his confidence greatly. So from then on the students took turns sitting in the middle of the circle and getting compliments.

Conferences

Discussion

Too often conferences are intimidating. Parents and teachers are both afraid of being blamed and criticized if the student isn't doing well. The students who aren't doing well feel discouraged. And the students who are doing well feel intense pressure to maintain a high academic standard as proof of their worth.

Expand the idea of what conferences can be. Remember that an atmosphere of mutual respect is essential for a successful conference. Consider moving beyond the tradition of having only the parent and teacher discussing the student. Even when the intention is to help, it is disrespectful to talk about students, set goals for them, and make decisions about them when they aren't present and involved. It is more respectful and beneficial to include the student in the circle of discussion. The purpose of parent–teacher–student conferences is to encourage and empower the student, the parents, and the teacher as a team with the same goals.

Suggestions

1. Appreciate both the student and parent(s) for participating in the conference. Take some time to share the purpose and the benefits of working as a team.

2. First discuss what the student is doing well. Allow everyone to take a turn suggesting one of her strengths. Invite the student to begin.

3. Next discuss what needs improvement. Again, ask the student to speak first. Students know where they need to improve and feel safer when they are the ones to mention these areas.

4. Brainstorm ideas to enhance what is going well.

5. Brainstorm ideas to encourage improvement.

6. Choose one of the resulting ideas, on which all can agree, for enhancing what is going well, and choose one idea, on which all agree, for encouraging improvement. Don't forget to ask the student which of

the ideas he or she feels will be the most helpful.

7. Remember to use this book as a reference either before the meeting or during it to enhance the brainstorming and understanding of a particular concern or problem.

Planning Ahead to Prevent Future Problems

1. Set the tone in advance. Tell the student and her parents, "We can work together to help and encourage each other."

2. Give each parent and student a form to fill out in advance:

Parent–Teacher–Student Conference Preparation Form

Things that are going well: _____

_____

Things that need improvement: _____

_____

Ideas to enhance what is going well:

_____

Ideas that will encourage improvement:

_____

3. Be sure the student truly agrees to the chosen suggestion and isn't just saying okay to get you off her back.

Inspirational Story

The book *Soar with Your Strengths*[13] begins with a delightful parable about a duck, a fish, an eagle, an owl, a squirrel, and a rabbit who attend a school with a curriculum that includes running, swimming, tree climbing, jumping, and flying. Of course all of the animals had strength in at least one of these areas, but they are doomed to failure in other areas. It hits close to home to read about the punishment and discouragement these animals encounter when parents and school personnel insist they must do well in every area to "graduate" and become well-rounded animals.

A major point of the book is that "excellence can be achieved only by focusing on strengths and managing weaknesses, not through the elimination of weakness."[14]

Teach students to manage their weaknesses and soar with their strengths. Students learn mediocrity when their teachers insist they try to earn all A's. Sometimes teachers even penalize students by taking away the time they spend on their best subjects (where they feel encouraged) until they do better in their weak areas (where they feel discouraged). Instead, teachers should coach students to spend enough time on their weak areas to maintain progress and most of their time building on their strengths.

---

13. Donald O. Clifton and Paula Nelson, *Soar with Your Strengths* (New York: Dell, 1992).
14. Ibid., 11.

PART 2

Positive Discipline Solutions

Abuse

Discussion

According to the congressionally funded 1991 National Incidence and Prevalence of Child Abuse and Neglect Study, 22.6 per 1,000 children in the United States are victims of abuse. This number is based on cases actually reported, so the real number is probably even higher. It is unlikely that a teacher will never come into contact with a student experiencing abuse

Many abused children's best chance of receiving help and intervention is through the efforts of a teacher. The approachable teacher who creates an environment of trust is a potential confidant for students.

Most states bind teachers by law to report suspicions of abuse. As frightening as this issue is, think of how the support and actions of an alert teacher can change lives.

Clear definitions are important. *Abuse* occurs when a person responsible for a child's welfare causes, allows, or creates physical injury to the child that may lead to impairment of physical or emotional health, loss or impairment of any bodily function, disfigurement, or death. Included are excessive corporal punishment, torture, and any sexual offense. *Neglect* occurs when a person responsible for a child's welfare abandons the child or fails to provide the proper or necessary support, education, medical care, or other basic care. Most states define a child as any person under eighteen years of age.

The other side of abuse is the ever-present fear of accusations against a teacher. It is important to be aware of this and to act accordingly.

Suggestions

For Children's Safety
1. Make it clear that a child is welcome to approach the teacher with a personal concern. Explain that help and support are available and that abuse must be reported.

2. Learn about child protective laws in your community, and have a clear plan of how to proceed in the event of a disclosure or if you suspect abuse.

3. Learn to identify signs of abuse.

4. Always make a written notation of any injury you see on a child.

5. Keep dated documentation of any unusual behaviors or conversations that arouse your concern.

For Adults' Safety
1. Try to avoid being alone with a child, especially in closed or isolated places.

2. When working with young children, if there is a need to change their clothing, first ask whether they need assistance or can handle it by themselves. If they need help, make sure two adults are present.

3. Document all injuries that a child has upon arrival at school. (Regular documentation will protect teachers against parents who might falsely claim that an injury occurred at school.)

4. You may be a hugger, but to be respectful, first ask whether they would like a handshake, a high-five, or a hug. A child may not want to be touched.

5. Maintain confidentiality. Do not discuss your students outside the professional setting.

6. Avoid mixed messages by being clear with your students about the nature of your relationship with them. If you are uncomfortable about a student who may be approaching you in an inappropriate way, share this information with your supervisor or school counselor, and ask his or her advice.

Planning Ahead to Prevent Future Problems

1. Create an environment where children feel free to talk openly.

2. Educate children about abuse and the steps they can take to protect themselves and others.

3. Children need to feel that they have power. You can empower them by facilitating matter-of-fact discussions that present

them with options to exercise on their own behalf.

4. When children feel helpless and victimized, they usually can't see a way out of the situation. The knowledge that an adult is available to listen and provide support and assistance is truly a lifeline.

5. Adults can foster a safe environment by demonstrating respect for others and themselves. It's important to teach children that self-respect includes making sure their own needs are met.

6. For very young children, provide dollhouses with adult and child figures. When children are playing, stay alert to the situations being acted out, especially by any child whose behavior is disturbing.

7. Build a library of children's books that address various kinds of abuse; read and discuss them at story time. For older children, include literature that addresses these topics in your reading plan. Such stories help children understand that they are not bad or at fault in their own situations and may open the door to questions or disclosures.

Inspirational Story

Five-year-old Suzy was attending kindergarten. She had trouble playing with the other children. She often singled out another child, Diane, as a playmate. During this "play," Suzy frequently hurt Diane physically or hurt Diane's feelings. Each time, Suzy's behavior was addressed through the use of positive time-outs (see "Positive Time-Out") or problem-solving or role-playing sessions on how to play cooperatively.

Yet, over a period of weeks, the situation worsened to the point where none of the children wanted to play with Suzy because she always hurt them. Suzy's teacher, Lauren, decided to bring up the problem at a class meeting. First Lauren talked with Suzy and asked how she felt when the children didn't want to play with her. Suzy felt very sad. She was very willing to have this problem brought to a class meeting.

At the meeting, Lauren explained that Suzy was feeling left out and needed some friends to play with. Lauren said that Suzy wanted to work on learning how to play without hurting others and asked which children were willing to be her friend. Several children volunteered, and for the next two weeks the children included Suzy actively in their play.

In spite of these efforts, which included lots of support and feedback, the hurting continued and, in fact, escalated. In addition, Lauren noticed that sometimes Suzy would get a dazed look in her eyes, as though she were not present at all. Lauren carefully recorded what was taking place.

Suzy's behavior deteriorated further, and it was about this time that Suzy was found with Diane, whose pants were pulled down. Diane said that Suzy had threatened that she wouldn't be Diane's friend if she didn't pull her pants down. Equipped with her previous documentation and concerns as well as the implications of this new behavior, Lauren reported the potential problem to the child protective services in her area. Eventually the likelihood of sexual abuse was identified, and Suzy was put in a special program that included counseling and active therapy.

Suzy was lucky that Lauren recognized her behavior as more than misbehavior. Without Lauren's intervention, Suzy was unlikely to have received relief from her situation.

Arguments

Discussion

Whether students quarrel among themselves or bicker with a teacher, arguments have three basic causes: (1) a need to conceal feelings of not belonging (a defense mechanism), (2) a lack of communication skills, and (3) a lack of problem-solving skills. The supposed issue of the argument isn't as important as the opportunity to help students feel that they belong and to teach them ways to communicate and solve problems.

Suggestions

1. Invite the students to take a positive time-out. Point out the need to cool off in order to discuss an issue respectfully.

2. Facilitate a discussion among the students involved. Guide them in using effective communication tools, such as expressing their feelings and wants in words and brainstorming for solutions on the spot.

3. If the students are unable to settle the argument by themselves, invite them to put the problem on the class meeting agenda.

4. If the argument is with you:

A. Listen carefully, and reflect the student's statements and feelings back to her, so that you both understand what's troubling her.

B. If you are too upset to discuss the matter respectfully right away, share your feelings. Tell the student you need to take some time out to cool off and feel better. "I'm feeling angry and overwhelmed right now. I want to be able to deal with this respectfully, so I'll meet with you after school."

C. Tell the student you would like to put the matter on the class meeting agenda so you can both get help from the whole group.

D. To avoid a power struggle or retaliation, allow the student to have the last word.

Planning Ahead to Prevent Future Problems

1. At the beginning of the year, put two posters up in your classroom, one saying, "We're here to help, not hurt!" and the other saying, "Look for solutions, not blame." Explain to your students that you will all be working as a team to live those attitudes in your classroom.

2. Have regular class meetings, so that all students can experience a sense of belonging and practice their communication and problem-solving skills.

3. During a class meeting, have a discussion about arguing—why people argue, how people argue, what are people thinking and feeling during an argument, and how they may respond. Common responses to highlight and practice with the students are to attack, defend, or withdraw. Then have students practice more respectful and healthier responses, such as using I-messages.

4. Teach students about the four mistaken goals of misbehavior (refer to "Mistaken Goals [Hat Messages]" in Part 1). Brainstorm with them about productive ways to get attention, positive ways to use power, how to deal with hurt feelings, and how to get help when they feel like giving up.

Inspirational Story

Tom and Marco got into an argument over the use of the basketball at morning recess. Before the afternoon recess, Mr. O'Leary offered to help the boys figure out what had gone wrong that morning. He allowed each child to state the problem in a sentence or two. Tom said, "I got the basketball first, and I want to use it." Marco said, "The fourth graders are playing against the fifth graders, and we need the ball for our game."

Mr. O'Leary then asked each boy to practice reflective listening by restating what the other had said. Marco said, "Tom wants to keep the ball because he got it first." The teacher checked that Tom agreed with this perception: "Tom, do you want to keep the ball because you got it first?" Tom nodded.

Next Tom repeated Marco's reasons for wanting the ball. (Considering the other's point of view is part of clear communication as well as the first step toward a peaceful solution.) Marco and Tom proceeded to work out a plan for sharing the ball that involved Tom joining in the proposed fourth- and fifth-grade game. Cooperation replaced arguments.

Class Meeting Solution

Carl and Jaime had argued over a pen, each boy saying it was his own. During a class meeting, each boy was given the opportunity to tell his side of the story (each claimed his mother had bought it for him), and then each had a chance to come up with a solution.

When neither boy could think of a fair solution, the problem was turned over to the class for help. The class struggled to find a solution that both parties would consider fair. The problem stayed on the agenda for several meetings while students discussed it and brainstormed for solutions. During this time, the class decided to put the pen away and to allow Jaime and Carl each to borrow a pen from the teacher. (The teacher agreed to this idea.)

On the third day, as the students again began to discuss the problem, Carl said he had a confession to make. He owned up to taking Jaime's pen and tearfully apologized for lying and stealing. Carl told the other students that the way they had focused on looking for solutions without blaming him or Jaime helped give him the courage to speak out.

Assignments, Not Turned In

(see also "Homework, Nontraditional"; "Homework, Traditional"; and "Failing")

Discussion

Whether they teach first graders or high schoolers, teachers struggle each year with students who dawdle over—or just don't do—their in-class assignments or homework. Educators variously hope that rewards, incentive plans, grades, or punishments will promote the completion of assignments and homework. However, the research clearly indicates that these extrinsic motivators don't work in the long term.[15] To make a real difference, teachers need to understand that they cannot control students but they *can* influence how students motivate themselves.

Teachers should also be aware of the reasons students choose not to turn in their class assignments or homework. Some do it for the attention (even if negative); others do it because they see their refusal to do assignments as way of being in control in an environment that gives them few choices. Some students refuse as a way of getting back at the teacher or their parents. Others are afraid of making a mistake or believe they are incapable of completing the task, so they just don't try. (Refer to "Mistaken Goals [Hat Messages].")

---

15. See Alfie Kohn's *Punished by Rewards*, chapter 11, and *Positive Discipline in the Classroom*.

Suggestions

1. Create a safe classroom climate in which mistakes are seen as wonderful opportunities to learn. Emphasize that the academic task is a way for students to learn for life rather than a way for teachers to evaluate a student's performance. Ask students to make a big poster that proclaims, "Mistakes are wonderful opportunities to learn."

2. Model this axiom by welcoming mistakes in front of students. Admit it when you don't know something, and emphasize the knowledge we gain from errors made on a task rather than focusing on how well it was performed. When you design an assignment poorly, for example, tell the class, "I discovered by your response [or lack of response] to this assignment that it could have been more applicable to what you are learning. I suspect it seemed to you like busywork that was just meant to produce something to put in the grade book."

3. Ask your students for feedback about assignments. Ask for their help in designing relevant homework and class work.

4. Ask the student who is having trouble with assignments whether she would find it helpful to work with a buddy.

5. Set up a conference with the student and parent. (Refer to "Conferences.") During the conference, address specific needs for completing assignments and steps necessary to take between home and school. Brainstorm ideas about where to keep materials in the home and classroom, especially for long-term assignments.

6. Use the Mistaken Goal Chart on pages 12–13 to determine the belief behind the misbehavior and for suggestions to help you deal with the belief instead of just the behavior. Use the last column of this chart for ideas on how to encourage the student.

7. Check with yourself to make sure that you have taken time for training. Help your students break down the successful completion of assignments into small steps.

   A. The first step is making sure that the assignment is clear and if it is for homework, that it has been written down by teacher and student in a consistent place.

   B. Students need to know what materials they need to have assembled to work on the assignment (e.g. paper, compass, markers, poster board, etc.).

   C. Help the students understand that an assignment is not complete unless it has been turned in. For some students it may be helpful to have them create a chart that lists boxes to be checked off by them, titled "I WROTE IT, I DID IT, I PACKED IT." This will help you and parents to avoid nagging.

8. *When it's due, it's due.* Follow-through is essential. Respectfully require that unfinished work be completed. Perhaps students

may miss recess or need to make arrangements before or after school to complete the assignment, but they are learning that they are accountable.

Planning Ahead to Prevent Future Problems

1. Involve your students in brainstorming on in-class assignments and homework related to what they are learning.

2. Instead of using the word *homework*, begin a shift in conventional thinking by changing the term to *investment time*. Then be sure to follow up on students' suggestions as to making their investment time relevant to their learning.

3. As much as possible, eliminate grades from student assignments and homework. Instead, develop a portfolio for each student in which to place his or her work. Make sure that one student's work isn't compared to another's.

4. Begin the school year by incorporating class meetings into your classroom schedule. This process emphasizes collaboration and gives students choices within boundaries that show respect for all. This approach also has proven to foster a lasting involvement in the learning process that spills over to class assignments and homework.

5. Be aware that the use of external rewards or punishments for turning in or not turning in assignments may work temporarily with some students, but it won't work for long. When you offer rewards, the students do the assignment for what they can get, not for the purpose of lifelong learning.

6. Tell your students the purpose behind each in-class or at-home assignment. To be motivated to do an assignment, students must at least have a clue as to how it can contribute something to their education. Make sure it's not simply to get a grade for your grade book, to keep the students busy, or to easily fulfill a requirement of your school system. (Remember how you feel when required to do something for which you see no need.)

7. Consider creating a before- or after-school study program. One school calls their program "FIA," which stands for Flowery (name of school) Intelligence Agency. This type of program can take many forms. It is designed to assist students' study habits or help complete long-term projects, or it can be used as a referral for students to get the specific help they need.

Inspirational Story

Each month, Mrs. Andrews assigned her fifth graders a book report. The books were usually short, and most of the children read them the week before the reports were due. Mrs. Andrews frequently reminded the whole class of the upcoming assignment in the hope that one student in particular, Steven, would take the hint. Steven never turned his reports in on time, even though he often showed her the book he had chosen well in advance of the assignment's due date.

At first Mrs. Andrews did nothing about Steven's late reports. When he continued to turn them in after the due date, she sat down with him, and they agreed that if he didn't turn in his next report on time, he wouldn't be allowed to go on the next class field trip. (This wasn't a consequence that seemed related or appropriate, but Mrs. Andrews didn't know what else to do.) The following month, Steven despondently spent field trip day in the next-door classroom, trying to concentrate on reading his book while his classmates went to the zoo with their primary-grade buddies. It didn't take long for him to make some decisions about himself. He decided that his inability to get his assignments in on time proved that he was a very stupid person.

This was certainly not the message that Mrs. Andrews wanted Steven to receive. Now they both felt discouraged. Mrs. Andrews decided to take a fresh approach. This time she sat down with Steven at the beginning of the month and asked whether he would like some help on planning how to get his book report done on time. Steven was worried that this time he would have to miss more than just one field trip, but he really wanted to do better, so he agreed. He showed Mrs. Andrews the book he had se-

lected to read. She asked him how many pages the book had. He looked puzzled but figured out that there were eighty pages. Mrs. Andrews got out a copy of the month's calendar and placed an X on the date the report was due. She asked him how long it usually took him to write his reports. He said two days. She then made a mark two days before the due date and suggested they add one more day just in case there was some reason he needed additional time. Then she and Steven counted how many days there were between this day of their discussion and the mark three days ahead of the due date. There were thirteen days. They divided thirteen into eighty (the number of pages in the book). The answer was just over six, so Mrs. Andrews suggested they make it seven. If Steven read seven pages of his book each day, he would finish in time to write his report and turn it in on time. Did he think he could read seven pages every day? Steven eagerly said that he could.

At the end of the week, they sat down together again, and Steven proudly announced that he had been reading seven pages every day and that, in fact, he had read ten pages on each of the last two days. He beamed with pleasure. Well ahead of time, Steven finished his reading, and he turned his report in two days before it was due.

Attention Deficit Disorder (ADD) and Attention Deficit with Hyperactivity Disorder (ADHD)

Discussion

It is a rare classroom without that one child who seems to be everywhere at once, though seldom in his seat. He is the child who never stops going; he talks, fidgets, and continually causes commotion. Some days teachers wish they could press the off switch, or at least turn down the volume. By now most teachers are nodding their heads and saying, "Yes, that's Malcom [or Jessica, or Bill, or Maria] to a tee."

In some ways, children who have attention deficit disorder, with or without hyperactivity, suffer from something akin to a phantom illness. No teacher would think of admonishing a blind child that if she would only try harder she would be able to see, yet teachers respond to children with ADD by trying repeatedly to extinguish the specific disruptive behaviors.

A child with ADD almost certainly knows that something is different for him than for his classmates. Because he gets in trouble so frequently, the child logically concludes, based on his experiences, that he is bad. Children are good perceivers but poor interpreters. One of the first and most helpful steps for a child with this disorder is an acknowledgment of the influence that ADD has on him. Children need more understanding of themselves. A child with ADD needs to know that his phantom has a name and that he can learn strategies to minimize its effects. What a relief to learn that you have some special challenges rather than to go on thinking that you are bad or stupid. As a teacher, you can become an ally rather than another adversary to a child whose day is often filled with struggle and discord.

The most current research, which uses brain wave imaging, has shown that chemicals in the brains of children affected with ADD are distributed differently, during a variety of activities, from their distribution in the brains of those not affected. ADD should be diagnosed by a professional licensed to do so. This ensures an evaluation that considers similar disorders, for which treatment might vary. Teachers need to make a special effort and take the time to educate themselves about the needs and characteristics of children with ADD.

A lot of information about ADD is available. An excellent resource is the national headquarters of CHADD (Children and Adults with Attention Deficit Disorder); call (800) 233-4050 or go to their Web site at www.CHAD.org.[16]

---

16. For additional tools and classroom suggestions, refer to Dr. John F. Taylor's *Helping Your Hyperactive Child,* revised second edition (Roseville, CA: Prima Publishing, 1994).

Suggestions

1. Form a working partnership with the child. Meet with her privately, and ask what she finds most difficult about being in this particular classroom. If she says there isn't anything, ask whether she would like to hear some of your observations. If she agrees to listen to your comments, mention one or two things that you've noticed are difficult for her—for example, "I notice that you often seem to have trouble standing in line without bumping into others or pushing. Have you noticed that, too?" When an issue is brought up in this respectful manner, the child is less likely to feel threatened or accused. Now you may say, "How might I help you with this? Let's see if we can think of what is really hard for you about standing in lines and find some ways to make it easier."

Offer her your support. Engage in a dialogue rather than attempting to plan consequences or attach blame. Remember that the goal is to help a child who is having a difficult time in the classroom find ways to meet her special challenges. Perhaps together you might decide that she will be the person in charge of closing the door, so she doesn't have to stand in line. She will line up at the very end but will have a special role. This solution could transform her bone-deep difficulty with standing still into a way she can make a positive contribution to her class.

2. Seek solutions to recurring problems, working on one problem at a time. Here are some ways to reduce distractions:

A. Provide a quiet space in the classroom with a partition (a filing cabinet or even a cardboard box attached to a desktop can form a carrel). Call this "the office," and make it available to an ADD child at work times to help screen out distractions. (Involve the child in developing this area, and make sure she sees it as a helpful refuge rather than as punishment. Using the office can be a privilege that other children are allowed to share.)

B. During math work, show the child how to cover the page except for the current problem.

C. Minimize classroom clutter. Simplify the environment to provide a soothing and muted background.

3. Provide outlets to release excess physical energy. Here are two possibilities:

A. Invite an older child to bring in a squeeze ball, or place a band of stretchy exercise hose between the legs of the child's desk. The child can handle the ball in his lap or inside the desk, or press his legs against the band. He thus has an acceptable, non-disruptive way to move during lessons.

B. Plan regular opportunities for the child to get up and move around. You may want to agree in advance that he can go to a specific spot, such as a clay table if he is really having a difficult time. Decide on a signal so that he can leave quietly. You may be concerned about what the other children will say. Of course, they will all want to do it, too. But remember that your job as teacher is to help each child get what she most needs. The child with ADD may

need to move about at times in order to work better in the classroom. Children are perfectly able to understand that each person has unique needs that can and should be met in different ways, especially when they discuss it together during a class meeting. However, if this arrangement becomes an issue, perhaps you need to evaluate whether your whole class actually needs more opportunities for movement.

4. Note how the child does in the first ten minutes of an assignment. If she is getting all of the answers correct but after thirty minutes turns in a paper filled with mistakes, this is a strong clue that her ability to keep focused deteriorates rapidly. If your goal is for each child to learn the material, doing extra or longer assignments may defeat that goal in the case of an ADD child. Agree to reduce the number of problems as long as her accuracy rate stays high. This will result in a more encouraging learning environment, and she will be evaluated on her strength, which is her intelligence, rather than on her weak-

ness, which is her long-term attention span. One child with ADD said that the words began to blur after the first three pages of an assignment. She therefore learned to do her work in increments, with time for physical activity in between. Whatever arrangements you must make, the bottom line is that learning is truly taking place.

5. Discover the child's interests or strengths, and build on them. Focusing on strengths encourages healthy self-esteem and improved behavior.

Planning Ahead to Prevent Future Problems

1. Welcome the child's parents as part of his support team. Most parents of ADD children experience censure for the child's behavior and blame themselves, perhaps even feeling that they are failing as parents. Furthermore, they live with this child every day, simultaneously loving him and being driven to distraction by him.

2. ADD is usually not the result of inadequate parenting or teaching methods. Start with a respect for differences instead of seeking to assign blame to yourself, the child, or his family. The phantom is real.

3. Envision yourself as a coach with the ADD child on the team. Remain open and flexible to various learning arrangements. Not all solutions succeed with all ADD/

ADHD children. Work together to find the best combination of resources.

4. Use class meetings to discuss the different needs of each person in the class. Help the children recognize that differences exist and that they are not cause for ridicule or embarrassment. Use role playing to explore what it might feel like to be in a wheelchair or unable to hear. Develop the children's insight into the perspectives and needs of others.

5. Take loving care of yourself. Many children and families rely on you. Every teacher will have a child with ADD at some point (between 5 and 10 percent of the children in the United States are estimated to experience the combination of traits associated with ADD). The daily rigors of the classroom drain your energy, and a child with ADD often takes an additional reserve.

6. Celebrate the chance to know these wonderfully gifted and often creative young people. When the focus shifts to what they can do rather than what they should not be doing, there is a real change in the classroom atmosphere. The goal of educating a child to feel good about his abilities and develop skills for living with his impulses is far more worthy than teaching him how to obey, conform, and sit still.

7. Just as you would provide books in braille for the sightless child, make an effort to provide an environment that takes an ADD child's needs into account. Don't overlook these needs simply because the obstacles to his learning aren't as obvious as blindness.

8. Support parents in researching nontraditional settings that may better meet the needs of their children.

Inspirational Story

A story from Donna Presti, second- and third-grade teacher, Flowery Elementary School, Sonoma, California

In my eleven years of teaching in elementary school, I have had the experience of teaching many different grade levels. I have taught a culturally, academically, and emotionally diverse group of students, including students who have been diagnosed with attention deficit disorder.

In working with students with ADD, it can be quite challenging to keep them focused and ready to learn. After many years of trying the usual strategies, such as squeeze balls, clay, beanbags, and special seating, I have found something that works not only for my ADD students but also for all my special needs students. I use a microwavable moist heat neck roll. When worn around the neck, this neck roll provides weight, heat, and tactile stimulation. I have had students with ADD, ADHD, and autism respond well to the calming, stress-reducing effects of this method. When they are relaxed and grounded, their focus shifts to what they *can do*, rather than to off-task behavior. All students are attracted to the beautiful fabric and benefits, so there is no stigma attached to its use. In fact, it is a rare occasion that I don't have one around my own neck!

Bathroom Issues

Discussion

The school bathroom is often unsupervised, so it becomes a hideout for students who haven't developed social interest; have never learned to make thoughtful, independent choices about their actions; or have not learned constructive ways to experience a sense of belonging and significance. These students act out in the bathroom—festooning the stalls with toilet paper, throwing wet paper towels at the ceiling, intimidating other students, or just staying there longer than they need to—with the goals of earning undue attention, power, or revenge. (Refer to "Mistaken Goals [Hat Messages]" for more understanding about mistaken goals.)

Go to any elementary, middle, or high school in the country, and you can discover how much self-discipline the students have by the way they behave in the bathroom.

Instead of blaming students, we need to find ways to help them develop self-discipline. Use problems there as another opportunity to teach students social interest and valuable life skills.

Suggestions

1. Mistakes made in the bathroom are an opportunity to educate students about respect for people, privacy, and property. Take time to discuss bathroom etiquette and the basics of plumbing.

2. When students complain about situations in the bathroom, invite those involved to work on a solution and report back to you, or to put the problem on the class meeting agenda for help from all the students.

3. If you want to be involved, ask "what" and "how" questions: What happened? What caused it to happen? How do you feel? How do you think the others feel? What ideas do you have that might solve the problem?

4. Remember to work for improvement and not perfection. Sometimes students need to discuss a subject and brainstorm for solutions several times.

5. Ask the custodians to describe their responsibilities with the class. Lead a discussion about how students' actions in the bathroom affect the custodians' job. This will spark the students' empathy for others and their responsibilities.

Planning Ahead to Prevent Future Problems

1. A discussion at a class meeting is the best way to increase students' awareness of concerns surrounding use of the bathroom and to help them see how misbehavior affects individuals and the learning environment.

2. Role-playing the situation can deepen awareness of a bathroom issue.

3. Invite students to brainstorm for solutions. When students have participated in establishing the rules and routines, they are motivated to follow them.

Class Meeting Solution

A story from Heather Jubenvill, third-grade teacher, Caernarvon Elementary School, Edmonton, Alberta, Canada

A student in our class brought up a concern about our washroom policy. When the issue was discussed, we found that everyone had similar concerns.

We talked about the problems that occur when students leave the classroom and about inappropriate behavior in the washroom. The students brainstormed ways they could make sure that each student only went to the washroom and didn't become involved in other activities.

After a few minutes of discussion, the students began to realize the dilemma a teacher faces when a student leaves the room, because the teacher can't leave all the other students to keep tabs on the one who left. In just a few more minutes, the students had developed a better understanding of problems that occur in the washroom. One student suggested that we maintain our current policy, which was to go to the washroom at recess and lunch and to go during class time only if it was an emergency. When the students took a vote, they unanimously determined that they would be responsible to follow this policy.

Because of the discussion, the class now has a greater understanding of the washroom issue and students have made an effort to make use of the washroom during recess. We have very few emergencies, and when children do leave the class, they are gone for only a short time, so they don't disrupt the learning environment. The children were very pleased with their decision and felt that they had a voice in classroom policies.

Inspirational Story

Victor, frequently a scapegoat for problems in his early school years, entered Ms. Owen's fifth-grade class. Ms. Owen and her students had regular class meetings. Her students had found that the emphasis in this classroom was to help each other and to look for solutions rather than blame. Shortly after the beginning of the school year, her students returned eagerly from their bathroom break to tell on Victor. He had stuffed the toilet with paper towels and made it overflow.

After Ms. Owen confirmed that Victor had indeed done this, she sent a note to the custodian, Mr. Leal, asking whether he could attend a class meeting as soon as possible to help solve this problem. (Mr. Leal had previously been informed of the class meeting process and had agreed to help whenever possible.)

When Mr. Leal joined Ms. Owen's class meeting, she began with appreciations. She asked the students to think about all the ways he helped them and to share these thoughts with him. Ms. Owen led into a discussion of the immediate problem—the overflowed toilet—by reminding her students that they were there to help each other while finding solutions, not to hurt each other with blame and punishment.

Victor was asked first whether he had any suggestions. He asked Mr. Leal whether he could help clean up the mess he had made. Because Mr. Leal had already cleaned up the mess so that no one would slip and fall, he and Victor chose another cleanup activity with which Victor could help. They discussed an appropriate time to do the activity, and Victor decided to do it during his free time. Ms. Owen then complimented Victor on how well he accepted responsibility for his actions. As the class followed suit on the compliments, Victor beamed. This was the beginning of Victor's transformation from class scapegoat to a student with a sense of belonging and purpose.

After this incident, Victor often used his free time to find some way to help in the classroom. During compliment time in class meetings (when students commend one another for good deeds or displays of good character), the other students' recognition of his helpfulness encouraged his sense of belonging in the class. His behavior and class participation improved throughout the year.

Blaming

Discussion

Students live what they learn. They are often raised with blame, which gives rise to the painful emotion of shame. In this kind of atmosphere children quickly learn that one way to avoid shame is to avoid accountability by pinning the blame on someone else or on circumstances. They also learn to belittle others or deflate others' accomplishments as a method of puffing themselves up; this is an unfortunate by-product of our competitive society. Teachers can help stop the habit of blame and denigration by creating an atmosphere where students aren't afraid to be responsible and accountable.

Suggestions

1. Avoid using blame, shame, or humiliation when speaking with a student. When students are confronted with these attitudes, they often respond with defensiveness and then use blame themselves. Be aware of the power of your words and tone of voice.

2. Redirect the blame to personal responsibility. Ask the student, "What was your part in this?" Think of this as an opportunity to take responsibility that has nothing to do with blame.

3. Focus on showing your understanding of how difficult it can be sometimes to accept responsibility. Share a personal experience you may have had either of blaming or of being blamed.

4. Invite students to put problems on the class meeting agenda, so the whole class can focus on finding solutions, rather than resorting to blame.

5. When a problem occurs, have the student fill out a "what/how" form. A sample form appears here:

"What/how form"
What were you trying to do or
    accomplish?

What happened?
What caused it to happen?
How do you feel about what happened?
What did you learn from what happened?
What suggestions do you have for solving
    the problem?
How can you use what you learned in the
    future?

Planning Ahead to Prevent Future Problems

1. Every chance you get, teach that mistakes are wonderful opportunities to learn.

2. As an art project, have students make posters and banners on the theme of seeking solutions instead of placing blame. Their signs may say, "Are you looking for blame, or are you looking for solutions?" or "We are not interested in blame, only in solutions," or "We don't need to hurt each other through blame because we know how to help each other through solutions."

3. Always model the behavior you are expecting from your students. They learn more from what you *do* than from what you *say*. Before each class meeting or when one student is trying to place blame, refer to the posters about seeking solutions that the class made. Have the courage to ask your students to refer you to the posters when you forget to look for solutions instead of placing blame.

4. Teach students about the "what/how" form as a valuable tool to help them learn from experiences. Present this as a positive and valuable activity. (If your attitude or

tone of voice is punitive, it will sound like a punishment.) Let them know that they can fill the form out just for their own information and benefit, or the class could use the form later as a guide to solving problems.

Class Meeting Solution

When Sai Ling scrawled, "Boys," on the class meeting agenda followed by her name in capital letters, her teacher, Mrs. Wilson, recognized a hot issue. As Sai Ling explained her problem at the next day's meeting, she bristled with outrage. The boys had made her late for class because they had hidden her lunch box, and now she had a tardy mark.

Mrs. Wilson asked how the boys managed to get to her lunch box since the class policy was that students should store all lunch things inside their desks before going out to the playground. Sai Ling pouted that she didn't have time to put the lunch box inside because another girl wanted her to play tetherball right away.

Mrs. Wilson agreed that no one should hide another student's lunch box but asked Sai Ling who was responsible for placing her lunch box in her desk after lunch. Sai Ling acknowledged that storing her lunch box was her responsibility. Rather than blaming the boys for her tardiness, Mrs. Wilson inquired whether Sai Ling could think of what she might have done differently to prevent the problem and the resulting tardy slip. Sai Ling recognized that putting her lunch box away should take precedence over joining a friend in play and that she could have prevented the problem. She agreed that she was accountable for being in class on time and that it was unfair to blame the boys for her tardy slip.

Mrs. Wilson appreciated Sai Ling's careful reflection on the issue. Mrs. Wilson also wanted to work on solutions to students' taking property that wasn't their own. The class discussed hiding anything that belonged to another person. Many children indicated that this was a problem for them at times as well. The focus shifted away from blaming the boys for Sai Ling's tardy mark as the children talked about how to treat other people's property respectfully. Instead of brainstorming for solutions, the class decided that the discussion was enough to help them remember to be respectful of other people's things.

Bothering Others

Discussion

"Mary's bothering me." If you're a student, be sure to put the emphasis on *bothering* and to draw out the first syllable as mournfully as possible.

To the groaning student, it is, of course, always the other person's fault that she is being bothered. When a student has a pattern of complaining about bothersome behavior, someone is almost certainly sending a message about a mistaken goal (refer to "Mistaken Goals [Hat Messages]"), but it could be the botherer or the botheree. Perhaps the person who is bothering wants attention; perhaps the person who is complaining wants the same thing. If neither student is pursuing a mistaken goal, the issue is then likely to be one student's lack of awareness of how her particular behavior affects her classmates.

Suggestions

1. Clarify the problem. Speak with the complaining student first and find out what she sees as the problem. Then find out whether the student doing the bothering is aware that she may be causing a problem. If she is truly unaware, she will probably be surprised and willing to work out a solution. If she denies doing anything bothersome, mistaken goal information may be buried here. Proceed to step 2.

2. Use the Mistaken Goal Chart (pages 12–13) to identify your feelings, which are your first clue to her goal. Once you identify the goal (or even if you aren't sure), use the last column of the chart for ideas both to encourage students to change their behavior and to solve the problem. Whichever feelings and behaviors are identified will lead to a different path for solving this problem. Hence you can address the real problem (the discouragement) rather than one symptom of the problem or the particular behavior.

3. Use goal disclosure. Refer to the last section of "Wandering" for an explanation of this process.

4. Teachers need to address not only the belief behind the behavior (the mistaken goal) but also the behavior itself. To meet the needs of the situation, you may need to temporarily ask the bothering student to relocate themselves. "Sarah, it looks like you're having trouble sitting next to Jenny today. Let's have you sit over by Tara for now."

5. Maybe Mary isn't doing anything bothersome. By complaining that Mary taps her on the shoulder twenty times a day, Sally may be simply trying to get Mary in trouble. This is a classroom version of sibling fighting and probably a veiled bid for the teacher's attention. A teacher might suggest that Sally collect some data for the next two days to learn just how many times Mary does tap her on the shoulder. The two girls can then schedule a time to share Sally's data and figure out a way to handle the problem. This removes the teacher from the situation and assures both girls that she has confidence in their ability to work the problem out themselves. No sides are taken; no judgments are made.

6. Ask the student being bothered how the behavior in question makes her feel. Listen carefully, and then ask her what she could do to solve the problem. Perhaps she could ignore it, or move away from the student bothering her, or use her own words to ask the botherer to stop.

7. Ask the student being bothered whether she would like to work out the problem with the student bothering her and then let you know how they decide to solve the problem. (See the problem-solving suggestions in the third item under "Planning Ahead.") Or offer the student being bothered the option of putting the problem on the class meeting agenda.

Planning Ahead to Prevent Future Problems

1. Teach your students how to resolve issues on their own. Give them some hypothetical situations, and let them brainstorm for solutions.

2. Make it a classroom goal that students will seek solutions to individual problems with one another or seek help during a class meeting.

3. Teach your students about the four problem-solving suggestions:

    A. Ignore it.

    B. Talk it over respectfully with the other student.

    C. Work together on a win–win solution.

    D. Put it on the class meeting agenda.

    Once you have taught these options through role play and discussion, ask a student to make a poster to display in the classroom. When a student complains that someone is bothering him, refer him to the poster and ask him which of the suggestions he has tried or is willing to try.

Inspirational Story

Jeff complained to his teacher that Nancy, his seatmate, was always singing. Mrs. Murray asked Jeff what he meant by "always." "Well," said Jeff, "she sang just now, and she sang yesterday in the lunch line." Mrs. Murray considered this and asked Jeff whether two times meant always. Jeff looked up in surprise and then smiled, and they both laughed.

    Sometimes a sense of humor can lessen problems quickly. It is important that the humor is shared and not sarcastic. Mrs. Murray remained respectful and watched for Jeff's reaction. Although not belittling his problem, she helped him see it differently.

Class Meeting Solution

A story from Lorn Henker, sixth-grade teacher, Caernarvon Elementary School, Edmonton, Alberta, Canada

    I received a call from a parent saying that three boys were picking on her son when he was on the way home for lunch. The counselor talked to all four boys and worked out some strategies for how they would deal with their difficulties.

While the boys were out of class with the counselor, the rest of the students held a class meeting about this problem. Many of the students were upset with the boy who was complaining about being bothered. His behavior was turning quite a few people against him.

We listened to individual concerns; then we discussed the concept that when people are unsure about whether they belong in a group, and their needs aren't being met when they behave positively, they will misbehave. (A misbehaving child is a discouraged child who doesn't believe he or she belongs.)

I asked the students to think of ways they could help the boy who was complaining. At the start their tone was negative, but as they talked it shifted to become positive and helpful. They either said positive things about the boy or suggested things they were willing to do that would help him feel better about his role in the group. The class's efforts made everyone involved feel good and empowered.

Bullying

Discussion

According to SuEllen and Paula Fried, authors of *Bullies and Victims: Helping Your Child Survive the Schoolyard Battlefield* (New York: Evans, 1996), there are more than two million bullies and nearly three million victims in American schools. Without intervention, the problem can become epidemic.

Bullying is a means of forcing other people to act or agree to a course of action. It frequently includes disparagement, physical aggression, insulting language, and threats or intimidation. It is important to realize that a bully is a person who feels inferior to those around him. At a subconscious level, bullies believe that their only significance in life, their way to belong, comes from making themselves more powerful than others.

Bullies seem to have an instinctive ability to find and pick on weaker people. There is a type of fish, known as the puffer, that frightens off enemies by puffing itself up to a greater size. A bully is like a threatened puffer fish—that is, all puffed up and full of air. The best tool at the bully's disposal is the willingness of other people to be victims. When a bully meets weakness, he thrives. When a bully encounters dignity and assertiveness, he often deflates into nothingness.

Suggestions

1. When you become aware of bullying behavior either through observation or

through report, you need to address the situation directly. You need to stop the behavior and take steps to assess the degree of bullying. If this is an isolated incident, you may speak with the student about his behavior and the effect he is having on others. If it seems to be an ongoing problem, you may need to deal with it in a more formal way. Schools and school districts have guidelines that can be consulted when dealing with behaviors that constitute harassment.

2. Let the victims know it is not their fault and that they can learn some skills and get some help to deal with it.

3. Put the problem of bullying on the class meeting agenda for students to work on together. Hearing the opinions of classmates often takes the wind out of a bully's sail.

4. Focus on the ways in which the students are currently reacting to bullying. Tell them about the puffer fish. When they learn to change their response to bullying, the bullying is likely to cease.

5. Seek positive outlets through which the person used to bullying others can use her power to contribute to the classroom. Remember that you want to deflate the bullying behavior and not the person doing the bullying. Brainstorm with your students about ways to foster a healthy sense of belonging and significance in people who use power in a hurtful way.

Planning Ahead to Prevent Future Problems

1. Discuss with your students reasons why people use bullying behaviors. Make a list of their reasons. If it hasn't already come up in the discussion, let them know that bullying is learned.[17] Let students know that no matter what happens in other parts of their lives, in your classroom everyone will be learning respectful ways to solve problems, and that it is not okay to treat anyone disrespectfully.

2. Read stories in which some characters bully others. Children's literature and folktales are rich with bullies. The witches, trolls, dragons, and monsters of fairy tales all disintegrate when other characters stand up to them. Be sure to note that force or violence isn't necessary to deflate those who seem powerful. After all, the Wizard of Oz turned out to be hardly more than a figment of the community's collective imagination after the man behind the curtain was revealed.

3. Teach children how to assert their opinions and ask for what they want or need in a respectful manner. For example, children can learn to state, "I do not want to smoke

---

17. Leonard Eron, a psychology professor at the University of Michigan, believes that bullying is learned in part from viewing too much violent TV, but largely from bullying parents.

a cigarette." Children who rely on bullying to get what they want can learn to say, "I would like to use the tetherball at recess today." Learning to state views and desires clearly is important for all children.

4. Role-play different responses people have to bullying. Help your students see which are effective responses and which are ineffective. Explore how an assertive response differs from an aggressive or violent response. You may want to teach some basic tools, such as setting clear limits, ignoring a provocation, staying with groups of friends where a bully may be encountered, problem solving, asking for help, and using other Positive Discipline methods described throughout this book.

5. Explain to your students that the most challenging bully of all is that voice that discourages and intimidates each and every person from the inside. Encourage them to discuss the messages they receive from their inner critics and ways they can deal with the "inner bully."

6. Remember that bullies are discouraged and have found a mistaken way to deal with their discouragement. It can be very interesting to invite students to discuss how they could encourage a bully. Bullying often becomes less of an issue when schools are engaged in class meetings in which students are learning to give and receive compliments and when they are learning to focus on nonpunitive solutions.

Class Meeting Solution

A story from Kerri McCaul, sixth-grade teacher, Everett, Washington

I was first introduced to Positive Discipline by a colleague who suggested I read the book, *Positive Discipline in the Classroom.* I had been sharing my discouragement and despair about the behavior and attitude of a particular sixth-grade class; they were "my class from hell." It was only December and I had already run through my entire "bag of tricks" to get them to cooperate with each other and with me. I was developing a strong dislike for this class and knew the feelings were mutual.

I read the book over Christmas vacation and came back to school with a new attitude. The theories challenged the very core of my teaching philosophies and practices, even my own personal family upbringing. Until then, I was a staunch "assertive discipline" manager. I was in control—I was the boss! But none of this was working, and I figured I had nothing to lose.

We jumped right in and tackled a "building block" a day for the first week. By the second week, we were ready for our first class meeting (or so I thought). It lasted ninety minutes. I couldn't get my students to stop talking! They had so much to say. They felt they weren't important, I didn't listen, I was mean, and I didn't care! I was devastated, bruised, and heartbroken by their responses. But not about to give up, I recognized that something important was happening. I observed a class meeting of the colleague who had loaned me his book, and I left impressed and determined. We could do this! I knew we could!

The agenda became a powerful tool. We discussed (sometimes argued) homework assignments, classroom rules, school rules, harassment, and grading policies. After recess, they would line up at the agenda to write down complaints. Some meetings the agenda was two pages long. Our role plays were invaluable. A turning point came when, during a role play, a girl told the class bully how much it hurt when he called her terrible names. When she role-played the name-calling, his mouth dropped open and he hung his head. He agreed, with the class, that his restitution should be a sincere apology. This was a really tough kid. I doubt he had apologized much in his life, but he did it. The girl accepted, the class cheered, and we began to work with him on controlling his hurtful behaviors.

Bus Behavior

Discussion

Problems on the bus seem to arise at every grade level, from kindergarten through high school. Behavior on any school bus, anywhere in the world, is a good measure of students' internalization of life skills and social interest.

The bus driver is busy driving the bus. This leaves students with an opportunity to show what they do when not directly supervised by adults. When the students behave disrespectfully, we usually blame them, instead of looking at the ineffective-ness of those adult methods of directing behavior that are based on control. Too often adults do not understand the importance of dealing with the belief behind the behavior (the discouragement) instead of just the behavior.

How much does bus misbehavior reflect a student's need for attention because he feels insignificant and isolated? How much is due to a student's need for some kind of power in her life and a lack of training in how to use power? How much does hurtful behavior on the bus reflect the hurt and discouragement students feel because no one listens to them and no one validates their ideas by taking them seriously?

Bus misbehavior gives us a clear view of our need to improve the methods through which we teach children internal control and social interest. We can welcome this view. Furthermore, we can learn that involving students in formulating guidelines and finding solutions is an effective way to deal with problems.

Suggestions

1. Bus drivers can decide what they will do instead of what they will make students do. When children act disrespectfully, the driver can pull to the side of the road and say, "I don't feel it's safe to drive when disrespectful behavior is distracting me or hurting others. I'll continue driving as soon as you're ready." If students complain that they'll be late for school, the bus driver can say, "You might be." Bus drivers should stay calm, refraining from lectures or putdowns.

2. When a bus driver has a specific complaint about a student or students in your class, invite him to come to your class meeting at a time which is convenient for him. At the class meeting, the driver and students can discuss and find solutions.

3. If you are aware of a problem, you need to meet directly with the student or students involved. Share the information you have received in a nonjudgmental way. Ask them what their picture is of the situation. Take this as an opportunity to review safe and respectful bus behavior. Show faith that they can follow these guidelines. Sometimes students simply need to be reminded of the rules. Set up a time to meet to check in about their progress.

4. Use your class meeting time to discuss bus behavior in general. You may encourage students who have been involved in an incident to share and discuss what they have learned as a result of their mistake.

5. When students complain about problems on the bus, ask them to put their concerns on the class meeting agenda. This keeps you out of the role of mediator and doesn't set you up as the person who will solve all problems. Then allow students to work on solutions when that item comes up on the agenda. Let the students involved choose the brainstormed suggestions they think will help the most (even if two or more students make different choices).

6. Review your school's policy on bus behavior, and follow through with firmness and kindness. Sometimes a student's behavior may result in suspension of bus privileges. You can encourage your student by helping him see the connection between his behavior and the loss of the privilege. Sometimes asking for assistance from your administrator and the student's family may help the student deal with his discouragement. If this step is left out, often students may find ways to retaliate, give up, or show others they can't control him.

Planning Ahead to Prevent Future Problems

1. Treat students with respect by listening to them and inviting them to participate in solving problems that occur on the bus.

2. Facilitate a discussion on bus safety issues. Let the students come up with the problems. Once they have produced a list, encourage brainstorming for solutions to each problem.

3. Invite bus drivers into the classroom to share their feelings and concerns, as well as their guidelines from the school district, and to ask the students directly for their help. Include some role playing of various problems so students can experience the bus driver's point of view. The bus driver may enjoy role-playing a student to see what it feels like to be treated disrespectfully.

4. When students are involved in discussing safety issues, the bus driver's responsibilities, and possible solutions to problems, their awareness and motivation to cooperate are much stronger than when they receive lectures or are simply instructed to follow teacher-initiated rules.

5. Discuss the concept that privilege equals responsibility. Invite students to discuss which responsibilities go along with bus privileges. Ask for a volunteer to record their ideas. This can be followed by a discussion of the concept that unwillingness to accept responsibility equals loss of privilege. Let them suggest the appropriate consequences of not responsibly following the guidelines. (This is a good example of logical consequences that are related and reasonable. Students who don't want the responsibility lose the privilege.)

6. Invite students to write notes of appreciation to the bus drivers. Form a committee to learn and keep track of their birthdays, so students can send cards.

Class Meeting Solutions

Stories from Cathy Binns Ater, fifth- and sixth-grade teacher, Elk Grove Elementary School, Elk Grove, California

Sofia and Mindy

This took place in a second-grade class in an international school in Germany. During a class meeting, Sofia brought up the problem of older boys sitting behind her on the bus and kicking her seat. The students came up with the following suggestions for Sofia:

1. Sit away from them.

2. Sit behind them.

3. Ignore them.

4. Watch where they sit, and then sit somewhere else.

5. Trick them by putting your bag in one seat and sitting somewhere else. As soon as they get on the bus and sit behind you, move to where your bag is.

6. Ask them to stop kicking your seat.

7. Trade places with someone.

8. Tell them how you feel when they kick your seat.

It is amazing how many wonderful ideas can come from brainstorming with students. Sofia chose the second suggestion.

Mindy, who was in the same class, brought up the problem of students pushing her when she got off the bus. The students came up with the following suggestions for her:

1. Ask them to please stop.

2. Tell them that you don't like it and that it hurts you.

3. Be the last student to get off the bus.

4. Hang onto the bars.

5. Get off first.

6. Get off from the back of the bus.

Mindy chose to be the last off.

Mark

This story is about Mark, a boy with Down's syndrome, who was in a special education class at an international school in Belgium. Mark continually exhibited unsafe behavior on the bus by hanging on the bars and running up and down the aisle while the bus was in motion.

This had been going on for a year when I came to teach his class. Adults and students alike excused the behavior, saying that Mark didn't understand the rules and couldn't learn. I took exception to this opinion. I sat down with Mark and talked to him about appropriate behavior on the bus. For safety reasons, I told him, he would be removed from the bus if he didn't follow the rules.

I then invited his parents to participate in a conference with Mark and me. His parents agreed to drive Mark to and from school if he lost bus privileges by refusing to follow the rules.

The next day, Mark chose to exhibit unsafe behavior on the bus. When he got to school and I was informed he had been running in the aisles, I told Mark that he wouldn't be allowed to ride the bus home. At the end of the day, his mother picked him up from school. She had been coached to show empathy for his dilemma and not to lecture or punish him.

Mark loved to ride the bus. It was one of his favorite times of the day, so he was not at all pleased when his mom showed up to drive him home.

The following day, when he was allowed to get on the bus, the same behavior occurred. We followed through and kept him off the bus for the rest of the week. Each day we talked to him about safe behavior. On Monday we were ready to try again. That morning Mark displayed no misbehavior and stayed seated during the entire trip to school. He didn't have any more problems on the bus for the rest of the year.

Cheating

Discussion

As with most problems, teachers will be more effective if they deal with the mistaken goal or belief behind cheating and not just the behavior. Why would a student cheat? The obvious answer is that he wants to do well on tests and get good grades, but the desires are deeper than that. Some students may be afraid they won't have value if they don't do well. Others may be afraid of punishment if they don't live up to their parents' expectations. A student may believe that disappointing her parents and teacher would mean that *she* is a disappointment. Many students are motivated by rewards (monetary rewards from parents, other rewards from teachers) and will do anything to attain them. Adults need to be aware of their own attitudes and actions, which may motivate students to cheat; adults can then use interventions that help students learn responsibility and life skills that will inspire them to achieve long-range goals.

Suggestions

1. If a student is involved in cheating, speak to him directly and in private. Begin the discussion by naming the behavior you have observed ("I notice you cheated on this test") instead of trying to trick him into a confession. Then invite him to work with you on a solution so that he can succeed without cheating.

2. When you observe a student cheating, don't wait to intervene. Quietly speak with the student and let her know that you will discuss the incident after class. At that time, let her know what you observed. If the student denies cheating, calmly repeat what you saw. Remember to show respect by your behavior. A cheating student is someone who is afraid.

3. Be curious. Let the student know that you are interested in helping him find out the purpose of his behavior. You may say to a student, "Students cheat for lots of different reasons. For instance, sometimes students cheat when they are not prepared and don't want anyone to know; sometimes they're convinced that there's no way they could know the answers. I'm interested in knowing what is going on for you."

4. Follow through with your established policy for dealing with a student who has chosen to cheat. Make sure your policy is reasonable and respectful and is related to the behavior. Many teachers simply lower the grade and let the student know that they have faith in the student to do better next time. Remember to help the student preserve her dignity as you are dealing with the behavior.

Planning Ahead to Prevent Future Problems

1. Stop offering rewards for high grades on tests or assignments. Help students understand the intrinsic value of their work.

2. Consider strategies that help eliminate competition. Let students test each other (when ready) on subjects that require memorization, such as multiplication tables. Give open-book tests. Hand test questions out in advance so students know what to study.

3. Teach good study habits, and allow students to practice in pairs or teams.

4. Involve students in a discussion (that comes mostly from them) about the relevance or long-range benefits of what they are learning.

5. During class meetings, lead a discussion on cheating. Invite students to talk about the long-term results of cheating. Ask "what" and "how" questions about cheating: "What do you think causes people to cheat?" "How do you feel about it?" "What do you learn when you cheat?" "What pressures do you experience from parents and teachers that might motivate cheating?" "What kind of character traits or skills could help you be stronger than the pressures from parents and teachers?"

6. Have students brainstorm on how to solve cheating problems. Make three lists: suggestions for students, suggestions for parents, and suggestions for teachers. Ask for volunteers to type the lists for parents and teachers in petition form, so all the students can sign them and present copies to their parents and teachers.

7. Have a clear policy about how cheating will be handled within your class. Possibly you may want to consult with other teachers on their ideas and their procedures, keeping in mind that your goal is to have a policy that is respectful, reasonable, and is directly related to the behavior. Share your policy with your students.

Class Meeting Solution

A story from Cathy Binns Ater, fifth- and sixth-grade teacher, Elk Grove Elementary School, Elk Grove, California

Someone put "cheating" on our class meeting agenda. This student didn't give the name of the person who cheated so as not to embarrass him.

As we went around the circle for comments or suggestions, the students were making statements similar to those that adults make when they lecture children about cheating: You don't learn anything when you cheat. You might copy from someone who has the wrong answer. It isn't fair to people who took the time to study.

The discussion turned to solutions. Several suggestions were made, but the class decided that the most helpful idea was for the student who cheated to take the test over again when no one was around.

An amazing thing happened. The boy who had cheated said, "I was the one who cheated, and I would like to take the test over at recess."

We went around the circle once more for comments. Several of the students congratulated the boy for his courage in admitting what he had done and for being willing to take responsibility.

Class Meetings, Disruptions

Discussion

The class meeting enables students to learn about and practice mutual respect. However, students may be unaccustomed to handling the respect and power they have in this setting. They may be used to teachers trying to solve all the problems through punishment and rewards. They may be used to seeking blame and excuses for problems rather than seeking solutions. They may think that punishment is the best way to motivate each other.

Until students have learned the skills of effective class meetings and the value of re-spectful solutions, teachers can expect disruptions during class meetings.

Suggestions

1. If you find yourself nagging students about their behavior in the circle, stop. Ask questions to redirect the process: "How many of you think we're being respectful now?" "How many of you can hear when more than one person speaks at a time?"

2. Name the problem and simply ask for help to solve it.

3. Say what you see: "I notice that our circle is getting wrinkled."

4. Refer to the class's list of acceptable behaviors during class meetings. (See the first item under "Planning Ahead.") Let the list

be the boss. Ask, "Who can see which agreement we are breaking right now?" When an item on the list isn't working, ask the students to discuss it and find solutions that might work better.

5. If a student is continually disrupting class meetings, speak to him privately: "Tim, I notice that you bother the people sitting next to you in the circle and that I'm always asking you to stop. How can we work this out so that I can stop nagging?"

6. If the disruption continues, ask the student whether moving to another place in the circle would help him be respectful or whether it would help for him to have some positive time-out until he feels ready to be respectful.

Planning Ahead to Prevent Future Problems

1. Take time for training. Engage students in a discussion of behavior problems that could occur when students are seated in a circle for a class meeting. Be sure they talk about why these potential behaviors would interfere with the process. Have the students generate a list of acceptable ways to behave (and talk about why these behaviors are appropriate or nondisruptive), and then have them role-play these behaviors. Post the list.

2. Ask the students for suggestions about how to arrange the circle to mini-

mize disruptions. Listen to their ideas, and review their proposals. Let them be creative. If their first try doesn't work, discuss it and let them come up with some new possibilities.

Inspirational Story

A story from Barbara Evangelista, kindergarten paraprofessional, Rocky Mount Elementary School, Marietta, Georgia

We tried several solutions to help everyone get ready (bring chairs into the circle, sit comfortably, and quiet down) for class meetings. We then decided to sing the following song (to the tune of "If You're Happy and You Know It"). When the students finished singing, everyone was in his or her chair in the circle, ready to begin exchanging compliments.

If you're ready for class meeting, please sit
    down.
If you're ready for class meeting, please sit
    down.
If you're ready to help each other, solve
    problems, and give compliments,
If you're ready for class meeting, the room
    will sound like this!

When the song ended, there was silence and the students would start their meeting. They enjoyed the song and often sang it while doing other activities. It was a positive, fun way to get everyone ready.

Class Meetings, Refusal to Participate

Discussion

Sometimes a student will resist taking part in class meetings and even try to sabotage the process for others. Students are used to disciplinary methods that create a one up/one down situation: a teacher tells a student what to do, and the student either complies or rebels without thinking. Hence students may find it difficult to shift to a more respectful, horizontal way of relating. It usually takes time for students to see the class meeting as a vehicle for participating in decisions and finding belonging, personal significance, and positive uses of power. We tell teachers over and over, "Trust the process. The long-range benefits are worth the time it takes."

Suggestions

1. Treat the refusal to participate as a class problem rather than a teacher–student problem. Invite the students to share their reactions and their ideas for a solution.

2. Don't assume that you know the reasons a student isn't participating. Become curious; ask "what," "how," and "why" questions. Have students discuss why some of their peers might not want to participate in class meetings and what the class could do to make the meetings more inviting for everyone.

3. Remember that a class meeting is part of the curriculum and not an optional feature for students. Because they can't choose not to attend, let your students choose something about the structure of class meetings. Students could have input as to when meetings will be held and how long they will be.

Planning Ahead to Prevent Future Problems

1. Incorporate fun into the class meeting. Students should look forward to these meetings not simply for solving problems but also just for enjoying being together as a class.

2. Talk to your students about how the school usually handles discipline with punishments and rewards. Introduce class meetings as an opportunity to practice making decisions and having positive power, as opposed to another experience in which adults decide for them or overpower them.

Inspirational Story

Ari listened as Mrs. Gonzalez told him and his mother about the curriculum at his new school. It all seemed familiar except for this one part of the day called the class meeting. His mom asked questions and was excited that Ari was going to be part of a discipline process that was very different from the one at his previous school. As Ari listened to the adults talk, he was already deciding not to participate in that stupid meeting.

On Ari's first day in Mrs. Gonzalez's class, he sat in the circle for the class meeting, but he refused to speak. He wouldn't offer a compliment or even acknowledge compliments that other students gave him. Eventually Ari approached Mrs. Gonzalez before class and told her that her meetings were stupid and a waste of time. He said that he could use this time better and wanted to spend it in the library.

Mrs. Gonzalez told Ari that she appreciated his taking the time to let her know how he felt about the meetings, and she said that she had noticed that he hadn't been participating. She explained to Ari that class meetings were similar to any other subject and that attendance wasn't optional. She said, "Ari, since attendance is mandatory, you may feel resentful. But I would like you to know that you do have a choice around this. You may attend the meeting and still choose not to speak or choose to comment and talk." Mrs. Gonzalez again thanked Ari for sharing his feelings with her. She suggested that he might want to put his thoughts on the class meeting agenda and share them with others.

For about a week Ari continued to feel resentful about class meetings. But then he started to become intrigued with what was going on. Before long he was participating as though the whole thing had been his idea in the first place.

Cleanup

Discussion

When teachers assume that students know how to clean up, when to clean up, and what to clean up, everybody ends up feeling discouraged. When teachers take time for training, see cleanup as part of the curriculum to teach life skills, and get students involved in the planning process, they meet with success.

Suggestions

1. Take time for training. With the students' help, develop a list of steps that they need to follow when cleaning up, whether they're doing an everyday chore or straightening up after a particular activity or project. (See "Take Time for Training.")

2. Make visual aids with the students to help them remember the cleanup routine that they created together.

3. It can be fun to use a timer and play "beat the clock," as the students try to complete the cleanup in a certain amount of time.

4. As one of the classroom jobs, have a student or a few students monitor cleanup and be available to help complete tasks.

5. Decide on a start time and an end time for the cleanup, and indicate these clearly.

6. Give limited choices, no matter how small or insignificant they may appear: "Would you like to clean up before or after recess?" "Would you like to do that task alone or with a partner?" When students have choices, they experience positive power and are more likely to complete their tasks. Remember, not participating is not one of the choices.

7. Use logical consequences when discussing follow-through for certain tasks. Sometimes the clearest consequence is that another activity cannot begin until cleanup has been accomplished.

Planning Ahead to Prevent Future Problems

1. Students respond favorably to routines. Once routines are in place, the routine is the boss and the teacher doesn't have to give orders continually. The teacher can simply refer to the routine chart and ask, "What do we need to do now?"

2. Through class meetings, involve students in establishing all steps of the cleanup process. Discuss who cleans up what, how long each task will take, and how to rotate monitors and other jobs.

3. Schedule time for daily cleanup as well as weekly cleanup.

4. Role-play and discuss cleanup problems during class meetings as they arise. Remember that difficulties will continually arise. Look at them as opportunities to teach rather than punish.

5. Be aware of the influence that birth order may have on skill levels and willingness to participate. An oldest child may jump in and enjoy the tasks as well as the responsibility. A middle child may see the whole experience as unfair. A youngest child may feel that others should do the tasks for him. An only child may have difficulty in dealing with others.

6. Avoid gender biases in job selection.

Class Meeting Solution

A story from Betty Ferris, sixth-grade teacher, St. Eugene's Elementary School, Santa Rosa, California

Students in my sixth-grade class were having trouble keeping their cupboard tidy. Jackets and book bags were spilling out onto the floor. Several students put the problem on the class meeting agenda because their things were getting stepped on or crushed in the mess. During the meeting, they opened the cupboard so everyone could look at the situation. They decided that they weren't using the space wisely and that it would make sense to assign sections and hooks to correspond with their seats in the classroom. One student pointed out that I was using a section of the cupboard for storage and that perhaps I could move the items there to another part of the classroom. During a follow-up the next week, all the students agreed that the cupboard was no longer a problem and that our classroom looked a lot better.

Clinging

Discussion

"I teach third grade. This year I have a little girl in my classroom who clings to me constantly. She will not let me out of her sight. As soon as she arrives, she is at my desk telling me about what she did the night before. During class time, she seeks my help for every little question. Even at recess she stands by my side most of the period. It is driving me nuts."

This student's need for attention is obvious. Teachers can give attention in ways that are respectful and caring while fostering independence. It's important to set clear and firm limits and then to follow through on these limits. When the student's requirement for attention is being met in a consistent way, she will feel that you care and see that her needs are important to you. She can also learn to respect your needs. With this reassurance, the courage to stand on her own will gradually develop.

Suggestions

1. Give a clingy student your undivided attention when she arrives. Greet her and listen thoughtfully to what she has to say for thirty seconds or so.

2. Plan together what she intends to do in the day ahead. Taking a moment to visualize with her in this way will give her a feeling of security.

3. Set clear and reasonable limits for your interactions. Explain to her that you won't be able to come over and answer all of her questions throughout the morning. Ask her whether she can think of a classmate to whom she may turn for help when you are unavailable.

4. If necessary, decide on a specified length of time you will make available to her at recess or the maximum number of times she may ask for your help during class.

5. Ask for her help immediately. Assign a task, such as holding the door open, so she can feel important without clinging.

Planning Ahead to Prevent Future Problems

1. Involve a clinging student in helping someone else in the class. This fosters her development of social interest; when she feels concern for another person, she will stop focusing exclusively on her own needs.

2. Invite other children to join this child in group projects. She can thus enter a social situation even if she doesn't have adequate social skills to attempt doing so on her own.

3. When she arrives in class or during recess, assign her a special job that both gives her an independent role and helps her experience belonging in the group.

Inspirational Story

It was the middle of October, and Miss Taglia realized that she needed to find a new way of dealing with the behavior of one of her first-grade students. Lisa had had a very hard time on the first days of school. She cried and didn't want her mother to leave her at school. Eventually, Lisa was comfortable with her mother leav-

ing but had taken to clinging to Miss Taglia every morning. Aside from feeling irritated and pressed for time, Miss Taglia wanted to encourage Lisa to be more independent.

She wanted to find a way to help Lisa contribute and feel important and see herself as a part of the class, rather than depending only on Miss Taglia for attention and comfort. She decided to take advantage of an upcoming project for the class. There was a lot of preparation to be done such as paper sorting and distributing items into separate containers. She talked to Lisa about taking on this job and asked her to choose a partner to help her. Lisa was excited about this project. She immediately felt important and useful. She was thrilled to be able to choose someone to work with and asked Miss Taglia if Jenny could be her partner. Miss Taglia agreed and asked both of the girls to meet with her during recess to show them what needed to be done. She reminded them that they would need to come directly to their classroom after getting off the bus the next morning to begin the project.

The next morning, Miss Taglia was pleased to see two smiling faces at her door. It was a different way to begin the day. During that day and the days that followed, Miss Taglia noticed a marked change in Lisa's relationship to her and to the rest of the class. Lisa no longer focused only on her teacher but looked for ways to be involved with her classmates.

Cruelty

Discussion

Cruella is going to drown those darling Dalmatian puppies. How dastardly!

Will Lex Luthor manage to destroy Superman in this episode?

The theater erupts into applause when Luke Skywalker succeeds at blasting the enemy into oblivion.

Movies offer satisfying villains. We cheer their demise without a twinge of guilt. Of course, teachers face real-life children, not mustachioed evildoers.

Classmates hit, punch, and call each other names. Children squash bugs and torment small animals. Sometimes children are cruel for lack of knowledge. Sometimes hurtful actions reflect inner pain.

More is not better. This is a good rule of thumb for responding to cruelty, especially if your gut reaction is outrage. Responding to cruelty with cruelty teaches children to lash out. It's more effective to look directly at the misbehaving child and say in a quiet but clear voice, "I need your help to be sure everyone is treated with respect." Screeching does not improve communication. It's just louder. More is not better.

Children are not bad guys or villains. A child who hurts another child tells us that she is hurting. We do not ignore the damage a child does, but neither children nor adults benefit from punishment. Children do better when they feel better.

Suggestions

1. Take a moment to calm down and regain your composure before approaching a situation that brings your blood to a boil. Teachers also do better when they feel better.

2. Address hurtful behavior. Help hurting students. Do not confuse the two. Until everyone has calmed down, a rule of using ten words or fewer keeps you from wanting to retaliate through your words or actions. You may say, "Stop. This behavior is not acceptable." Let all parties know that the situation will be addressed at an arranged time. When speaking with the student who uses cruelty, be clear that the behavior is not acceptable, that he will be held accountable, and that you are still there to support him in making better choices.

3. Usually a student who engages in using cruel behavior may have the mistaken goal of revenge. She has the mistaken belief that she is not likable and will behave in ways to prove that this belief is true. Consult the Mistaken Goal Chart (pages 12–13) for ideas on ways to encourage this student.

4. Help a student whose behavior is hurtful feel a sense of belonging in the classroom. If a student makes enemies more easily than friends, seek support from her classmates. Ask her whether she would be willing to find out what her classmates

appreciate about her and use that information to increase the nice times she shares with them. For example, Becky usually spends recess taunting the other students. New information helps her make better choices. When Becky hears that several students enjoy jumping rope with her because she knows so many rhymes, she brings in a jump rope the next day and invites these students to join her at recess.

5. No one is perfect. If you respond with anger, punishment, and your own cruelty, use the Three R's of Recovery: *Recognize* that you made a mistake. *Reconcile* by apologizing. *Resolve* by working on a solution together.

Planning Ahead to Prevent Future Problems

1. Classrooms where misbehavior and punishment are connected don't produce peaceful students. Keep in mind the desired long-range results. When students focus on solutions during class meetings, they develop compassion and tolerance.

2. Discuss the needs of all living creatures. Help students feel empathy for their fellow beings. It makes sense to a student to carry an insect outside to the garden rather than smearing it on the rug if she comprehends the contribution of even small creatures to her complex world.

3. All behavior has meaning. Students treating others with cruelty may be experiencing cruelty. Students who hit are often being hit. (Refer to "Abuse.") A student's actions may be a cry for help. Behavior that persists and isn't altered by positive interventions deserves closer examination. Thoughtful scrutiny changes the focus from "How can I make this student behave?" to "What help does this student need?"

4. When behavior doesn't improve, another possibility is that the child has been pampered and doesn't know how to deal with not getting his way. Parents of an overindulged child need support and encouragement. Blame and guilt don't inspire adults any more than they do students. The teacher's approach to the child's family should be one of collaboration and teamwork: Mrs. Smith enlists the assistance of John's parents in dealing with the problems John has at school. She is not blaming them for John's problems or judging their effectiveness as parents. She suggests a parenting class in which they can learn the same principles the teacher is using and finds helpful.

5. Teach and model a positive attitude toward mistakes. We all make them, so use mistakes as learning tools rather than branding irons.

6. Use role plays instead of lectures to help students understand the results of cruel behavior.

Inspirational Story

During a workshop, a teacher asked coauthor Jane Nelsen what she could do about a little boy kicking a bird. Jane cautioned her not to give free rein to her indignation about it, not to focus on making the child feel guilty, and to remember that it's a crazy idea to think we can make children *do* better by first making them *feel* worse. She persisted, "Well, what would you do?"

Jane confessed that she would feel angry and indignant and would probably scold and throw in some guilt. Then, when she calmed down, she would use the Three R's of Recovery by first recognizing that she had been just as disrespectful to the child as he had been to the bird. She would then reconcile by apologizing and sharing with him that when she was hurting him, she was doing the same thing he had done to the bird. She would get into his world and guess that he didn't like being hurt by her, check it out with him to see whether that was true, and help him feel validated for his feelings.

Jane's experience of using this process is that it will create an atmosphere of mutual respect and understanding that promotes the last step: working together on a resolution. She would begin by asking "how" and "what" questions: "How do you think the bird felt?" "What did you learn from this experience?" "How could you help instead of hurt the bird?" "What will you do next time?"

A mother in the workshop shared how grateful she was for hearing this answer because she had just spanked her child for hitting the cat. She felt that she could now go home and use the Three R's of Recovery to apologize for treating her child as disrespectfully as her child had treated the cat, and she and her child could work on a solution together. We all need to know that, as human beings with human frailties, we will continue to make mistakes no matter how much we know. What better opportunity do we have to continually teach our children that mistakes are wonderful opportunities to learn?

So don't try to be perfect. Make lots of mistakes, and learn from them in such a way that your life and relationships are better because of the mistakes than they would have been without them.

Crying

Discussion

Crying is a natural, healthy process for relieving distress. Students should be allowed to cry in the interest of their mental health. However, if you think a student is using the power of tears to manipulate you, acknowledge his unhappiness without buying into his manipulation.

Suggestions

1. If you notice a student is crying, ask him whether he would like to take a break and talk to you after he feels calmer: "Carl, would you like to go get a drink of water, and I'll talk to you at noon?"

2. Without words, walk over to the student, hand her a tissue, and lightly touch her back or give her arm a reassuring squeeze. Continue with your instruction to the class. A truly sad student deserves to have her feelings respected. Don't mini-

mize them or try to stop her tears. Dignify her sadness by allowing her to feel and release it. Quietly offer support and comfort.

3. Offer a limited choice. Ask the student whether he would like to talk with you about the tears for a few minutes now or after class.

4. If a student habitually uses tears to manipulate situations, speak to her privately: "I notice that when you are upset or angry, you begin to cry. When you are crying, I can't help you. Do you have any ideas about what we can do the next time this happens?"

Planning Ahead to Prevent Future Problems

1. Be aware that crying is one of those displays, such as laughter, that will impact a group. Acknowledge the feelings not only of the student who is crying but also of those around her. During a class meeting, allow students to share how crying impacts them and to offer their ideas about how to help.

2. Be aware of the four goals of misbehavior (refer to "Mistaken Goals [Hat Messages]"):

   A. It could be that the student has received undue attention at home that led her to believe others should take care of her. (The goal is attention.)

B. Tears might indicate that last night she managed to prove to her parents that they can't make her do her homework, but today she regrets that decision and has decided to exercise her "water power." (The goal is power.)

C. A student who is still smarting from the lecture she received at recess may see an opportunity to make her teacher feel guilty. (The goal is revenge.)

D. Crying could also indicate that the student feels inadequate to accomplish the task. (Her goal is assumed inadequacy, and she wants to give up.)

3. Remember that a misbehaving child is a discouraged child who needs encouragement. In this case, the teacher can encourage the student by teaching her effective life skills and helping her see that the overuse of tears isn't an effective way to resolve problems.

Inspirational Story

Manuel came into class after lunch with his stomach in knots. He hadn't studied for his math test, and he knew there was no way to get out of taking it. Mrs. Sarantino handed out the tests and asked the students to begin. Manuel put his name at the top of the paper and felt his eyes well up with tears. He became even more nauseated. Within three minutes, tears were rolling down Manuel's cheeks, and he was quietly sobbing. The entire class was aware of what was going on with him. Mrs. Sarantino slowly walked over to Manuel and asked him whether he would like to take a break for five minutes, get some water, and then resume taking the test.

Mrs. Sarantino was sad for Manuel. She realized that it was important for him to take a break to regain his composure. She also realized that it was important for him to complete the test and not learn to escape through tears.

Manuel came back and finished the test. He didn't do well. Mrs. Sarantino invited him to see her after school. She asked him what happened.

Manuel said, "I failed the test."

"What do you think caused that?" Mrs. Sarantino asked.

Manuel sheepishly admitted that he hadn't studied.

Mrs. Sarantino asked, "How do you feel about that?"

"I didn't like it," Manuel said. "It made me sick to my stomach."

Mrs. Sarantino continued, "How will you use what you learned in the future?"

"I'm going to study," Manuel said.

Mrs. Sarantino said, "It's up to you. Remember our class discussion about mistakes being wonderful opportunities to learn. It sounds like you have learned a lot."

Death

Discussion

Death is something of a taboo subject in Western society, particularly in the United States. Yet death is just as much a part of life as is birth. We prefer to ignore its presence because of our fear of dying or our reluctance to deal with our pain from the loss of a loved one.

We also usually avoid dealing with another's personal loss (for a teacher, this may be the student's loss), because we feel inadequate and powerless to cope with it. Finding the right words and actions seems almost impossible, making it easier to sidestep the issue and hope the student will heal with time. Meanwhile, the student is often struggling alone, possibly with guilt, and is understandably falling behind in his studies. This can add discouragement to the grieving process and prevent the student from learning until he has dealt with the loss forthrightly. The sense of loss needs to be faced in one of the many ways suggested if the student's emotional growth and academic learning are to continue.

Suggestions

1. Don't avoid the situation. Feel your discomfort, and do something anyway.

2. Say something like, "I can't even imagine how painful this must be for you, but I want you to know my heart aches for you. I'm here for you if you want a shoulder to cry on or someone to talk to."

3. If the student chooses to talk, don't try to offer solutions or answer unanswerable questions. Just listen with empathy. An exception is the child who feels guilty or to blame. You must refer this student to a trained counselor in case the student is contemplating suicide.

4. Ask the student whether she would like to hear about the feelings of other people who have experienced the death of someone they loved. If the answer is "yes," during a class meeting ask students who have experienced a loved one's death whether they would be willing to share their experiences and feelings.

5. Ask the student whether he would like to choose a buddy in the classroom who has experienced losing someone. If the student feels this would help, he can choose a buddy from a list of people who have had some training for this job. (See the fifth item under "Planning Ahead.")

6. Explain to the student that intense feelings of grief can occur at unexpected times

for months. Let her know that, if and when this happens, she can quietly leave the room or go to a special place in the room, with or without a buddy. Assure her that crying is nothing to be ashamed of.

7. If a classmate or teacher dies, provide time—during a class meeting or other special time—for all your students to express their feelings and concerns. One asset of the class meeting format is that every student gets a chance to speak or pass upon receiving the talking stick (or other item) that is passed around the circle. Having the item in their hands encourages students who might not otherwise speak up. The teacher could first invite the students to express their feelings, go around the circle once, and then go around the circle again so they can express their fears or concerns. They can go around the circle a third time to share ideas for comforting themselves and others. (Death can be very frightening to students. Encourage them to talk about their fears instead of keeping them inside.)

8. Create a celebration collage as a tribute to the classmate or teacher who died. Invite students to write short statements about what they appreciated about this person or some way in which he or she influenced them. (If the students are too young to write, invite older students to help by taking dictation.) Your students might also want to decorate the collage with drawings or pictures from magazines that remind them of the person who died.

9. Plant a tree in memory of the person who died.

Planning Ahead to Assist with Future (and Past) Problems

1. Incorporate the study of death into your school curriculum through social studies, history, geography (culture), or health. An open discussion of how various cultures throughout history have viewed and treated death can begin to eliminate the fear of this normally taboo subject. Scientists have reported in the *Journal of the American Medical Association* that fear of death may produce enough stress to have a serious detrimental effect on a person's physical and mental well-being. Through a study of death, students may begin to treat their own lives and others' with more respect.

2. Have your class read inspirational stories of people dealing with loss due to death. You might assign older students to do a book report in cooperative learning groups.

3. Have older students research how people throughout history have offered comfort to those dealing with the death of a loved one. Students may discover clues in books, movies, and poems. (One Native American chief told a young man suffering

from the loss of his mother, "My words are dust, but my heart shares your pain.") The point is to strengthen your students to deal with the inevitable.

4. A teacher, psychologist, or counselor can facilitate a support group for people (students and teachers) who have experienced the loss of a loved one. Even when the loss isn't new, survivors still need opportunities to express their feelings and experiences.

5. Social interest can be healing, so take time for "buddy training." Students and teachers in the grief support group can learn to assist others. The buddy's job is to ask a student or teacher who has recently gone through a loved one's death what he or she needs—to share feelings, to listen to someone who has gone through a similar experience, or just to be with someone who can give silent support. Training is simple. Students can role-play in pairs, taking turns asking what the other needs from the three choices mentioned earlier and then offering what the person needs.

6. Have your students plan a project that assists or brightens the lives of some elderly people, and arrange a field trip so the students can visit the people and bestow the gift. (The late Dr. Leo Buscaglia told a wonderful story about a rich, spoiled college student who changed dramatically after Dr. Buscaglia persuaded him to visit a home for the elderly. Later Dr. Buscaglia

would see him leading several old people across campus to a concert or some other event.)

7. Teach the five psychological stages experienced in the dying and grieving process. It may be comforting to understand that denial, anger, bargaining, depression, and acceptance are normal stages that people go through when dying or grieving.

8. Don't expect someone who is grieving to "snap out of it" and get on with life. It's normal for intense grieving to last six months to a year, and continuous support is helpful. If intense pain or anger or serious depression continues longer than a year, therapy may be needed.

Class Meeting Solutions

In Memoriam

A story from Marti White, instructional support teacher, Educational Leadership Center, Orange County Public Schools, Orlando, Florida

A little girl who attended an elementary school in Florida was killed in a car accident. At a class meeting, her classmates were invited to celebrate how this little girl had touched them. Each student had a chance to share an appreciation for the girl who had died.

Then the teacher asked her students, "What are your concerns now?" Some of them were afraid to go home. Many had never dealt with death before and didn't know what to do. They brainstormed and came up with several suggestions. One was to set up a phone buddy system so they could call each other, even in the middle of the night. They made a list of people they could talk to during the day. The kids had different people they felt comfortable talking to during school hours: janitors, librarians, a lunchroom supervisor, counselors, teachers, the principal, and each other. The class decided that anyone could get a pass to go talk to someone whenever they felt the need.

They decided to paste pictures of the little girl on ribbon pins, which they wore for a week in her honor. They planted a tree in memory of the little girl, and they nurtured it throughout the year. The kids became role models for the school's adult personnel on the many ways to deal with grief.

An Unexpected Death

Corpus Christi, Texas, was where the Tejano music star Selena died suddenly. Born and raised in Corpus Christi, Selena was known and beloved by many there.

Word of her death by shooting surfaced during lunchtime and spread like wildfire through the city, including all five high schools. The high school students using class meetings called emergency meetings in their classrooms to deal with Selena's death. In one of the class meetings, students were able to give comfort and show empathy for their classmate, Claudia, who was Selena's first cousin.

Their teacher, Mrs. Biddle, was amazed at the students' understanding and compassion. Several weeks later, during the appreciation time of class meetings, Claudia thanked her fellow classmates for their support during a difficult time. She told them that she did not know whether she would have been able to cope with her loss and still come to school if it hadn't been for their support.

Inspirational Story

A class developed a plan for all of the students to honor those whose deaths had affected them. The teacher suggested to her students that they bring something to class that reminded them of a person or animal whom they had lost through death.

After the plan was implemented, a hair ribbon appeared on a corner of the blackboard. It had been given to a girl in the class, Sarah, by her grandfather. Only she and the teacher knew what it meant. If asked, the teacher would refer students to Sarah, as the teacher and Sarah had previously agreed. If she felt comfortable explaining, she would then do so.

The collar of Edgar's dog encircled the pencil sharpener. This had been suggested during a class meeting and chosen by Edgar as something he would like to do. All class members had known the dog, so they were able to share in this memorial. After several months, Edgar took the collar home and placed it on his dresser. When his teacher saw him two years later, she asked about the collar, and Edgar told her he had eventually buried it beside his pet.

Defiance

Discussion

It is difficult to know the cause of defiance. It could be that a student is being overly controlled or pampered at home, and his defiance is a display of undue attention or misguided power. He could be experiencing abuse at home, and his defiance is a way of seeking revenge in a safer environment. He could be acting out the influence he experiences from the media. It could be rebellion against the control and/or punishment he experiences at school—a way of saying, "You can't control me." And, it could be a simple lack of social skills and social interest. Most students prefer to cooperate and do what's in their own best interest, but if they are treated disrespectfully, they are willing to suffer great personal pain to show that they can't be bossed.

Suggestions

1. The first thing to do is to look at your own behavior because defiance is often a direct response to excessive control.

2. If your student is an arguer, she may have someone nearby who gives her arguing practice. If it's you, practice letting your student have the last word. (This is harder than you think. Try it.)

3. Get into your student's world and make some guesses to learn what is behind the defiance. Look at the Mistaken Goal Chart (pages 12–13). Check our your feelings as your first clue to the student's mistaken goal.

4. Use goal disclosure. (Refer to "Wandering" for an explanation of this process.) You might ask, "Could it be that you are angry because you think I boss you around too much?" "Could it be that you feel hurt because the others get more attention?" You can usually guess what is going on in your student's life that may be provoking defiance. Your student will feel validated and understood when you guess correctly. If you guess incorrectly, try again.

5. Let your student take the lead whenever possible by offering limited choices. (See the "Inspirational Stories.")

6. Some students will push and push until they are punished. Then they settle down. They have been trained not to settle down until they are punished. Instead of using punishment, say "I'm not going to punish

you. I am sorry I have used those methods in the past and wish to change our relationship. I'm not happy with what you are doing, but I care about you and would like your help so we can stop fighting with each other and work things out together." Then follow through with dignity and respect.

7. It is important not to ignore defiant behaviors or to give in to a student to avoid a confrontation. By following through, you are showing your student that you see him as someone who is capable of respectful behavior. (See "Follow-Through" and "Firmness and Kindness.")

8. Instead of *telling* your student what to do, try *asking* her what needs to be done. "What do you need to do before recess?" This often invites students to think and use their power to solve the problem instead of defying your direct orders.

9. Let your student know that you need his help: "I would appreciate anything you could do to help." This often invites cooperation instead of defiance.

Planning Ahead to Prevent Future Problems

1. This is an opportunity for you to learn how to invite cooperation. Pay attention to how much talking you are doing. Are you barking orders, nagging, and scolding? Your student may be "teacher-deaf" because you talk more than you act. Talk less and act more if this is the case. (See "Listen, Failure to.") Don't say anything unless you mean it, and if you mean it, give the matter your full attention. Say what you mean, firmly and kindly; then follow through on what you say. (See "Follow-Through.")

2. For a student who has a pattern of defiance, create time for training. (This includes training for yourself in being firm and kind.) Training could include class meetings, positive time-out, the Problem-Solving Wheel of Choice, joint problem solving, or simply your modeling mutual respect.

3. Give limited choices and ask questions instead of giving lectures. Ask for your student's opinion and input. Really listen to what he tells you.

4. Get your student involved in the planning of events and in problem solving during class meetings. Students are seldom defiant when they have been respectfully included in the decision-making process.

Inspirational Stories

Word Power

A story from Stephanie Corvese, second-grade teacher, St. Catherine of Sienna, Woodbridge (Toronto), Ontario, Canada

Last year, I had quite the "difficult" class. I had several behavior students and decided I was going to make the best of it. I had one particular student who just refused to do anything you asked him; he couldn't sit still and "bounced from wall to wall." He claimed he "hated school," and nothing I said would make a difference. At first, we had power struggles. I'd want him to get his work done, and he wouldn't. In fact, the more I pushed for him to get work done, the worse his behavior got. He'd shout at me, scream in class, kick his desk, and throw his chair.

The behavior resource team at my school put together a plan for me where he would have a time-out in the class if he didn't do his work, and if he still defied me, he would get sent to the office. If he refused to do any work at the office, he got sent home.

Well, he spent most of his days in the office having temper tantrums, and the parents were frustrated that he was getting sent home. After I was introduced to the idea of giving students choices, I decided to try it on him. Whenever there was work to get done, I would say, "Joey, you have two choices: you can do this, or you can do that. You decide which activity you want to do, and when you're ready, let me know."

Well, I'm not kidding—that phrase turned his behavior right around. At first he just sat there, probably waiting for me to get angry, but when he realized I wasn't going to push or get angry anymore, he picked up his pencil and got to work. I couldn't believe it. One simple phrase transformed our relationship. This child just didn't want to feel controlled. He

needed to feel like he was responsible for his own learning. This one change helped me make it through the year much easier. I'll never forget the last day of school when he hugged me and said, "I'll miss you a lot this summer." Wow! What a feeling to know I had made a difference.

Cody

A story from Therese Durston, second-grade teacher, St. Olivier School, Saskatchewan, Canada

Cody comes from a home that is very controlling. The dad is the boss, and you do as you are told. Cody spent a great deal of time in an isolated spot in the classroom in first grade. He wants to do what he wants when he wants. I have to be constantly thinking of choices for him. Do you want to use the red pencil or blue pencil? Do you want to do your work at your desk or my desk? I have tried to give him control whenever I could—dismiss students, choose game, and so forth. He was exhausting me. He'd try to defy me all day, and then at dismissal time he'd leave about twenty-five minutes after everyone left. He'd talk and talk and talk.

I decided to do a contract with him. The deal was that if he defied me, I'd give him a signal (he chose *choo-choo* whispered in his ear or a train motion if I wasn't near him). If he still defied me, he would stay after school five minutes for every time he defied me, and we would practice doing what the teacher told him to do. (This part worried me because he loved to stay after school.)

We just completed day one. He went off track a couple of times, but the signal got him back on track. At the end of the day, he came running up to me and literally jumped up into my arms and gave me a huge hug: "I did it. I did it!" We talked about how he felt, and then off he went home along with all the other students! I can't wait for day two.

Depression

Discussion

Depression is an extreme form of discouragement. People feel depressed when they have lost hope, are disappointed in themselves or others, don't have self-confidence, or lack the perspective and skills to see potential solutions to their problems.

Perfectionism can also cause depression. When a parent or teacher expects too much from a student or the student expects too much of herself, she may become depressed. Students can become depressed when they feel they have tried their best, but their best is not appreciated—only perfection is appreciated. In addition, depression may result when students can't handle serious personal problems, such as sexual or physical abuse, divorcing parents, an unplanned pregnancy, or rejection from a boyfriend or girlfriend. Other causes of depression include facing a serious illness, having to move away from friends, or losing a loved one. Students who feel teased or rejected by peers, or who are continually fearful of bullies, may also become depressed.

How often do teachers consider all the problems that may be heaped on the plates of their students? Those who do consider these problems may get depressed themselves if they feel helpless or hopeless about the situation.

Suggestions

1. Suggest professional help (perhaps from the school counselor or psychologist) when you notice signs of depression.

2. Spend special time with discouraged students. Let students know you care, so they can have at least one place in their lives where they feel a sense of belonging and significance.

3. If a student looks depressed, allow him to choose a listening buddy, go into the time-out area, and share his concerns while the buddy just listens. (This works when students have been taught the value of listening without giving advice as well as the

value of being able to share feelings without seeking advice.)

Planning Ahead to Prevent Future Problems

1. Teach social skills and give students opportunities to show caring for each other. The compliment portion of a class meeting does both.

2. Facilitate a discussion about depression. Allow students to share their ideas about what can cause depression and what they can do about it. Make lists of causes and solutions.

3. Be sure to teach that suicide is a *permanent* solution to a *temporary* problem.

4. Teach students that bad times pass. Share times when you have experienced depression, and describe how you overcame it—perhaps simply through the passage of time.

5. Provide many opportunities for students to build strength in social skills and problem-solving skills. Students are much less likely to feel depressed for long periods of time when they are strong in these important areas.

6. Class meetings are an excellent vehicle for building empathy and a support system in the classroom.

Inspirational Story

Mrs. Gunderson taught high school. She had noticed that one of her students, Amy,

seemed very depressed. Amy had lost interest in her schoolwork and was missing a lot of class. Mrs. Gunderson asked Amy to stop by after school—"because I really care about you."

When Amy came by after school, Mrs. Gunderson asked whether anything was bothering her. Amy started to cry, and Mrs. Gunderson said, "Amy, I remember going through a time in high school when I thought life wasn't worth living. My boyfriend left me for my best friend, and I was devastated." Amy hid her face and kept crying. Mrs. Gunderson continued, "I certainly didn't know it then, but he did me a big favor. I might have missed so much if he had stayed in my life." Amy nodded, and Mrs. Gunderson said, "I think it can be very helpful to talk to someone, so you don't have to struggle with whatever is bothering you by yourself. Our school counselor, Mrs. Latimer, is very good. Would you be willing to see her?" Amy nodded again. Mrs. Gunderson said, "Good. I'll walk over to her office with you right now. If she's busy, you can make an appointment."

It happened that the school counselor was busy with paperwork, which she happily set aside so she could spend time with Amy.

Amy didn't show it, but she already felt a little bit better because of the interest Mrs. Gunderson had shown and the personal things she had shared. Amy was ready to open up with the counselor. Drawing a large circle on a piece of paper, Mrs. Latimer added lines to make four pie-shaped pieces. She then said to Amy, "Let's look at the pie of your life. Each one of these four pieces represents a slice of your life." She labeled the slices "Friends," "Family," "School," and "Love." She asked Amy to rate how things were going in each of these areas.

Amy shared that she had had a fight with her best friend and felt rejected. When asked about her family, she admitted that her parents were talking about divorce. She wasn't doing well in school and was facing detention if she missed one more class. The only area of her life that felt good was love, because she was doing well with her steady boyfriend.

Mrs. Latimer said, "No wonder you're feeling depressed. Look at all the pieces that aren't feeling so good right now. Why don't we take one piece at a time and see what possibilities there might be?"

They started with the fight with her best friend. Mrs. Latimer role-played with Amy so she could practice how she might share her feelings with her friend. (That night, when she did this, she learned that her friend felt just as bad, and they made up quickly.) Next they tackled school. Amy had gotten so far behind that she didn't see the use of doing any work. They talked about the possibility of Amy temporarily going on independent study. (Amy pursued this possibility, with the help of the counselor, and did independent study for a semester. She worked diligently and received all A's. When she rejoined regular classes the following semester, she did well.)

When they discussed the family situation, Amy realized she couldn't do anything about her parents' decision, but she started to focus on the many good things about her family situation. She knew that both her parents loved her very much.

Later Amy shared with the counselor how much this session had helped her see that her problems were temporary and that she could do something about most of them. She also appreciated the help in focusing on what was going well in her life. She said how much it had helped her that Mrs. Gunderson had cared enough to approach her and had shared that she had experienced depression and that it didn't last. Others' care and help gave Amy hope and taught her skills so that she could overcome her depression.

Discouraged (Dysfunctional) Families

Discussion

Let's begin this discussion by changing the perceptions we have when we see or use the word *dysfunctional*. It's important to shift from using *dysfunctional* to describe individuals, families, or institutions to describing them as *discouraged* individuals, families, or institutions.

Dysfunctional describes behavior only. This word labels, neglects to incorporate wholeness, creates distance, and negates people's abilities to make changes. *Discouraged* means that people have lost their courage or never had enough courage.

Courage develops through the power of encouragement. Encouragement invites people to be connected and instills optimism about the ability to make changes. People feel encouraged when they learn effective life skills to replace their ineffective methods.

The term *dysfunctional family* is certainly overused. There's a cartoon that depicts an auditorium where a large banner is hanging at the front of the stage. The banner reads, "National Conference of Functional Families." The room is completely empty.

In spite of the overuse of the term *dysfunctional*, there is no denying that many children live in families ravaged by various social ills. Begin with abuse, drug and alcohol addiction, and poverty, and the list has only begun. Just what role does a teacher play in the lives of children who are in crisis and pain? Teachers are neither social workers nor counselors. Few teachers have the magical abilities we see portrayed in movies. Though many of us long to be all things to all people, we are not. What teachers can do is encourage students, listen to them without judgment, and not add to the burden of injustice in their lives. Schools can provide a troubled student with an environment where he feels safe, is encouraged to grow emotionally and intellectually, and can learn important life skills.

Suggestions

1. Offer compassion and understanding, but refuse to feel sorry for students who are struggling within discouraged family systems. To feel sorry for them negates their ability to change and choose a different path.

2. Listen, and accept what you hear. When a student is in despair, sitting with his head in his hands, the presence of someone to hear his story is healing. "My family is falling apart," he tells you. "My brother is in a gang. My sister died. My mother yells all the time." You can't fix this ten-year-old's life. But you can sit with him, listening and allowing his pain to surface, and

this may give him the strength to face the rest of his day. You haven't removed the burden from his shoulders, but you have lessened its weight.

3. Help a student who is feeling overwhelmed by his family situation focus on things over which he does have control. He may not be able to control what is happening at home, but he can focus his energy on his life at school and with his friends. Reminding him that these parts of his life are his "jobs" can be encouraging.

4. Punishment, blame, and shame do not improve behavior. When a student is suffering from conditions in her home, the last thing she needs is to suffer from conditions at school as well. You may not be able to improve her home life, but at least you aren't creating another set of crises for this child.

5. When responding to a student's misbehavior, ask yourself whether this particular misbehavior is interfering with learning. If a student is failing several subjects and getting into serious fights, is his taking off his shoes during class an issue worth focusing on? This student has so many opportunities for discouragement; try a lighter approach to a particular idiosyncrasy, and pick your issues carefully.

6. Remember that you aren't alone in dealing with discouraged families. Utilize the resources you have within your school and your community. Check with social ser-

vices, local newspapers, or the Internet for information on support groups, such as Al-Anon. These groups offer support for tots and teens.

Planning Ahead to Prevent Future Problems

1. Create a classroom environment of support, acceptance, and challenge. Each student should feel that he or she can depend on this refuge no matter what is happening at home.

2. Use class meetings to build skills and provide a healthy sense of belonging and significance for each student. The class meeting method answers the common complaint from teachers that they have too many students in need and too little time to care, because the process lets students help and encourage each other. High school teachers with 150 students find that, by creating a supportive network among their students through class meetings, many more of those who are struggling receive attention and assistance than teachers alone could provide.

3. No matter what life experiences a person has, she can choose her own actions. Teach students about choices by offering them choices and helping them brainstorm about various choices in difficult situations.

4. The flip side of choice is responsibility. Neither rescue a student from his choices

nor punish him for poor choices. Consequences (good and bad) result from choices. Help a student explore the consequences of his choices through "what" and "how" questions to help him learn about the role his choice had in the outcome he experienced: "What were you trying to accomplish?" "What did you do?" "What happened as a result of your choice?" "What did you learn?" "How might you approach this situation next time?" Notice how different this approach is from imposing a consequence. When students make poor choices, your compassion can help them have the courage to move on to the next step.

5. Teach your students, "It's not what happens to us that effects us so much as how we choose to perceive it and what we choose to do about it." Find, share, and discuss examples of people who have experienced great difficulty in their lives and have managed to triumph. (This could be a classroom assignment.)

6. Teach students to act on situations rather than reacting to them. A teacher can model this by choosing not to yell when angry or by not demanding immediate retribution for a misbehavior. By controlling her own behavior respectfully, the teacher is modeling a response that many students never see. She may follow this up with a class meeting discussion to identify a desirable response.

Teacher: When Jack crumpled up his paper and threw it down, what did you see me do?

Students: You turned around and walked away.

Teacher: Did walking away mean that I thought it was okay for papers to be treated in that way?

Through such a discussion (for which the teacher should have attained Jack's permission to use his example), the class learns a new process. Jack picked up the crumpled paper later in the day, after he was calm enough to sit and discuss the problem with his teacher. Along with taking responsibility for the paper, Jack learned several additional ways to respond the next time he feels frustrated. He was treated respectfully, his behavior was addressed, and the entire class was able to examine a new model of behavior.

7. When you know that a student in your class is part of a family in which members suffer from chemical dependency or are in a stage of recovery, educate yourself about the stages of dependency or recovery. Your awareness and knowledge will help you during interaction with both your student and his family.

8. Remember to do all you can within your sphere of influence. You may not be able to save all drowning children, but you can at least throw them a lifeline of skills,

care, and belief in their abilities until one day they can pull themselves out of the ocean of discouragement.

Inspirational Stories

Two Discouraged Boys

Two boys got into a serious fight during which one of them was injured. In their school such behavior typically resulted in a Saturday spent in detention. But their teacher, with the support of the administration, chose to get the students' agreement to meet with him the following morning for a problem-solving session. Their behavior was dangerous and needed to be addressed, but a day in detention wasn't going to improve the situation. These two boys had spent many days in detention.

What this teacher realized was that both boys were in terrible emotional pain. The upcoming Sunday was Mother's Day. The mother of one of the boys was in jail, and the mother of the other boy had a very abusive boyfriend. The school, in conjunction with social services, had been addressing these situations, but the teacher had never dealt directly with these boys about these problems. The teacher knew that children who hurt others are in pain themselves.

When they met the following morning, the first thing the teacher did was listen to each boy. Some strong feelings came up. Once those feelings had been aired, they all went on to discuss the fight and, in particular, the injury to one boy. They eventually agreed that the boys would spend four hours each helping out at a shelter for the homeless over the coming week. Given an opportunity to contribute to the well-being of others, the boys could see themselves as helpful rather than hurtful people.

That no more fights would occur between these boys certainly isn't guaranteed by this solution. But detention hadn't changed anything for the better, and the teacher's actions didn't add to the boys' burdens. He couldn't change their mothers or any other part of their home lives, but he could find a way to treat the needs of each boy with compassion and respect.

Encouraging Charlie

Charlie, a sixteen-year-old high school student, was doing poorly in school. During a class meeting in his world history class, Charlie shared with the other students that his home life was terrible. The students and the teacher, Mrs. Fernandez, brainstormed ways that they could show Charlie support and help him. Some students offered to tutor him in subjects with which he was struggling; others offered to call him once each day to let him know he wasn't alone; still others offered to pal around with him at school.

The group decided to implement their plan for one month and then check with Charlie to see how it was working for him.

Before the month was up, during appreciation time in a class meeting, Charlie thanked all the students for what they were giving him. He said he would have dropped out of school and run away if it hadn't been for them.

Discrimination

Discussion

"They're different from us, which means they can't be trusted. . . . We must sound the drums of war." In the Disney movie *Pocahontas,* the native people and the newly arrived English soldiers sing this refrain simultaneously. What a perfect depiction of discrimination! What is different and unknown is frightening. When people are frightened, they attack to protect themselves.

If you were asked to describe a student who comes into your classroom, you might say, "This is an Asian boy wearing a blue sweater." Skin color, gender, and clothing are details typically described. They are immediately visible. Racial, sexual, and class discrimination correspond to this list. We see differences, we fear the unknown, and discrimination results.

Education should enlighten students by transforming the unfamiliar into the known. A current trend in education is the antibias curriculum. The goal of this curriculum is to teach children that differences are not merely tolerated but represent viable lifestyles. A child whose head is covered by a white scarf isn't weird, nor is her religion stupid. Her family's beliefs lead to the use of such clothing.

In a class that has this type of training, when a student stumbles over the pronunciation of an English word or substitutes his native Spanish for the missing phrase, titters don't erupt throughout the room. The students have learned that Spanish is the language of many of the world's peoples and that their classmate has the good fortune to be bilingual.

Differences do not equal danger. Education is powerful enough to make discrimination as extinct as dinosaurs.

Suggestions

1. Bobby calls Kim a racially charged name. Kim is hurt and humiliated. When discrimination occurs, address it in three ways:

A. Clearly tell Bobby and Kim that such behavior isn't acceptable or allowed in this classroom. Kim doesn't deserve to be treated unjustly.

B. Ask Bobby whether he knows how it feels to be hurt by a classmate. Help him recognize that his words hurt Kim. Offer Bobby an opportunity to do something to help Kim feel better.

C. Plan classroom activities that validate Kim's culture.

2. Expect students to treat one another with respect. Take note of statements and actions that indicate distrust or a lack of information. Don't overlook them. Get the students involved in discussion and solutions. Blame and shame don't change beliefs or patterns of discrimination. Education does.

Planning Ahead to Prevent Future Problems

1. Lead a discussion of ways in which students are alike and ways in which they are different. Approach differences with curiosity and appreciation.

2. Use class meetings to address discrimination in the school setting. Come to a class agreement that all students in this school will be treated with respect.

3. Use examples from the media to help students learn to identify discrimination. Discuss how people feel when they are discriminated against. Ask class members to share their experiences.

4. Question the way books portray people. Are dentists ever female? Are there black police officers? Do men take care of children or cook?

5. Establish an environment in which many cultures are represented. Instead of putting up pictures of Native American peoples only for the month when the class studies the Plains Indians, keep a variety of pictures on display all the time. Pictures of an Asian doctor, an African American soldier, and a Navajo legislator reflect the diversity in the United States. Use fabric, musical instruments, and art from other cultures regularly. When you present cultures as normal and comprehensible, they change from exotic to familiar.

6. Expose students to a wide variety of gender roles, social statuses, and other types of differences as well. When teaching subjects such as government or social sciences, don't miss the opportunity to discuss discrimination and the value of diversity.

Inspirational Story

Mary Ellen and Tirome were playmates in the second grade. One day Mary Ellen announced to Tirome that she didn't like her because her skin was dark. Mr. Crane was shocked to overhear this comment. He told Mary Ellen that dark skin is beautiful and demanded that she take back such an unjust statement. Mary Ellen adamantly refused to retract what she had said. It was time for school to end, and all three of them went home upset.

The next day Mr. Crane decided to try another approach. First, he went to Tirome and told her that no one had the right to say unkind things about the color of her skin. He said he was sorry that her feelings had been hurt yesterday. With Mr. Crane's encouragement, Tirome practiced responses to such derogatory remarks. She learned to say, "What you said is untrue. I am proud of who I am." She rehearsed turning from her detractor and walking away with dignity.

Next Mr. Crane sat down with Mary Ellen and asked her whether she could remember a time she felt hurt. She nodded as tears begin to flow. Her daddy had moved out of their house this week. Mr. Crane put his hand on Mary Ellen's shoulder to comfort her while she wept.

When she was calmer, he asked her whether she thought Tirome felt hurt yesterday when she said she didn't like her because of her skin color. Mary Ellen agreed that Tirome probably felt hurt. Mr. Crane wondered if Mary Ellen was willing to think of a way she might help Tirome feel better again. Mary Ellen made suggestions with enthusiasm and then decided to write Tirome an apology for hurting her feelings.

Mary Ellen may have lashed out at her friend because of her own feelings about what was happening at home. When children feel hurt, they often take it out on whomever is in their path. Helping children empathize with the feelings of others is an excellent way to educate against discrimination.

Disorganization

Discussion

Organization skills may come more easily for some, but they are teachable to others. Oldest children naturally tend to put things in order. Youngest children often flounder and expect others to provide order for them. Middle children may be organized in some areas and not in others. Only children may have unique styles of organization. These possibilities are presented neither as absolutes nor as stereotypes. They are meant to show that individuals' different priorities aren't a matter of right or wrong; they are styles people have adopted. Keeping this in mind may help you teach (or learn) organization without attaching judgment.

Suggestions

1. Be aware of the importance of modeling organization. Your approach and the structure of your classroom will provide direct

examples of the importance of organization and the process itself.

2. Take time for training. Whether it is how to organize a paper, a desk, a group project, daily work, or a game on the schoolyard, students need to be shown the steps needed to take them to their goals. (See "Take Time for Training.")

3. If a student is having difficulty in this area, you can say, "I notice that you are having some trouble getting yourself organized. I've got some ideas I'd like to share with you. I'm available Wednesday after school. Can you meet me then to get some help?"

4. Don't assume total responsibility for keeping the classroom organized. Every student should have a job that contributes to this. (Refer to "Jobs for Everyone in the Classroom.")

Planning Ahead to Prevent Future Problems

1. Post a written daily schedule to help students get in the habit of seeing the whole day and the parts that make up the day. They can transfer this skill to times when they need to see what they need to accomplish and the steps they need to take to get there.

2. Schedule a weekly period of time for getting organized. Some students may need to work on their desks; some may

need to organize their notebooks; some may need to check their progress on a long-term report.

3. Allow students to choose between organizing their desks individually or accomplishing the task with a buddy for company and ideas. Older students may opt to receive help in organizing projects or study time from another student or from their teachers.

4. During a class meeting, facilitate a discussion about disorganization. Let the students make suggestions as to solving the problems that result from disorganization.

5. As part of the discussion of disorganization, let the students brainstorm to come up with a list of tips on getting and staying organized. Ask a volunteer to make a poster of the tips.

Inspirational Story

Sometimes a simple solution can go a long way. Mrs. Lenox had some concerns about a student in her class. She noticed that although Phil's in-class work was satisfactory and his test scores were excellent, he had many missing homework assignments. When Mrs. Lenox spoke to Phil about this, he replied that he was positive that he had done them. Mrs. Lenox set up a short meeting with Phil and his parents to discuss how to solve this mystery.

When they all met, Mrs. Lenox began by sharing some of Phil's strengths and asked his parents to also add their thoughts. She asked Phil to share his impressions of how he was doing in her class. He said that he thought he was doing fine and didn't understand why they had to meet. Mrs. Lenox explained the problem to Phil and his parents and how missing assignments were affecting his grades. Although there was confirmation from his parents that assignments were being completed, they all noticed that the missing link was getting them turned in. Mrs. Lenox asked Phil whether he had ever tried using a filing binder that has separate pockets for keeping papers organized. Phil hadn't used one but knew that several students in his class used them. His mother said that she would be willing to buy one this evening and to help Phil label the individual slots.

Phil was excited to bring his new binder to school the next morning. He showed Mrs. Lenox how he had organized the pockets alphabetically. He was beaming as he pulled out his homework and proudly placed it in the basket.

Disrespectful Behavior

Discussion

When a student is disrespectful to teachers or classmates, the first source to consider is the behavior of the adults in this student's life. Children who aren't treated with respect have no model for respectful behavior. Joe's parents call each other names, belittle Joe, and sneer when he objects to anything. When Joe behaves similarly at school, it is unacceptable. Joe needs training, experience, and examples of respectful behavior.

Self-respect is the other important aspect here. The teacher who passively allows a student to sneer or engage in sarcasm isn't modeling respect for herself. She must calmly tell the student, "We have spoken about respectful behavior in our classroom, and we have agreed what that looks like. Your choice of words is showing disrespect and I'd like to speak with you at the next break." This statement needs to be followed up with a dialogue when both teacher and student are calm again. Contrast this response to lecturing, blaming, and threatening, and then decide which response you would prefer if you were the student.

For another important clue to the source of this misbehavior, consider how widespread the displays of disrespect seem to be. One wise administrator said that if a classroom has two or three problem students, then there are probably two or three students with problems; if a classroom has five, six, or more problem students, then there may very well be a problem teacher. A wise university professor stated that all teachers have problems with students. Conversely, all students have problems with teachers.

Every teacher knows that some classes are more difficult than others. Whatever the situation, a teacher's best tool is control over his or her own behavior.

Suggestions

1. Model respectful behavior. Before approaching a situation that's making your blood boil, take a moment to calm down and regain your composure.

2. Give lessons on respectful behavior. Demonstrate respectful ways to approach and respond to others, and let the students practice them.

3. Encourage students by letting them know when you notice their efforts to practice new behaviors. Be specific: "Mary, you explained to Susan how much her whistling during lunch was annoying to you. That shows respect for Susan as well as respect for your own needs."

4. Use the Mistaken Goal Chart (see pages 12–13) to decode what a student's behavior is telling you. A teacher's intuition may offer the best clue. Typically a student who is hurting others is feeling hurt herself; the goal is then revenge. Some students may be disrespectful to get attention or to show

power. Identifying the likely hidden message helps the teacher figure out the best way to respond.

5. Avoid lectures, shaming, and blaming students. Such adult tactics incite disrespectful responses.

6. Practice mutual respect. That means remembering to respect your own needs as well as the students' needs.

Planning Ahead to Prevent Future Problems

1. Take time to connect with your students. It's easy to be disrespectful to a person you perceive only as an object of your control or manipulation. Similarly, it's difficult to be disrespectful toward someone who is an asset to you or who sees you as an asset. Middle and high school teachers who use Positive Discipline class meetings have discovered that taking time for giving compliments, appreciations, and encouragements contributes to a mutually respectful atmosphere in their classrooms.

2. At a class meeting, discuss the students' understanding of disrespectful and respectful behavior. Share your own thoughts. Identify and role-play ways in which people can behave respectfully in specific situations. The class might formulate a plan with a chosen focus, such as ways in which they can show respect for one another when standing in line waiting for lunch. In

a few days or a week, students can discuss how the new plan is working.

3. Take time for training. Role-play a problem situation with a student individually or during a class meeting. Allow the student to play the role of the adult and to practice both unacceptable and acceptable responses. Then encourage the student to express the feelings he experienced when in the adult role. Reverse roles, and go through the process again.

4. Develop an atmosphere of trust by helping students see that you are more interested in solutions to problems than in identifying or punishing those who misbehave.

5. Learn to trust the process of working *with* students, rather than trying to control them.

Inspirational Story

Peter had always been on the fringe and never quite belonged to any particular group in elementary school. When he started in middle school, he found that he had a talent for coming up with quick comebacks and sarcastic remarks in the classroom. The response from some of his classmates was positive, and he found that he was gaining new status.

A common response from Peter's teachers was to lecture and to threaten with disciplinary measures. This did nothing to stop his behavior. Mr. Lovitt, who had once taught Peter in the second grade, was now his math teacher. He was surprised and disappointed to see the changes in Peter. At first, he tried to ignore Peter's remarks. He soon realized that this was not effective and noticed that a general climate of disrespect was growing within the class.

Mr. Lovitt decided to bring up the issue of respect at their next class meeting. During this time, he shared his observations and some specific kinds of disrespect that were being practiced in the classroom. In fact, he set up a role play asking for a volunteer to play the teacher and positioned himself as one of the students. During the role play, he demonstrated some of the behaviors he had witnessed in the class. Afterward, he engaged the students in a discussion about what people were thinking, feeling, and deciding about being part of this classroom. He was glad to see the discussion naturally move in a direction of coming up with solutions aimed at creating a respectful classroom.

After this meeting, Mr. Lovitt approached Peter and asked him what he thought about the discussion. He shared that he noticed that Peter had been using some of those disrespectful behaviors and that his classmates always responded with approval. Mr. Lovitt pointed out Peter's leadership potential, expressing his wish to have Peter find other ways to get the recognition that we all want from our classmates. He asked Peter to think about this and told him that he would be looking forward to checking back with him. Before they parted, Mr. Lovitt and Peter exchanged a high-five.

Peter's behavior changed dramatically for two reasons: (1) After the class meeting discussion, he knew disrespectful behavior would no longer be received favorably. (2) He gained a sense of belonging when Mr. Lovitt treated him respectfully.

Disruption

(see also "Class Meetings, Disruptions")

Discussion

A single method will never be appropriate to dealing with all disruptions because the causes are so varied. Disruption offers a vivid example of a teacher's need to understand and respond to motives instead of dealing just with behavior. This section will present possible motives (purposes behind the behavior) and methods of dealing with them for long-range results, as well as methods of dealing with the immediate behavior.

Teachers can cope more effectively with disruptions when they understand the belief behind the disruptive behavior. When the student believes that he or she has no value, significance, or belonging, the disruptive behavior represents one of the mistaken goals: undue attention, power, revenge, or giving up.

Disruption frequently arises from seeking the goal of undue attention. This is beautifully illustrated by a few lines from the song "Attention" by Wayne Frieden and Marie Hartwell Walker:[18]

Oh I can tap my pencil, scrape my chair, drop my books, comb my hair, whistle and hum, act real cute, make funny faces, yell and hoot, ask for a drink of water ten times, sharpen my pencil, start to cry, wear my jacket inside out, when I have to hang it up I pout, go to the bathroom every hour, use flash cards to build a tower.

Students who are seeking power or revenge can be extremely disruptive. Power attained through disruption can be used to defeat a teacher or to lead other students in disruptive behavior. Revenge may be directed against other people or their property.

If the whole class is disruptive, the students may feel discouraged by adults who try to have too much control, don't have enough faith in their students' abilities, and don't treat them with respect. Disruption can also be due to a lack of training in cooperation and solving problems.

---

18. From *Behavior Songs,* available from Empowering People Books, Tapes, and Videos, (800) 456-7770.

Suggestions

1. If the disruption annoys you, and if the student usually stops the behavior for a while when reminded, the mistaken goal is probably attention. Get the student involved. Remember the message hat for attention that says, "Notice me! Involve me." (Refer to "Mistaken Goals [Hat Messages].") It's very effective to redirect this student immediately to something constructive: "Sheila, would you please be our light switcher today, and switch the lights when it gets too noisy?" Teachers who fear that this action rewards the misbehavior may be surprised when they try it. The student who doesn't feel encouraged is much more likely to continue her disruptive behavior than the student who feels encouraged because she's making a contribution.

2. If you feel challenged or threatened by the disruptive behavior, and if the behavior intensifies into a power struggle (passive or active) when you intervene, the student's goal is most likely power. Try responding in one of these ways:

A. Voice what is happening, and ask for help: "I see we are in a power struggle. I really need your help to get out of this. Do you have any ideas about what might work better?" (Remember the message hat for power that says, "Let me help! Give me choices.")

B. Without mentioning the power struggle, use distraction by acknowledging your need for help and immediately offer-

ing a choice: "Jenny, I need your help. Which job would you like, passing out these papers or taking the roll to the office?" This redirects the use of power from disruptive to helpful while providing a sense of belonging and contribution.

C. If you need a cooling-off period, tell the truth: "It feels like we are in a power struggle, and I'm too upset to deal with this right now. Should we put this problem on the class meeting agenda or make an appointment to talk later when we feel better?"

3. If you feel hurt or disgusted, and if the student reacts with more hurtful behavior when you try to help, the goal is revenge. It takes a lot of courage to break the revenge cycle. Awareness helps. Try these responses:

A. Tell the truth: "I feel hurt, and that tells me you may be feeling hurt by something." Then deal with the hurt feelings in an empathetic way. (Remember the message hat for revenge that says, "Help me. I'm hurting. Validate my feelings.")

B. Make a guess as to what may be hurting the student. Or ask, "Would you like to talk about it?"

C. A cooling-off period may be needed. See 2C.

D. If you were angered and reacted with some revenge of your own, use the Three R's of Recovery—Recognize, Reconcile, and Resolve. (See page 41.)

E. If a student has already hurt someone, it's easy to feel disgusted and distance ourselves from that student. We may then move into punishing and perpetuate the revenge cycle. The teacher must remember that the student who displays hurtful behavior is hurting, too. He may say in a firm and respectful way, "I'm here to make sure that everyone at our school feels safe. I can't allow this kind of behavior to happen to anyone, including you." The goal should be to prevent the hurtful behavior from happening in the future by helping the student have the courage to face the consequences. Encouragement does not reward misbehavior. Encouragement helps prevent future misbehavior.

4. Use the class meeting as a tool to solve specific problems. You may ask for the students' help in finding solutions to the disruptive behavior of one student or of the entire class.

5. Remember that disruption could also be caused by many of the other subjects discussed in this book, such as divorce, ADHD, death, or depression. See those subjects for other ideas on dealing with disruption.

Planning Ahead to Prevent Future Problems

1. Take time to train students in nonverbal signals that help them respond to disruptions by the whole class or by individuals. The upcoming inspirational stories give some examples of nonverbal signals.

2. Use class meetings to teach students social interest and problem-solving skills and to help them feel belonging and significance. (Giving students opportunities to experience giving and receiving appreciations and helpful suggestions is powerful encouragement.)

3. After a cooling-off period, invite the student to see you alone and use goal disclosure to discover the purpose of the disruptions. (Refer to the last section of "Wandering.")

4. Spend special time getting to know any student with whom you are having trouble. This may help him feel encouraged enough to stop misbehaving. Invite the student to stay after school to talk about fun topics, such as the activities that each of you likes to do.

5. Many students have a pattern of disruptive behavior. Take time to train these students in conflict resolution, peer tutoring, or cross-age tutoring to redirect their use of power into contribution. Consult with your administrator or school counselor for additional help with students who seem resistant to change.

6. Trust the process of class meetings and encouragement. It can take time—as the following story illustrates.

Class Meeting Solution

A story from Marti White, instructional support teacher, Orange County Public School System, Orlando, Florida

Matthew was almost always on the class meeting agenda for hitting, cursing, taking other children's things, or just generally causing trouble. I sometimes used the agenda and the problem-solving format of the class meeting to help me with Matthew's disruptive behavior in the classroom.

The special area teachers were fed up with Matthew and had begun to report his outbursts and hitting to the principal. The principal informed me that the next time Matthew hit another child, he would be sent home for three days.

Although I continued using class meetings with Matthew, I was beginning to wonder whether they could actually help him. At this time a new student who couldn't speak a word of English arrived in my class. For some reason he took an instant liking to Matthew. Because this new boy couldn't speak English, he decided to get Matthew's attention by hitting him between the shoulder blades as hard as he could. Normally Matthew would have retaliated with a vengeance, and I would have had to report the incident to the principal. Instead, Matthew did nothing to the boy, walked proud as a peacock to the agenda, and reported the incident.

This alone was an event to celebrate, but what happened next was truly amazing. Matthew described the problem in great detail in his own terms. My aide, who is bilingual, asked the new student to explain his side of the story. He cried at first,

not understanding that we were there only to help him. We finally came to understand that he was just trying to get Matthew's attention so he would play with him and thought he had no other way to accomplish this mission than by hitting Matthew.

I asked Matthew whether he was still feeling the same way about the problem as he had at first. He said that he felt differently and that from now on he would help the new kid. Matthew volunteered to go to lunch with him, sit next to him during seat work, be his buddy at recess, and in general look out for him. The new student was as thrilled as I was, and the rest of the students saw a side of Matthew they had never seen. Students started complimenting Matthew on the thoughtful things he did in class. Matthew made the most remarkable change that I have ever seen a student make.

Inspirational Stories

Success without Words

Mrs. Reed liked to use nonverbal signals in her fifth-grade classroom. She taught them to her students almost as a second language on the first day of school. Sitting quietly with their hands clasped on top of their desks, for example, was the signal that they were ready to listen. When she wanted them to turn around and sit down during class or an assembly, she would raise her right index finger and make two small circles followed by two up-and-down motions to the rhythm of the words "Turn around and sit down."

She also taught her students a signal for quiet during extreme noise. She would clap her hands once. Everyone who heard the single clap would clap once. She would then clap twice. Several students would have heard the echo clap of their classmates and would be ready to join the two-clap response. Two claps were usually enough to get everyone quiet. Once in a while it would take three claps before everyone would hear and echo with three claps.

Children respond to and enjoy these signals. Furthermore, the use of nonverbal signals tends to create a bond of positive conspiracy within a class.

Stop Signal

A story from Therese Durston, second-grade teacher, St. Olivier School, Saskatchewan, Canada

Suzy moved into our school last May. Her mother started a job in the fall. It was mainly evenings so Suzy saw her a little bit in the morning and that was all. Her father had emergency kidney surgery and was hospitalized for a long time. Things were not going very well for Suzy. Every time the teacher wanted quiet, Suzy would get louder. She did very immature things such as crawl down a hallway, come in late after breaks, go to the bathroom for long

periods of time, scribble on her desk, read when she was to listen, make noises when she was to read, and so forth. She is a student with average intelligence and average abilities. She is an excellent reader. She started to "not understand" her work, so I would have to help her.

I tried to give her "positive" attention. I noticed everything she was wearing. I gave her special jobs to do. I had her helping me. It made a difference, but she was still a huge distraction to the other students.

I finally decided to set up an agreement with her. I took her to another room and asked her how I could help her cooperate in class. She told me that she wanted a play schedule with the girls in the class. She also told me that if you want someone to be nice to you, you have to be nice to them. There was a mirror in the room. I had her look at her reflection. I told her to smile. What happens? I get a smile back. I told her to scowl. She got a scowl back. Then I told her to smile again, and she did.

Then we talked about losing control. I asked her whether there was a signal I could do when I saw that she was losing self-control. She told me to hold my hand up in a "stop" position. We wrote everything down, signed it, and then returned to the class. I had a meeting to discuss the play schedule with the girls. They were great, and everybody volunteered. It's only been a few days, but the disruptions have been few and the signal works great.

Divorce

Discussion

Many factors may interfere with students' learning, including personal problems such as a divorce in the family. Although teachers can't control the home environment, they can provide an encouraging school environment that may ease the way for students who are experiencing stressful times.

Suggestions

1. If you know that a student is experiencing some kind of trauma, ask her which of the following would be most helpful to her: time to talk with you after school, time with a counselor, or time with a listening buddy. (See the second item under "Planning Ahead.")

2. Allow some slack. Students sometimes need emotional encouragement more than academic excellence. They can catch up on academics when they are feeling better. On the other hand, don't be overprotective, as the student may start to use his problem to receive special service. A combination of kindness and firmness is the key. In this case, kindness may translate to empathy. Firmness may translate to having faith in the student to keep up with his schoolwork after a short mourning period.

3. Encourage your student to go to a divorce support group for children, if one is available.

4. Children often assume that something they did caused the divorce. If you have an opportunity to talk privately with a student whose parents are divorcing, assure her that the divorce isn't her fault. Hearing this from an adult can help.

5. Don't expect instant adjustment. Adjusting to divorce is a process.

6. Often a student whose parents are divorcing feel that she has no control over her life. Be aware of this perception, and consciously provide opportunities for the student to make choices and to have a voice in her classroom.

Planning Ahead to Prevent Future Problems

1. Communicate with both parents that a common problem for the student is the challenge of juggling two households. Suggest that parents provide a system for their child that will help him to complete and return necessary schoolwork. Ask parents how they would like to handle receiving communication from the school.

2. Share with students that we all go through painful experiences in life and that sometimes it helps to share feelings with another person. Teach listening skills, and then invite students who are experiencing personal problems to choose a listening buddy. Set up guidelines for students going into the positive time-out area (see "Posi-

tive Time-Out") for a few minutes of sharing and listening. (The importance of confidentiality should be stressed.)

3. Have faith in your students to deal with the pain in their lives, especially if you are providing a stable, loving classroom environment and teaching important life skills, such as solving problems and learning from mistakes. This doesn't mean they will resolve serious problems instantly, however.

4. Students pick up on your attitudes. If they sense your empathy and faith in them, they will have more self-confidence than if they sense that you find their situation tragic.

5. Hold regular class meetings so students learn the skills for dealing with life's challenges.

Inspirational Story

When Mrs. Keller, a sixth-grade teacher, heard the news that Jeff's parents were divorcing, she asked for a parent–teacher conference with both parents. Jeff's mother refused to come. However, Mrs. Keller met with Jeff's father to open up communication and to share some information that she thought might be helpful. Mrs. Keller shared a passage from *For the Sake of the Children,* in which Kris Kline and Dr. Stephen Pew point out:

In divorce and separation, the children are often left out, or used by one or both parents to get back at the other, or to carry messages, so that each parent can keep track of what the other parent is up to and still can avoid dealing directly with each other. The roles children find themselves thrown into, often by default, are not always healthy. The adults are too often caught up in their own emotional upheaval, and don't take the time to think about or shape the role children play in the divorcing process.[19]

In this book, the authors offer effective ways to break the behavior patterns that lead to further pain. In preparation for writing the book, they asked children whether they had any recommendations for divorcing parents that might make the process of divorce less painful for other children going through it. Here are some of the suggestions they received:

- "Try not to talk about each other in a negative way in front of your kids. Keep your problems between yourselves."
- "Even though you're going to be apart, make an effort to get along, I mean, like anybody else; if you needed to get along with somebody at work or whatever. You know, just for the child, so the child can have both parents around. Just make an effort to get along."
- "It isn't fair when your mom says that if you love her you won't love your dad, or

---

19. Kris Kline and Stephen Pew, *For the Sake of the Children: How to Share Your Children with Your Ex-Spouse in Spite of Your Anger* (Rocklin, CA: Prima Publishing, 1992, p. 18).

you have to love her more than you love your dad."

- "Allow the children to like the other parent. Make it okay to like the other parent. And if you don't like them, so what? Grin and bear it."[20]

If one strong theme consistently emerged from conversations with young people, it was the desire to be allowed to love both parents equally without having to take sides.

Mrs. Keller said to Jeff's father, "I know how difficult it can be to remember what is best for our children when we are suffering so much emotional pain ourselves, especially when one parent is breaking all the rules for an amicable divorce. However, I know that if even one parent is willing to consider the needs of the child, it can make a tremendous difference."

Jeff's father was touched by Mrs. Keller's concern. He made a vow to remember the suggestions of other children who had gone through divorce.

From that time on, he refused to fight fire with fire and stopped allowing his son to be used as a pawn. He was somewhat surprised that the divorce became less hostile. He behaved respectfully toward Jeff's mother, no matter what she did, and she eventually started behaving more respectfully herself.

Jeff's father was most gratified as he watched Jeff lose much of his anxiety and start to blossom again. Jeff still felt pain over the divorce, but he was reassured that he was loved by both parents, which made it less frightening and sad.

Faces, Making

Discussion

When an eighteen-month-old makes a funny face, everyone in her world stops to

---

20. Ibid., 202.

applaud with delight. She learns that this is a way to get attention and feel special. When this same child is in school and makes what she considers a funny face, her classmates may still applaud, but her teacher is far from delighted. This child still wants to get attention and feel special, and how the teacher responds can help her feel significant while behaving in ways that are appropriate to school.

Suggestions

1. Ask the student to draw that face on paper, and let her know that you are interested in her drawing and her thoughts. Set up a specific time to look at the drawing and to talk with her about it.

2. Stop the lesson immediately. Ask your students to make as many faces as they can in thirty seconds. Have the class applaud at the end of the time. Then carry on. This will be effective only if done with a fun—not disparaging—attitude.

3. Ask for help during a class meeting by putting this issue on the agenda. Sometimes simply sharing how you feel about students making faces while you are teaching and involving the students in a discussion is sufficient to end the behavior.

4. You may choose to ignore the student when he's making a face. By ignoring inappropriate behavior and giving attention at appropriate times, teachers can often redirect the energy of the attention-seeking student.

Planning Ahead to Prevent Future Problems

1. Use class meetings to explore the issue. Ask students how face making affects the class. Leave judgment out of the discussion, so that you can collect more information. For further discussion, have students guess as to whether the behavior is about getting attention, wanting to be the boss, hurting people, or not knowing what else to do.

2. Try goal disclosure with a student who continues to make faces. (Refer to "Wandering" for goal disclosure guidelines.) You may ask, "Do you think you make faces because you want people to notice you?" "Or could it be that you want to show that you can do as you like?" "Or perhaps you're making faces because you feel hurt and want to hurt others?" "Or could it be that making faces is something you do because you don't know what else to do?" Look for the recognition reflex—a smile that says *yes* even though the student says *no*. When goal disclosure is done in a friendly manner the student often feels understood and encouraged.

3. Have a private discussion with the student, and ask for his help in formulating a plan to change the behavior.

4. Consider the possibility that the facial movements may be medically related. Speak to the student's parents if you have concerns.

Inspirational Story

Matthew, a student in Mr. Robb's first-grade class, had a talent for making his eyes roll up into his head, his cheeks puff out, and his ears wiggle—all at once. The other students preferred watching Matthew to listening to Mr. Robb.

Mr. Robb talked to other teachers about how to deal with Matthew's performances. They suggested that he ask Matthew to draw the special face and tell him about the face. Mr. Robb did this, and then he asked Matthew whether he would like to hear how he feels when Matthew makes the face during class.

Listening intently, Matthew realized how much his teacher liked him. They talked about when it would be appropriate to make the face and agreed that recess and lunch were great times, but class wasn't a good time. Mr. Robb hung Matthew's picture beside the teacher's desk. Matthew stopped making faces during class.

Failing

(see also "Homework, Nontraditional"; "Homework, Traditional"; and "Assignments, Not Turned In")

Discussion

When a student is failing, the teacher needs to deal with the belief behind the student's behavior as well as the behavior. Students may decide that by failing they can secure special attention. They may refuse to do their work to show that they are in charge. Sometimes students feel they can take revenge on parents and teachers by failing. Finally, they may decide not to try to do their work for fear of not being perfect or of showing that they lack some necessary skills.

Suggestions

1. Remember the power of encouragement. It can be given at any time, whether a student is doing well or poorly. (Refer to "Encouragement.")

2. Ask "what" and "how" questions: "How do you feel about your grades?" "What happened?" "Do you have any ideas about why your grades are dropping?" "What would you like to accomplish?" Avoid all lectures and just listen. This helps the student develop an inner locus of control and is very encouraging.

3. Ask the student whether he would like some help improving his grades: "I would be happy to help you with your math, or can you think of someone else who might be helpful to you?" This helps the student

feel a sense of belonging and significance, and it motivates him to change his habits.

4. Make sure the student knows that you like her and don't see her as an "F." Find things that you like about her and continually share your appreciative feelings with her.

5. If the student is failing because she lacks a skill, allow her to choose a buddy for peer tutoring from a list of qualified students. If problems continue, arrange for the appropriate testing to determine whether she needs specialized help. Don't delay: The younger a student is when intervention occurs, the more successful the results will be.

6. Your attitude toward the student who is failing should never add to his humiliation.

7. Ask the student whether he would be willing to get help and suggestions during a class meeting. Alternatively, you could present failing as a general topic for discussion. A frank talk about what causes academic failure and what the future consequences may be is often enough to inspire change. Students may hear the same things they have heard from lecturing adults, but it seems to have more impact when it comes from their peers.

8. Schedule a conference with the student and her parents. This is a time to help the student see that she has the support of both you and her parents. When making the initial contact with the parent, clarify that the purpose of the conference is not only to discuss the academic status of their daughter but also to find ways to work as a team to support her. (See "Conferences.")

Planning Ahead to Prevent Future Problems

1. Continually communicate the requirements for achieving a passing grade to both students and their parents.

2. Take every opportunity to let students know that they are making choices, that you respect these choices, and that you are available if they want your help. Ask in advance, "Will I *give* you a good or poor grade, or will you *earn* it?" and "How will you earn your grade?"

3. Focus on helping students see what they need to succeed and how they can take small steps toward it. Treat each completed step as a success.

4. Use goal disclosure (refer to the last section of "Wandering") to help the student understand his own hidden goals: "Could it be that you want to keep people busy with you?" "Could it be that you want to show that no one can make you do anything you don't want to do?" "Could it be that you feel hurt, and that failing is a good way to hurt someone back?" "Could it be that you believe you can't succeed and so you are giving up?" Use the student's answers to discover the purpose of

his behavior. Based on this, work with him to devise a plan. If a student has been failing in classes with the goal of receiving special attention, you may want to set up a day to go to lunch with her or involve her in a task through which she earns attention for contributing. If she wants to show that no one can make her do something, you may want to admit that you can't force her and sincerely ask for her help in devising a plan that will work for both of you. If she feels hurt and wants to get even, take time to listen as she talks about her hurt feelings. If she doesn't have the necessary skills, help her take small steps for success and arrange for tutoring or specialized help.

5. Take a moment to look at your own beliefs and the messages you may be sending about mistakes. Are mistakes acceptable? Are mistakes forgivable? Are mistakes opportunities to learn?

6. Students feel encouraged when the teacher appreciates improvement. They feel discouraged when they have to strive for perfection. You will help them by pointing out any improvement, no matter how small.

Inspirational Stories

Sara

Sara, a senior in high school, was failing her English class. Her parents were worried that she wasn't going to graduate, which meant that she wouldn't be going to her fa-

ther's alma mater. Knowing her abilities and her history in school, her English teacher began to ask Sara about the purpose of her behavior. What the teacher discovered was that Sara was resentful about being pressured to attend her father's school. She felt powerless, and as graduation approached, she thought that her only alternative was to fail and not be admitted.

The teacher asked Sara whether she wanted to have a conference with her parents to share this information with them. She decided to do so. When Sara's parents heard her express her feelings, they were able to let go of their plan for her, despite their disappointment, and allow her to make her own choice.

Nils

Nils was beginning fifth grade. In the past, his teachers had allowed late assignments to receive full credit, and he had frequently taken advantage of this loophole. At the beginning of this school year, however, his new teacher, Mr. Wang, explained that late assignments would not be accepted. Arrogantly ignoring this new expectation, Nils continued his habit of procrastinating, and midway through the quarter he was dismayed to discover that he was failing several subjects.

He complained to his parents that this wasn't fair and maybe Mr. Wang just didn't like him. Who did Mr. Wang think he was, trying to force Nils to follow some stupid time schedule? His parents refused to complain to Mr. Wang but agreed to join Nils for a conference with him.

At the conference, Nils immediately declared that he had turned all of his assignments in and couldn't understand the failing marks. Mr. Wang acknowledged that Nils had turned in his assignments, but as they were usually late, he had received no credit for them. Nils bristled and said Mr. Wang couldn't make him fail when he had done all of the work. Mr. Wang asked Nils whether he remembered the discussion about late assignments that took place the first week of school. Nils confirmed that he remembered it but lamented that he didn't know what to do about his marks at this point.

Mr. Wang asked Nils whether he was interested in working out a way to improve his grades for the current term. When he said that he was, Mr. Wang suggested that Nils either turn in a series of extra-credit projects or do additional book reports. Nils chose to do additional book reports. His parents asked Nils how he planned to get his work in on time in the future. Together they worked out a study plan that included a daily assignment list from which Nils could check off items each afternoon.

Nils thus accepted responsibility for seeing that his work was turned in on time. Mr. Wang was careful to avoid the power struggle that Nils's early remarks had invited him to enter. Both Mr. Wang and Nils's parents showed respect for the class requirements while showing compassion, support, and encouragement for Nils in developing new skills.

Fairness

Discussion

Keep in mind that when a student complains about fairness, he may actually be seeking a mistaken goal, such as undue attention or revenge (refer to "Mistaken Goals [Hat Messages]"). Fairness may not even be the issue. Complaints about unfairness provide an excellent example of what psychiatrist Rudolf Dreikurs taught: A misbehaving child is a discouraged child.

When students don't perceive that they have belonging and significance they get discouraged and choose mistaken goals of behavior to achieve it. They may seek undue attention by complaining about unfairness. They may seek power by making sure they get the largest share. They may feel hurt by their perception that they lack belonging and significance and seek revenge by hurting others in their bid for fairness. They may avoid the problem of fairness because they adopt a belief about their inadequacy and would rather give up than seek fairness.

Students who feel encouraged don't worry about fairness, they seek solutions. Students can learn that fairness is not as important as finding out what people need and helping them achieve it.

Suggestions

1. Give up your own "fairness button." Kids become very aware of our "buttons" that they can push to get us involved in a rescue mission or to secretly enjoy the payoff of watching us react unreasonably. One teacher was amazed at how quickly her students quit complaining about unfairness when she simply said, "I don't do fair."

2. Develop positive steps to address injustice when it occurs in the school setting. Encourage students to find win–win solutions so everyone gets what he or she needs instead of worrying about what is fair.

3. Develop positive steps to address injustice in the world. Teach students that they have influence by encouraging them to write letters to the editor, legislators, or other people with authority over situations the students find unjust.

4. When a student feels that she has been treated unfairly, let her know that you understand and care about how she feels. Using "what" and "how" questions, invite her to tell you more and to come up with her own solution. If she has difficulty in doing this, suggest that she put the issue on the class meeting agenda to get her classmates' help.

5. Notice whether *fairness* is something that you are looking for. Your actions or words may be inviting more of this behavior in your classroom. When students come to you with a complaint about fairness, are you emphasizing the injustice, or are you able to guide the students toward finding a solution?

Planning Ahead to Prevent Future Problems

1. During a class meeting, facilitate a discussion about fairness. Make a list of situations perceived as unfair, and discuss whether they are in fact unfair and represent true injustices.

2. Facilitate a class meeting discussion about separate realities. Give an example such as this one: Lucy thinks it's unfair that Kate has a pencil box. Jane, on the other hand, doesn't care about having a pencil

box, so she doesn't perceive the situation as unfair. What one person perceives as unfair may seem either fair or a nonissue to someone else.

3. Be aware of the effect that birth order has on a child's perspective of what's fair. Fairness is often not an issue for only children, oldest children, or youngest children. However, a middle child may have a strong sense of justice and fairness. In fact, many middle children's motto is "Life is unfair." These children are often champions of the "underdog." With this in mind, be sensitive to a student who is a middle child. Help that student to channel his sensitivity to injustice in a positive direction.

Class Meeting Solution

One of the new books in Mr. Feldt's classroom library had been torn, with several pages missing. No one would admit to having done this. He was so disappointed that he announced to his students that the classroom library was now off limits to all students for the rest of the year. He heard several students complain that this wasn't fair and that they needed to use some of these books as references.

Mr. Feldt gave this some thought and decided to put the issue on the class meeting agenda. After explaining what he had heard and acknowledging that there might be another way to deal with this situation, he told the class that he would like their help. The students decided that they would hold a fund-raiser and use the proceeds to purchase a replacement book. The solution seemed fair to everyone because they were working together to replace a book that they would all be able to use.

Favorites

Discussion

Students usually know when their teacher has favorites and who they are. Even if the teacher feels he doesn't show favoritism, the students can often point out his pet. When teachers stress competition, which emphasizes comparing and judging instead of cooperating, they create the potential for favoritism to emerge.

Suggestions

1. Be conscious of comparing students or of preferring one to another. Simply making an adjustment in your behavior and thinking helps equalize the climate.

2. It's natural to feel a special connection to certain students or classes. The danger is in using it as a tool to motivate other students or classes to perform at a certain level: "My class last year always entered the auditorium quietly."

3. Make sure that each student has his own special time or connection with you sometime during the week. This could take the form of an individual greeting to each student daily, perhaps at arrival and departure times. To be certain you get to everyone, unobtrusively make a check mark by the names on your class roster.

4. If you perceive a student as an underdog and try to protect or rescue him, you'll only make the situation worse. Find ways to empower that student, such as engaging him in problem solving, through which he can discover new ways of behaving. (Refer to "Victims.")

Planning Ahead to Prevent Future Problems

1. Teachers often find themselves repeatedly drawn to certain students when assigning tasks. For selecting students to do special projects or errands or to speak for the class, devise a system that ensures rotation.

2. Enter into your students' world. What you may perceive as needed encouragement for a certain student may be interpreted by the rest of the class as favoritism. Check out your students' perceptions by giving them an opportunity to share what they are feeling, thinking, and concluding about special treatment.

3. Facilitate the "Do They Know You Care?" activity (see page 77 of the *Positive*

Discipline in the Classroom Facilitator's Guide): Separate the students into groups of six, and have them brainstorm about how teachers can demonstrate that they care about students. Let them share and post their lists. Keep their lists to give you ideas on ways to show caring.

4. During a class meeting, let students devise a plan for the rotation of special jobs and projects. This approach will eliminate the perception of favoritism that results when the teacher does all the choosing.

Class Meeting Solution

It was Thursday morning. The bell had just rung. Lizzy knew that today was the day that students were going to be selected to participate in creating a mural for the school music room. She was feeling hopeful yet anxious, because she kept having the nagging thought that Tom and Laura would once again be chosen to represent their class in the project.

Nine o'clock came, and Mrs. Timble, all too predictably, announced her decision to appoint Tom and Laura as the artists from their class. Lizzy was upset, mad, and hurt. She didn't want to speak to Tom, Laura, or even Mrs. Timble. Lizzy had never used the class meeting agenda, but she had noticed that other students put items on the agenda about having angry or hurt feelings. She decided to use the agenda to let Mrs. Timble know how she was feeling.

During the class meeting, Lizzy felt worried. When her item came up, Mrs. Timble asked Lizzy whether this remained a problem for her. Lizzy said that she still felt bad that she had never been chosen for any special art projects. Mrs. Timble was shocked and immediately thanked Lizzy for having the courage to bring this issue up. She asked the other students whether they had similar feelings. To her surprise, others voiced their thoughts about not being selected for projects. Mrs. Timble shared how difficult choosing students was for her.

After the discussion, the class brainstormed ways to involve more students in special projects. Some of the suggestions were to pick names from a can, to go alphabetically, to rotate opportunities by birth dates, and to allow others to make the selection rather than always having Mrs. Timble designate people.

The true value of this process was not only that it led to a solution but also that it helped both the students and Mrs. Timble become more aware of the feelings involved in the issue.

Fighting

Discussion

Why do kids (or adults) fight? What are wars fought over? Insults (producing a desire for revenge) or greed (leading to a struggle to attain more power) or some misguided claim to virtue (wanting the power to say who or what is right and wrong). Similarly, kids fight about insults, who gets to have the toy or sports equipment, and who is right or wrong about some issue.

Of course, another major reason kids fight is that the adults in their lives haven't taught them other possibilities—either by setting a good example or by developing the children's problem-solving skills. Children live what they learn.

Suggestions

1. If real danger is imminent, keep your mouth shut and act. When a student is about to throw a rock at another student, move quickly to stop the throwing. At the

high school level, you may have to send for help to deal with a fight immediately. Later you can use any of the following approaches.

A. Intervene in a fight by asking the students whether they would like help right now or prefer to take some time to cool off in the classroom's positive time-out place. (Refer to "Positive Time-Out.") A group of Texas high school teachers have found that establishing a designated cooling-off place in the room with pleasant things to do has greatly reduced the number of student fights. The teachers model this technique for regaining self-control by using the time-out spot themselves. One high school teacher even has a rocking chair for the cooling-off place.

B. If the students would like help, offer them the option of sitting down with each other to work their difficulties out and including you in the process.

C. Refer them to the four problem-solving steps (see the third item under "Planning Ahead to Prevent Future Problems").

D. Another way to help is to ask "how" and "what" questions after the students have cooled off: "What happened?" "What caused it to happen?" "How do you feel about it?" "What did you learn from this experience?" "What ideas do you have for solving the problem?" "How can you use what you have learned to prevent the problem in the future?" (Sometimes it's helpful for students to answer these ques-

tions on paper so they can collect their thoughts before discussing the issue.)

E. Intervene in a fight by asking the combatants whether one of them would be willing to put the problem on the class meeting agenda. Students learn to understand differences and work on nonpunitive solutions in class meetings. Furthermore, regular meetings are an excellent way to assure students that they will be heard.

F. Adopt the attitude that fights, like any other problem, present wonderful opportunities for learning. Teach students that there are respectful ways to handle conflicts.

Planning Ahead to Prevent Future Problems

1. Build trust, empathy, and an understanding of separate realities among your students. Respect for differences eliminates many fights.

2. Develop problem-solving skills through regular class meetings.

3. Teach students the four problem-solving steps:

A. Ignore it. (It takes more courage to walk away than it does to stay and fight.) Ignoring the dispute can take the form of doing something else for a while—finding a game or activity that distracts you from the fight. It can also mean going somewhere else to cool off.

B. Talk it over respectfully. This means four things: (1) telling the other person how you feel, (2) listening to how the other person feels, (3) acknowledging to one another how each person contributed to the problem, and (4) telling each other what you are willing to do differently.

C. Agree on a solution. This may simply involve one or both of you offering an apology, or you may have to work out a plan together for sharing or taking turns.

D. Ask for help if you can't work the problem out together. You can put it on the class meeting agenda. Or you can both approach a teacher, parent, or friend and ask this person whether he would talk the problem over with the two of you.

4. Have students role-play typical fights, such as shoving in line, scuffles over playground equipment, put-downs that escalate into fistfights, and arguments over a boyfriend or girlfriend. Then let them practice brainstorming for solutions.

5. Some schools have students who are trained in conflict resolution or peer counseling. However, this is often unnecessary when the whole class is participating in class meetings.

Inspirational Stories

Two stories from Suzanne Smitha, school psychologist, Sharon School, Charlotte, North Carolina

A Son's Guidance

The mother of a student in Beth Brewington's second-grade class shared this story with Beth. One evening the student's mother and father had an argument, and shortly thereafter the mother and son left the house. Riding in the car, the son asked about his parents' angry outburst. His mother explained that Dad was very tired and that perhaps they had both not used the best self-control in the situation. The boy, who had been participating in class meetings for the past three school years, said, "Well, you know, Mom, you need to go back to Dad and apologize for losing your temper like that. Then you need to shake hands, hug each other, and talk about the problem in order to solve it."

His mother was somewhat surprised at the maturity of his comments but thanked him and admitted that his advice was good.

When they arrived home, she went into the house and approached her husband. After she apologized, her husband put out his hand to shake hers, just as the son had told his mother to do. The parents burst out laughing at that point, because they realized their son had given Dad the same advice at an earlier time. Both parents were impressed with their son's ability to put the Three R's of Recovery into practice. (*Recognize* a mistake, *Reconcile* through apology, and *Resolve* problems together.) The boy's intervention was a great example of the far-reaching effects of Positive Discipline in the classroom.

Three Students Solve It Themselves

A very upset teacher brought three fifth-grade boys to my office. She was completely outdone by their misbehavior and needed some time away from them. The boys sat around my table and began talking about what had happened.

Within a few minutes, one of the boys commented that he thought he could understand why their behavior had upset the teacher so much, and he went on to explain. The other boys and I listened, and a few minutes later, one of these two came up with a suggestion for how they could handle such situations in the future. Soon another suggestion was made, and there was a little discussion among the boys. Then one of them said, "Ms. Smitha, we think we should separate ourselves from each other anytime the class is lining up to go somewhere for a while. We want to try this plan for a couple of weeks, and we'll get back with you to let you know how it worked."

I had given them only a listening ear. In return, they had given me another indication that, at our school, we are on the right track with our students, equipping them for solving problems throughout their lives.

Forgetfulness

Discussion

Everyone forgets things from time to time, but some students turn forgetting into an art. These students have discovered that their teachers will replace forgotten items, give them a lot of attention for being forgetful, or take over the responsibility for remembering.

Forgetting can also be a passive way to procure power. Students who would never openly defy their teachers by saying, "I don't want to," may find it easy to say, "I meant to, but I forgot." This problem presents many learning opportunities for both students and teachers.

Suggestions

1. Use an agreed-on nonverbal signal to help a student who chronically forgets classroom rules. A friendly gesture or expression may be the only reminder a student needs.

2. Talk to the student about using a buddy system so that she will go directly to her partner and not disrupt the entire class when she needs a pencil, a copy of the assignment, or something else she has forgotten.

3. Rather than launching into a lecture, use one word or a short phrase to remind students: "Math time." "Share." "Clean-up time." "Respect." "Are you helping or hurting?"

4. Avoid using individual rewards to motivate a forgetful student. Instead, help him by setting him up for success and focusing on appropriate responses to a specific situation. Ask, "What are we supposed to be doing now?" "How can we show respect in this situation?" "Who has ideas for solving this problem?" "What privilege will be lost if people choose not to be responsible for this equipment?"

5. Acknowledge the student's efforts and successes: "I noticed you brought your supplies today. Nice job!" "You lost your temper today, but let's acknowledge how many times you have controlled it."

Planning Ahead to Prevent Future Problems

1. Remember to consider the belief behind the behavior (refer to the Mistaken Goal Chart on pages 12–13). Interventions that would be effective for a student who's trying to keep people involved with him may not be effective for a student who's seeking to attain power or revenge or to be left alone.

2. You may decide to have supplies available that students may borrow when they forget certain things. This system is more effective when you require collateral or have them sign a checkout sheet.

3. Either during a class meeting or as you work with an individual student, ask for ideas about helpful reminder systems.

4. With a student who continually forgets, let her know that you've noticed that her actions and words do not match up. She continually promises to bring her books to class but habitually forgets. Together explore what the purpose of her behavior may be and what kind of encouragement she needs: "What are your ideas for solving the problem?" "Notice how many times you do remember?" "It's okay to ask for help from a buddy."

5. Acknowledge that everyone forgets and consequently feels embarrassed or fearful. Share your own experiences.

6. Help students see the consequences of forgetting by asking "how" and "what" questions: "How will this affect your grades?" "What will happen if you don't complete your project?" "How might forgetting this affect your friendship with Juan (if Juan may be angry or disappointed)?" But never ask questions that might add to the student's embarrassment.

7. Consider whether you tend to rescue forgetful students. Watch for ways in which you condone forgetfulness by excusing, by compensating, or by not following through on agreements.

Inspirational Story

Larry, a student in the third grade, came to school several mornings without his lunch. His teacher felt sorry for him and lent him money for lunch, but she found herself getting irritated when this problem continued. She said, "Larry, I seem to be spending a lot of time dealing with you about your forgotten lunch. I've decided that I won't provide lunch money for you any-more. I have faith that you can work this out."

Larry forgot his lunch every day for the rest of that week. The teacher followed through on her decision not to rescue him. Larry managed to convince his classmates to share their lunches with him, though they gave him only their least favorite foods. The following week, the teacher noticed that Larry was taking responsibility for remembering to bring his lunch.

Foul Language/ Swearing

Discussion

"Frankly, my dear, I don't give a damn." Movie audiences watching *Gone with the Wind* responded to Rhett Butler's words with gasps of disbelief. It was 1939, and a movie industry rule had been broken. Today movies, music, television, and all kinds of advertisements casually make use of words that were once forbidden. Teachers should have an awareness of the changing times, but what hasn't changed in dealing with students' use of language is the importance of mutual respect.

Suggestions

1. Swearwords usually get an impressive response. Rather than expressing dismay or anger, simply state that such language is inappropriate. Remind a student of school policy in a firm and kind manner (see the "Inspirational Story").

2. Use a class meeting as a forum to discuss swearing in an open and nonjudgmental way. Help students discern inappropriate language and its consequences by asking such questions as "What do umpires and referees do when people swear?" and "How does your grandmother feel about swearing?" and "This is how I feel about swearing."

3. Encourage students to share the impact that swearing has on them personally. Hearing other students' responses has a much stronger effect on the student who habitually curses than does listening to the usual lecture from the teacher or principal. (However, don't be surprised if some stu-

dents say that swearing is commonplace in their homes.)

4. Practice mutual respect: "I respect you, and I want to hear what you have to say. I respect myself, and I want to hear what you have to say without the swearing."

5. With younger students, say, "We do not use those words at school." Walk the child who has cursed away from the group, and invite her to return when she will use acceptable words. Ignoring inappropriate language fails to give young children guidelines for their behavior.

Planning Ahead to Prevent Future Problems

1. Students may swear to gain status with their peers or for its shock value with adults. Often teachers focus on the behavior and forget about the belief behind it. Be aware of the four mistaken goals of misbehavior. Students won't resort to swearing if they have positive ways to get attention, to have power, to deal with hurt feelings, and to get help when they feel like giving up.

2. Be aware of your own use of language around students. They are very sensitive to double standards.

3. Acknowledge that the use of certain swearwords is a way to express strong feelings. Have the class brainstorm for accept-able sounds or words that express intensity of feeling.

4. Teach students that the use of certain words borders on sexual harassment and racial defamation.

Inspirational Stories

The Girls' Song

A story from Suzanne Smitha, school psychologist, Sharon School, Charlotte, North Carolina

A boy in Kay Rogers's fourth-grade class came to her and said some girls had been singing a song that he found offensive because of the bad language. Ms. Rogers hadn't heard the song, so shortly thereafter she asked the girls to sing it to her. Although she didn't find it offensive, she told the girls her reason for asking them to sing it. Later that day on the playground, the girls asked her whether she thought the boy would accept an apology from them. Ms. Rogers encouraged them to ask him. She watched from a distance as two of the girls went to the boy and led him to where the group of girls was standing. They later reported to Ms. Rogers that they had apologized for offending him and agreed not to sing the song anymore. He accepted their apology, and the problem was solved.

Giving and Receiving Respect

A story from Kerri McCaul, sixth- and seventh-grade teacher, Everett, Washington

A student in my seventh-grade science classroom has been undergoing evaluation for admittance into the district's behavioral disorders program. He came into my classroom one day, threw his backpack on the floor near his table, and let out quite an explosive string of profanity. I asked him to join me outside the room, and in response, he let fly a few more choice words and followed me out into the hall.

My favorite Positive Discipline question to students is "What's going on?" Not "What's wrong with you?" "Why are you acting this way?" or "Who did this?" I find that asking, "What's going on?" invites students to share, without feeling defensive and threatened, and also lets them know that I am listening.

This boy explained that his previous class had been extremely rough, he'd blown his cool, and the teacher had written him a behavior referral. When I asked him about his swearing in my classroom, he replied that he "figured [he] was already in trouble" and was "going to see how many teachers [he] could get to write him up." He wouldn't look at me during this exchange but hung his head and fiddled with the drinking fountain. I asked him what I could do to help (my second-favorite Positive Discipline response), and we agreed that he needed a cooling-off period—a time to calm down and regroup.

We walked to the behavioral disorder [BD] teacher's room down the hall where he was invited to stay and agreed to meet in thirty minutes at my classroom door to talk about whether he should stay at school or go home. He showed up at my door right on schedule, as we had agreed, said he felt better, was ready to join my class, and wanted to stay at school. I saw him again that afternoon, in another class, and he was fine. At the end of that class, he came up to me and thanked me for letting him "blow off steam" and for giving him "a second chance." He told me, "I was ready to blow and planned to take you down with me. Thanks. You saved my day." When I checked in with the BD teacher, later that day, to see how this student had behaved, he told me, "It was really cool the way you handled the situation. I know this kid, and he was ready to explode. Most teachers have had it with his attitude and would've been more than happy to have kicked him out of class and written him up. But you didn't. I know he respects you."

Before I began practicing Positive Discipline, I would have fallen right into this student's trap and engaged him in the face-to-face conflict he was seeking. He wanted me to kick him out of class! Talking to him outside the classroom, in privacy, allowed him to maintain his dignity and respect; allowed him to be a part of the solution to go to another classroom to cool off; encouraged him to accept ownership for his behavior; and by keeping his appointment with me and regaining his self-control, he showed responsibility. And, his "thank you" at the end was the restitution I was expecting and hoping for.

Friendship Problems

Discussion

Teachers often find themselves involved in their students' friendship troubles. When teachers dive into the middle and try to fix or change a relationship, the situation may only get worse. It's much more helpful and respectful to students to honor their different styles and personalities. Provide a safe setting for them to discuss and practice friendship skills. The class meeting is an extremely good tool for helping students understand the feelings of fellow classmates and learn ways to solve problems and be helpful to each other. A discussion of friendship issues will also foster an awareness and concern for others, which leads to the development of social interest.

Remember that young students are learning how to make and be friends for the very first time. These early friendships present myriad learning opportunities, and mistakes abound. Keep in mind that social skills are learned and not inborn.

Suggestions

1. Listen empathetically to a student who is having friendship difficulties, but don't interfere. Listening gives the student an opportunity to vent and often leads to insight and solutions. Show faith in the student's ability to develop, maintain, or mend a friendship. Avoid feeling sorry for the student.

2. Invite the student with a problem to use the class meeting agenda, so the whole class can help her find solutions.

3. Help a student who is having friendship problems identify the friends he does have and what makes his friendships with them work.

4. Notice a student's positive attempts to make friends, and share your observation with him. Help the student see that common interests can be a basis of friendship. Ask about his special interests, talents, and hobbies. Suggest that he find others with similar interests, or prepare an activity to help all students with this.

Planning Ahead to Prevent Future Problems

1. Remember that the class meeting format provides an excellent opportunity for students to develop friendship skills. Through class meetings, students discover that others have similar experiences and feelings. They practice communication and experience cooperation in a safe setting. Moreover, they have fun with each other.

2. Avoid lecturing about cliques and leaving people out. Use role playing to promote discussion of how people feel and what they are deciding about themselves and others when they are left out as well as when they leave others out. Help them see the difference between a group, which allows for movement

of people coming in and out, and a clique, which is a closed system.

3. Be sensitive to the student who is always the last to be chosen for an activity or who is usually left out. Sometimes, instead of having students pick their partners or divide themselves into groups, make those assignments yourself, or have students count off and assemble by common number.

4. Group students so that they can achieve success working with others and have positive shared experiences.

5. Have faith that students will work difficulties out, especially if they are learning about respect and social interest during class meetings.

6. Set up a buddy system for compliments during class meetings. Every week each student draws a name. The students' job is then to notice their buddies' commendable attitudes and efforts during the week. In this way, everyone receives compliments.

7. Train students to be peer tutors or tutors of younger students, so that they learn concern for others and develop helping skills.

8. Help a solitary student develop friendship skills—hanging out with people, joining in, focusing on others instead of himself. Friendship Groups often provide a place where students can learn the necessary skills for enhancing relationships and have an opportunity to connect with other students. Some schools provide these groups for all students in the primary grades as part of their social curriculum. Other schools may provide them as a resource for students experiencing difficulty or who may be new to the school.

9. Enlist parental support in extending children's friendships beyond school. Encourage parents to take small steps: invite over one child at a time, arrange a limited length of time for the visit, and provide a structured activity for that initial visit.

Class Meeting Solutions

A Plan to Include Everyone

A story from Heather Jubenvill, third-grade teacher, Caernarvon Elementary School, Edmonton, Alberta, Canada

A student in our class had written in the agenda book that no one in the class liked her. This concern was presented at the class meeting, and I asked her whether she still felt this way. She replied that she did, so I asked her to expand on what was happening that evoked these feelings. After she gave her reasons, the class discussed their views on the situation.

The students then brainstormed about what might help this student feel like she belonged and what they could do to help. The students decided that for the next week they would make sure that no one in the class played alone at recess. They would invite students who were by themselves to play.

The following week the class evaluated the situation, and the girl reported that everyone was playing with her and she felt very happy. This, however, was just the beginning. The students had enjoyed carrying out their plan so much that they decided to do it for another week.

Now all of the students relate better to one another, and everyone feels accepted. Students are playing with different people at recess, and they are becoming more accepting of each other.

Groups, Not Cliques

A story from Betty Ferris, sixth-grade teacher, St. Eugene's Elementary School, Santa Rosa, California

It had come to my attention that cliques had become an issue in our class. I brought it up for discussion at a class meeting and was pleased with how open the students were with each other. They were able to talk about times when they had been lonely and isolated when their own group of friends had been absent. They made the point that, while they didn't think it was right to exclude people, they did think that

it is natural for them to be comfortable with some people and form a group of friends, often around common interests. What struck me was the observation they had that those who were in a clique felt they couldn't branch out to other people because they would then lose their place within the group.

I brought up the idea of looking at the difference between *cliques* and *groups*. We decided that a clique had rigid boundaries—no one in and no one out. A group, on the other hand, was more open, with people moving in and out and able to be parts of different groups. I asked them to be aware of this during the weeks ahead and told them we would check in about this issue at future class meetings. One student said that he felt hopeful that things could change, and the others agreed. When we did return to this issue, I was happy to hear that they now saw themselves as a class where *groups* had taken the place of *cliques*.

Gangs

Discussion

Young people join gangs for many reasons: they may suffer from low self-esteem (or

unhealthy high self-esteem), stressful home lives, peer pressure, poor academic performance, a discouraging environment, no adult support, a lack of awareness of alternatives, and feelings of helplessness and hopelessness. However, behind every one of these factors are the needs of young people to belong, to feel valued and important, and to have purpose in life. Looking at the four mistaken goals of misbehavior (refer to "Mistaken Goals [Hat Messages]"), it's clear that young people may join gangs for attention, for power, for revenge, and/or out of despair (when they give up on finding acceptance anywhere else in society). The gang is a family in which young people find a sense of identity, belonging, and purpose that they aren't finding elsewhere.

In the September 1991 issue of *Thrust for Educational Leadership*, Lilia Lopez writes:

The number of students involved in crime and violence is increasing nationwide; educators must take action to reverse this trend. Stiffer sentences for the perpetrators of crimes are not the answer. Instead, we must start convincing children at an early age that they are unique, special, and valuable. People with a healthy sense of self-worth do not tend to commit crimes or hurt themselves, their families, or communities.[21]

In the same article, Ms. Lopez goes on to say:

The school has a vital function in the lives of our youth. Educators must ensure that while students are in school, everything possible is done to serve not only academic needs but also social, emotional, and physical needs. Options for students must be made available so they can become productive, contributing citizens in our world.

The Positive Discipline system, featuring class meetings, serves students' social and emotional needs, and many of their academic needs. (Refer to the SCANS report in "Class Meetings.") This powerful process has the potential to prevent kids from going to the streets to develop a sense of identity, connection, and belonging. It also creates a strong sense of family at school—which lends emotional support and skill-building opportunities to the many kids who come from discouraged families.

Suggestions

1. Don't use punishment or controlling methods that incite resistance and rebellion. (Refer to "Rewards and Punishment" for more information.)

2. Regular class meetings will effectively provide a sense of belonging and significance. In class meetings, students experience what it's like to be listened to, to be taken seriously, and to have their thoughts and ideas considered. They experience belonging and significance.

3. Regular class meetings develop social interest. Students learn to help each other instead of hurting each other. They learn mutual respect. This has the potential to reduce or eliminate violence in gangs.

4. Regular class meetings teach essential life skills: how to communicate, solve

---

21. Lilia Lopez, "Keeping Kids Out of Gangs," *Thrust for Educational Leadership* (September 1991): 28–30.

problems, and find nonpunitive solutions. This teaches students to use words to solve problems instead of weapons.

5. See your students as the assets they are when you teach them social interest, mutual respect, and problem solving through class meetings. When students feel empowered and learn skills, their gang activity may be redirected to contribution (see the upcoming inspirational story).

6. Remembering that the goal of Positive Discipline is to find solutions and not to dispense blame, involve students who belong to gangs in some form of community service where they will have an opportunity to experience a sense of belonging and influence in a positive, productive way.

7. Don't make assumptions based on a student's clothing. Some students have chosen a style that may be typical gang attire. Get to know your students before creating a picture of who they may be.

Planning Ahead to Prevent Future Problems

1. Remember that the formation of gangs, whether they're called clans, tribes, or teams, is not new. Since human life began, people have been coming together to develop a sense of belonging, to achieve common goals, and to heighten each person's identity. Dealing with gang activity is primarily a matter of prevention through creating a classroom where students feel that they belong and have significance. Using class meetings creates a positive classroom "gang." All members are valued and respected for what they bring to the group.

2. Foster relationships of trust and respect with your students. Most students gravitate toward adults who show sincere interest in them. Once a sense of connection is established between students and at least one caring, wholesome role model, the likelihood of violent gang activity decreases.

3. Have your students discuss the reasons people join gangs and participate in violent or criminal activities. Sometimes an open exchange will give you more insight on how to deal effectively with a problem. Include in the discussion (without turning it into a lecture) questions about long-term consequences.

4. Don't neglect to review and discuss historic gang/group involvements that have had a positive influence on the world. The civil rights movement is one example.

Inspirational Story

Helen Medina's use of "Developing Capable People" with gang members: an interview with Jane Nelsen[22]

---

22. This article first appeared in the fall 1993 *Empowering People Books, Tapes and Videos* newsletter. Helen Medina received the Migrant Educator of the Year award in 1986.

The interview with Helen Medina focused on how the "Developing Capable People" (DCP) course changed her life and how she uses DCP to empower Spanish-speaking parents. I was mesmerized. When I heard her revolutionary ideas for working with gang members, I was in awe.

Jane: I hear you have been working with gang members.

Helen: I was going to use that as a success story because I think that if I had never run across the Developing Capable People concept, it wouldn't have opened up all these doors for me, and one of them is being able to give something to these high-risk students.

    Many times we tend to overlook the idea that not all people are really as capable as we think they are. We tend to think of all teachers as having the skills to share effective living skills with students. The mere fact that they're educators doesn't necessarily mean that they are equipped to give children all of the skills they need to become successful. I have been an educator for eighteen years, and after partaking in the Developing Capable People leadership training, I now feel that I have those skills.

    I wanted to start working with the very high-risk students. I'm talking about the super-high-risk, which, to me, are students who have been in jail and are active gang members. One of

them had just come out of jail, and, Jane, you don't know how this has changed my life. It has made me look at these special people with a different heart. They are in great need; I love them dearly. I don't look at their apparel (which indicates gang membership), and do you know that they have dreams? One of them in particular wants to be a teacher. I have taken him under my wing. I'm going to be taking two of these gang members with me for three days to a conference, and I know that after I get done with them they are on their way. It's just been, "Wow," for me. I have grown so much. I have learned so much from these two young men.

Jane: You make it sound so magical, and it is. How do you approach them and get them to trust you? Most gang members seem so belligerent and tough.

Helen: Jane, I think that one of the keys that has allowed me to reach them is that they can tell the difference when someone is just trying to talk to them because it's part of their job and when someone is coming across with all their love and respect and sees them as human beings. And that's what I do. As I said, I don't look at what they're wearing. I don't treat them as a gang member or a high-risk. I even call them *mijo*, which is a word that stands for "my son." And I use that a lot in speaking to my students; they're not

Johnny or Juan or Susan or whoever. To Mrs. Medina they're all *mijos* and *mijas*—"my sons," "my daughters." When I greet them, it's with a hug and, "I am so glad you're here. I really need you today! We're going to learn so much! And you know what? Mrs. Medina's going to learn a lot from you." And that's one of the things that I make them feel—that I need them. That they're there to teach me. When I make mistakes, I let them know that I am growing, I will always be growing, and that I am learning so much from them. That they help me to grow.

I guess they just can feel it. I just love it. I shared with someone that if I was offered a job working full-time with high-risk adolescents, I wouldn't think twice of leaving my classroom and going to them, because they are the ones that need it the most. And they are the future of this country. Yet they have been in hiding, and they need someone, and a concept like Developing Capable People, to help them habilitate themselves.

Jane: Do you think they'll be able to leave their gangs?

Helen: I don't see the concept of "gang" as being bad. Gangs offer them something that is missing in the home. What I do see as bad is the choices they make within the gangs. Gangs could be made positive.

Jane: What a great idea!

Helen: I encourage them to remain in their gangs, but say, "Let's go out into the community and help!" I never attack the gangs; to me it's a family. I see it as their "la familia," because they're validated, they're welcomed, and, hey, if I was feeling like they were and someone came up to me and said, "You wanna go someplace where we're gonna validate you, we're gonna love you and protect you?" I would go after it. I don't care if it is called a gang. What I'm trying to do is work within the gang and just redirect their energies.

Jane: That is fantastic! You started to talk earlier about a project where you work with gang members to teach them the Significant Seven and Developing Capable People.

Helen: Yes, I do. I thought, "How else can they internalize the concepts if they don't get an opportunity to practice them?" So I work with them on the Significant Seven [as outlined in Part 1 under "Self-Esteem"], one at a time. I teach it to them in three to four sessions. I do plenty of role modeling because I feel that if I'm going to sit there and just tell them about it, they will never really believe it. They won't internalize it.

Jane: What do you mean by role modeling?

Helen: Let me take you into the next step of our program. These four students who are the gang members, I am training them to become facilitators of Developing Capable People. I train them in one of the Significant Seven, and then, on Fridays, we meet with high-risk third- through sixth-grade children who have been identified at our school site. We break them up into teams that we call "tribes." These four boys are the leaders of each one of these tribes. They take full charge and responsibility of their children. And they must then model what I taught them and use it with these high-risk youngsters. I really build their self-esteem by lots of encouragement. Then they put it into practice when they meet with their tribes, and I walk away. And they are now in charge. You should see them! No put-downs. The right to pass or speak when going around the circle during discussions. What is shared here must stay here. And everyone is treated with respect and dignity. You would never believe that these were high-risk kids, because when they are in charge of their group, it's like, "Okay, guys, come on, let's get together. Let's start with our activities for the day." I leave lesson plans on the blackboard, but then I'm outside. Occasionally, I walk in, and I smile and go around, "You guys are doing a great job! I'm impressed with your brainstorming skills!" I walk around, and I affirm everyone. Again, it's just a way of letting them know I'm in touch; then I walk out.

They are the teachers. I think that the best way for them to internalize and truly believe in the Developing Capable People principles is by allowing them to use the principles with others.

Jane: What a wonderful concept. I love the idea of redirecting their activities in gangs instead of trying to eliminate "la familia."

"Good" Students

Discussion

Every classroom has a few students who never give the teacher any trouble: LaTonya always turns her work in on time and can be counted on to do it perfectly. Justin is attentive and wouldn't even consider violating a rule or talking out of turn. Always being good can have hidden costs.

The burden of being the good student may include perfectionism and isolation. Academic achievement and the ability to comply with rules are important. Just as important, however, are learning to work as a team member, to master communication and social skills, and to take risks. Programs that measure success only by academic achievement and obedience undervalue many other important skills that children will need throughout their lives. When social skills, problem-solving skills, and teamwork are also valued in the classroom, all students are encouraged to balance their strengths and weaknesses.

Suggestions

1. Be aware of the impact of labeling. If you label a student as good, then what's left for her to be when she isn't good? Often the student decides, "If I'm not acting good, then I must be bad."

2. Match the student who is academically advanced but has undeveloped social skills with a child who balances these strengths and weaknesses. Ask Marty to help Tom study his spelling words, and suggest that in exchange Tom could spend recess shooting baskets with Marty and giving him some tips. This method shows that you value both boys for what they can do. You aren't emphasizing one skill over another, nor are you disparaging any lack of skill.

3. Actively teach children that mistakes are opportunities to learn. Discuss learning

to ride a bike as an example. "Who fell off in the process?" "Was falling off a reason to quit trying?" "Falling is part of learning how to balance on a bicycle." Our mistakes are our own personal teachers and the way in which all of us learn new things.

4. Notice and encourage signs of risk taking, especially when it doesn't result in high achievement. A child may become so achievement oriented that she is devastated by a less-than-perfect paper. Help her understand that she can learn as much from failures as from successes.

Planning Ahead to Prevent Future Problems

1. Encourage the student to participate in areas that are new for him. The class math whiz might enjoy interacting with his classmates as a member of the volleyball team. Perhaps you can engage his parents' help in this effort. Unfortunately, some families see no value in nonacademic pursuits and therefore don't encourage their children to participate in them. Mary, a straight-A student, never took the art classes that interested her, nor did she join the high school swim team because her parents thought such activities were a waste of time. Consequently, Mary missed out on many opportunities to grow in different and important directions. Educating parents is sometimes the first step in furthering children's development.

2. Balance individual activities with group activities so that success in the classroom is

measured in different ways. The student who turns in an outstanding science report may be challenged when she has to work cooperatively with several other classmates to design a solar system mobile. Both types of learning are important.

3. Encourage students to take some reasonable risks. Role playing is a great opportunity for everyone in the classroom to behave differently than they typically do. Suppose that John is always in his seat on time and ready with his pencil not only on his desk but sharpened. At today's class meeting, when the students are discussing the problem of pencils not being sharpened, John might play the role of a student who never remembers to sharpen his pencil. It will be fun for him to safely do something he would be appalled to do during regular class time. For John, this is a small but healthful risk to take.

Cautionary Story

It was time for the school spelling bee. Each classroom champion would compete against classroom winners from other grades. In one day, all of the children in Miss Barry's fifth-grade class had been spelled down, with two exceptions: Jonas and Rita. The class "brains" were now one-on-one. For the next three days the whole class sat through the tennis match of words. Finally, Rita won.

Thirty years later, Rita can still tell you the winning word. She will also tell you that she refused to participate in a spelling bee or any similar competition ever again. She was so embarrassed and consequently felt so isolated by the experience that her willingness to participate in contests was permanently affected.

When children are pushed to perform, they pay a price. But in an unpressured situation they can experience the satisfaction of a job well done without feeling that they *need* to win. Perhaps Miss Barry might have had Rita and Jonas stay after school to spell against one another. Certainly when the contest extended beyond two days, the declaration of a tie could have allowed both students to move ahead and would have discharged the building pressure upon their performance. Imagine what the other students thought and felt during those three days. Did this experience endear Jonas and Rita to their classmates? Of course it didn't. In fact, such pressure is likely to further isolate those trying to cope with isolation.

All students need opportunities to excel and to fail. A positive attitude toward mistakes facilitates learning and frees children to take the risks that lead to discovery.

Gossip

Discussion

"Did you hear what she did?" "And then he said . . . and she said. . . ."

The psychiatrist Rudolf Dreikurs taught that people often deflate to inflate. In other words, a person may put someone else down so that he can feel up. Gossip is one way that individuals may try to make themselves feel better by finding fault with others.

On the other hand, gossiping can be simply offering and hearing information without judgment. Sometimes people share because they care. As with all behavior, teachers should look at the purpose, deal with the belief behind the behavior, and teach the skills of social interest.

Suggestions

1. Whenever students complain about gossip, suggest that they put the problem on the class meeting agenda. They may want to have a discussion simply to increase awareness, or they may want to work on solutions to specific problems. During that discussion, be aware of any information that comes to light that may warrant further investigation or action on your part.

2. Invite students to share how they feel when they are objects of negative gossip. Note when the gossip crosses a line and may become a form of harassment. (See "Bullying" and "Victims.")

3. Invite students to brainstorm for ways to feel belonging and significance besides putting people down. Awareness of other options makes harmful gossip less appealing.

Planning Ahead to Prevent Future Problems

1. Teach compliments and appreciations so that students have the skills and opportunities to focus on positive information about each other.

2. Invite students to participate in the "It's a Jungle Out There" activity (as explained in *Positive Discipline in the Classroom*[23]). In this activity students have fun exploring the desirable and undesirable characteristics of different animals. They can then apply this

23. Jane Nelsen, Lynn Lott, and H. Stephen Glenn, *Positive Discipline in the Classroom* (Roseville, CA: Prima Publishing, 2000), 76–81.

information to the fact that we are all different, with assets and liabilities. All of us have things to contribute as well as areas where we can improve. And sometimes what one person considers desirable is actually undesirable to the next person.

3. Emphasize the importance of helping each other instead of hurting each other. Have students make posters for the classroom: "We are here to help each other—not to hurt each other." "Are you looking for blame, or are you looking for solutions?"

Class Meeting Solution

A story from Wendy Goodfellow, sixth-grade teacher, Caernarvon Elementary School, Edmonton, Alberta, Canada

A topic that frequently appeared in our class meeting agenda was gossip. The students in this class were at the age when kids are starting to notice the opposite sex, so the gossip usually had a who's-interested-in-whom theme. The gossiping took many forms: notes, letters, chatting in small groups, and telephone calls after school. No matter the form, the results were the same: fights, name-calling, hurt feelings, and threats.

My students were very open and honest during class meetings. They kept in mind that their purpose was to help solve problems, and they never used the class meeting as a time to insult others. The discussions of gossip were sparked by entries in the agenda such as the following:

"People are spreading rumors about people liking other people, and usually it isn't true, and other rumors are being spread, too."

By talking about how certain rumors affected individuals, the students were learning to control their part in the gossiping. The class took this further by making gossip the focus of a health lesson. Students brainstormed and came up with three steps for dealing with gossip; they then performed role plays to demonstrate their understanding of the behavior.

1. Refuse to listen to the gossip.

2. Brainstorm for solutions to a specific problem.

3. Walk away if gossiping continues.

Knowing that gossip was a widespread problem, the students performed these role plays for other classes. They also made antigossip posters to display around the school. Students assumed a very active role in preventing gossip.

Once in a while the class meetings had no impact on the one or two students who appeared to be at the root of the problem. In such cases I had brief meetings at recess with four or five students, either those who had started the gossip or those about whom gossip was being spread.

The class was asked to come up with special options for students who continued to break the rules. The suggestions included the following:

1. Spend recess writing an action plan on what to do instead of gossiping.

2. Write a note of apology.

3. Give a talk on how and why gossip hurts other people.

The gossiper was invited to choose the option that would be most helpful to him or her.

Graffiti

Discussion

Graffiti is simply drawings and inscriptions made on walls or other surfaces where they'll be seen by the public. But most adults frown on graffiti and equate creating graffiti with vandalism. Young people, on the other hand, use tagging (a personal mark using letters or symbols) to make a statement of belonging and significance. Adults need to guide youngsters' need for self-expression and establish boundaries so that this art form doesn't become disrespectful to either people or property.

Suggestions

1. Don't create a problem where there is no problem. Saying, "We will have no graffiti or tagging at our school," when this behavior isn't an issue invites students to try it.

2. Provide an outlet. If students are creating graffiti in the bathroom, cover one wall with butcher paper and make it the designated graffiti spot.

3. Have students create murals in places where tagging has been a problem. Invite taggers and other interested students to participate in this project. Graffiti artists rarely deface murals that have been painted by other students.

4. Sometimes schools emphasize catching the culprits and making them pay. Instead, tell students that tagging is creating problems. Let them know that you don't want to put them in the position of tattlers, but you would like them to be involved in coming up with a solution.

5. Make students aware that there is a cost—sometimes a significant cost—to repainting walls or using solvents on concrete. Explain that funds for this will not come out of the general operating budget. Brainstorm with them about raising money, and involve them in the fundraising process.

Planning Ahead to Prevent Future Problems

1. Let students brainstorm to find ways to keep graffiti respectful, such as using butcher paper on designated walls, planning a mural on the playground fence, or creating a mosaic of children's ceramic tiles in an area that's vulnerable to graffiti. Instead of vainly attempting to extinguish graffiti, accept these messages and drawings as a means of expression that's here to stay. Remember that graffiti has taken different forms at different times. There may have been a time when your own similar behavior was seen as insolent or destructive—perhaps you drew all over a binder instead of a wall.

2. Have your students do an anthropological study of graffiti. They can collect samples of graffiti from different locations, compare the samples, and draw conclusions.

3. Organize cleanup projects in which students paint walls that have been used disrespectfully. This teaches them social interest and gives them an awareness of the cost and effort required to keep areas beautiful.

4. Prevent bathroom graffiti by involving students in designing and painting art murals on the doors and stalls in the student rest rooms.

Inspirational Story

When earning her master's degree from California State University, Sacramento, Ann Platt wrote about an incident with graffiti in her thesis titled "Efficacy of Class Meetings in Elementary Schools":

A school with a serious graffiti problem kept hiring painters to repaint the walls. Every time a wall was repainted, the kids put graffiti on it again. One of the teachers suggested asking the students for ideas on how to solve the problem. The students decreed that when kids were caught writing on the walls, they would be supervised by a student monitor while they painted over their inscriptions. It's no surprise that the graffiti problem disappeared.

Gum Chewing

Discussion

For students, chewing gum is one of numerous sources of classroom diversion—one that generates satisfying levels of teacher annoyance. A rhythmically chomping jaw is an excellent invitation to combat. Even if you don't permit gum chewing in your classroom, surely other, comparable activities irritate you, prompting a battle of wills. You may find your personal challenge in a baseball cap set backward above a defiant face or in a candy bar being surreptitiously unwrapped behind a desktop.

It is helpful to remember the Mistaken Goal Chart when faced with a young person who is chewing gum or engaging in other behaviors that fit the same category (see pages 12–13). Your response to the misbehavior will give you a clue as to the student's goal. What feelings surge in your breast when you are confronted with a situation? Maybe you are just irritated. If you are instantly angry, this emotion can escalate quickly into fury and a thought such as, "You are not going to get away with that behavior in *this* classroom!"

If your response is closer to irritation, the child in front of you wants attention. She believes that she can feel belonging and significance only when she is the center of attention. Gum is a tool with which she can meet her goal of keeping you busy with her. No matter what kind of attention she receives, even negative attention, she achieves her goal.

If you're angry and ready to do battle, then the student is pursuing a different mistaken goal, such as power. Whatever the purpose of the behavior, don't simply scold or reiterate the rules. Choose an encouraging response that helps the student feel a sense of belonging in your classroom and learn to get attention or use power in constructive ways.

Suggestions

1. If you notice a student chewing gum when it's against the established rules, you may use one of several approaches (any of which is more effective than lecturing, reminding, or scolding):

A. Describe what you see: "I see Laura chewing gum with a smile on her face."

B. Offer a limited choice: "Do you want to throw your gum in the wastebasket up front or in the one at the back of the classroom?" To continue chewing gum is not one of the choices.

C. Use one word: "gum" or "please." Then wait quietly until the student does what is necessary to abide by the rule.

D. Don't talk. Act. Pick up a garbage can, walk over to the student, and indicate without words that he is to put the gum in the can.

The following suggestions assume that there is no schoolwide policy in regard to gum chewing:

2. Consider minimizing the number of restrictions placed on students. Teaching them how to chew gum politely and dispose of it responsibly might work better for some classrooms than having to hassle frequently with gum chewers. If your goal is cooperation, listen to your students' ideas and decide together about will work best in this classroom rather than beginning the year with a preconceived list of have-to's.

3. If you aren't distracted by gum chewing and the kids figure out ways to resolve possible problems (such as gum stuck on desks), consider allowing students to have gum-chewing privileges as long as they

accept the responsibility that goes with the privilege.

4. If a gum-chewing student is seeking attention, ignore her misbehavior when the audience is present, but ask her to stay behind for a moment when the class leaves for recess. Ask her what the class rule about gum chewing is. Ask her why she chose to break that rule and what she might do to remember it in the future. Offer to give her a secret signal, such as pulling at your ear, if you notice she has forgotten the rule. That will be her personal cue to get up quietly and dispose of the gum. By involving her in a solution to the problem and respectfully giving her attention, you will diminish or eliminate her need to seek attention inappropriately.

5. If a gum-chewing student is seeking power, the good news is that a power struggle requires a minimum of two participants. Fortunately, you have complete control over one potential participant—yourself. Instead of charging in and demanding that the gum be thrown away *right now,* you can choose among several responses:

A. Announce to all the students that they may use the next two minutes to prepare for the upcoming lesson. Add that this is a good time to throw away gum, sharpen pencils, and clear desks. Without engaging in one-on-one combat, the gum chewer is given an opportunity to cooperate with dignity.

B. You may give a choice: "Jo, would you like to put gum chewing on the agenda, or should I?"

C. You may ask for help: "Class, I need your help. Would anyone who has forgotten about our gum-chewing rule please take care of that now?" Kids who want power often respond to a request for help, as this allows them to use power in a positive way. Furthermore, making the request a general one avoids a personal challenge.

Planning Ahead to Prevent Future Problems

1. Be familiar with your school's policy regarding gum chewing. Share this information with your students.

The following items assume that gum chewing is an issue to be decided in individual classrooms:

2. At the beginning of the school year, involve students in determining the rules for chewing gum, wearing caps, eating candy, and other distracting behaviors. (If gum chewing distracts you when you're teaching, give your input and ask for their help.) Facilitate a discussion of why gum chewing may be disrespectful or what problems it may cause. If you and the students decide on a "no gum chewing" rule, they can also decide on ideas for enforcement and solutions to any problems that arise.

3. Post rules where everyone can see them. It's nice to have the students make the rules poster, which can be titled "We Decided . . ." or "We Agreed Together . . ." Silently pointing to a rule can immediately halt the misbehavior of those who forget.

4. When you notice that the problem is on the rise, bring it to your students' attention at the class meeting: "Why is more gum chewing going on in the classroom?" Sometimes simply raising awareness will reverse a problem's growth.

5. When students understand the reasons behind rules, they are more willing to honor the rules. As a class, check out the bottoms of desks and spend a half hour scraping off the fossilized gum that is found. Then ask them to pretend they are giving a talk to a group of new students on the problems that gum chewing creates. Allow them to share what they have learned. (If one student uses this information to argue that teaching how to dispose of gum properly makes more sense than outlawing it, don't consider the lesson a failure. Remember that the goal is not to manipulate the students but to learn things together.)

6. If the real problem with gum chewing is that the teacher finds it distracting, then he can explain his problem to the class and ask for help. When children see themselves as able to contribute, they don't feel resentful or controlled. Involvement meets their need to feel that they matter and belong.

Inspirational Story

Barb Goble is a sixth-grade teacher at Beacon Elementary School in Montesano, Washington. During a training session on how to use Positive Discipline in the classroom, she took part in a role play that fo-

cused on a gum-chewing child whose goal was power. The task was to demonstrate how to avoid a power struggle.

For the role play, several teachers arranged their chairs to represent a classroom of students, with Mary, the gum chewer, in the front row. Barb, in the role of the teacher, began a lesson on prepositions. As the gum chewing became obvious, Barb said without missing a beat, "For instance, we can say that Mary has gum *in* her mouth." While she spoke, Barb picked up the trash can, walked over to Mary, and held it out. Again, with no break in her dialogue, while proffering the trash can, Barb continued, "We can also use this preposition in the sentence 'Now the gum is *in* the garbage can.'" (The student deposited the gum therein without a fuss.)

Mary was also wearing a hat (showing disregard for another rule). Barb calmly took the hat and placed it under the chair, saying, "The hat is now *under* the chair." The students were spellbound, and the gum chewer was too surprised to be defiant. As the discussion of prepositions continued, even Mary was listening, and the lesson was actually enhanced. No battle or negative attention disrupted the flow of class time.

Barb offered a beautiful example of doing the unexpected. She also demonstrated that a teacher can act kindly and firmly while maintaining the dignity of all of those involved. Instead of trying to make the student do something (remove the hat), she focused on her own actions and did what she could do (remove the hat herself). (Rudolf Dreikurs, the psychiatrist and child specialist, often said, "Decide what you will do, not what you will make the student do.") Because her action didn't express anger or try to control, the stu-dent wasn't invited to engage in a tug-of-war over the hat. In handling the gum situation, Barb modeled using humor and grace. She showed that kindness cou-pled with firmness is both respectful and effective.

Hitting

Discussion

The most effective way to respond to hit-ting depends on the student's age. Younger students are actively learning social skills. This process involves considerable trial and error. A big part of developing such skills is learning about feelings. Actually teaching about feelings and having students practice acceptable ways to express strong feelings are critical to fostering the development of social skills.

An older student who hits is almost certainly sending a coded message. This student is most likely feeling hurt himself. It's necessary both to address the underly-ing hurt feelings and to make it clear that hitting is unacceptable. This involves no punishment, suffering, shame, or blame. A student who is hurting others because he hurts is unlikely to mend his behavior as a result of being further hurt or humiliated. Remember, the goal is to change behavior, not to retaliate.

Suggestions

Because hitting is approached very differ-ently according to a student's grade level, the suggestions here reflect this. The initial suggestions are aimed at working with younger students who are developing social skills. The latter suggestions take into con-sideration the fact that schools have poli-cies that need to be considered.

1. Respond quickly and firmly by remov-ing the student from the situation.

2. State clearly that hitting is not accept-able: "I will not allow other students to be hurt."

3. Allow students to cool off and regain their composure. (Don't try to find out who hit whom. Send both students to cool off.)

4. After calm is restored:

A. Discuss what happened that led to the hitting.

B. Explore alternatives to hitting with the students involved.

C. Role-play the situation to try out the new responses.

5. Teach students to be assertive. Tell them to respond sternly with words if they are hit. A student who is hit needs to say, "No hitting!" or "Do not hit me!" very clearly to the hitting student. If this hasn't occurred before the student comes to the teacher for help, then the adult should stand by supportively while the student who was hit tells the other student not to hit him.

6. At a quiet moment, talk to a student who is repeatedly hitting others about what is bothering him. Books are a good tool for opening up a topic.

7. A five-part approach can be helpful:

A. Damage control: Don't let the hitting escalate. Separate the students.

B. Deal with the hurt feelings.

C. Address the issue of restitution: What can be done to help the student who was hit feel better?

D. Involve students in finding solutions besides hitting.

E. Remind the student of the school policy. Follow through with firmness and kindness. (Refer to "Follow-Through.")

8. Use the Mistaken Goal Chart (pages 12–13) to decode what a student's behavior is telling you. The teacher's own feelings are the best clue. Typically a student who is hurting others is feeling hurt herself, which means the goal is revenge. Hitting may also be a means of getting and keeping the teacher's attention (the goal of undue attention) or a form of control (the goal of power). Identifying the likely hidden message helps teachers figure out how best to respond.

9. Spend time alone with a student who frequently hits other students. Explore what may be causing this student to feel hurt. Sometimes an adult telling a story about a time she felt hurt will open the door to communication.

10. Encourage students by pointing out times when they handle frustration or anger in an acceptable way: "Jeff, I noticed that you walked away when you were provoked during that basketball game. That was a great way to handle your anger, and I congratulate you for making such a healthy choice."

Planning Ahead to Prevent Future Problems

1. Teach students about feelings. During a class meeting, explore and role-play acceptable ways to act when feeling angry, sad, hurt, or other difficult emotions.

2. Use class meetings to discuss how to help one another feel better and to brainstorm for ways to handle difficult situations other than hitting.

3. Ask students to suggest things they can do when they feel really angry or frustrated at school. They may want to designate items or activities that will absorb the physical energy such feelings generate (e.g., balls to squeeze). Some students find it helpful to put their hands in their pockets when they feel angry and want to hit someone.

Class Meeting Solution

A story from Suzanne Smitha, school psychologist, Sharon School, Charlotte, North Carolina

A little boy was always hitting the other children in his kindergarten class when they were walking in line to various places. The children had told him several times in class meetings that they did not like it when he hit them because it hurt. The problem continued, however, until they chose a clever solution to help him re-member not to hit when walking in line. There was a prized toy fire engine in the classroom, and one of the children suggested that if this boy was allowed to carry the fire engine everywhere, he wouldn't be able to hit anyone because his hands would be full. Everyone agreed that this was a great idea. He carried the engine for about a week every time they went somewhere, and he seldom hit anyone again.

Holidays

Discussion

Holidays bring a mixed bag of feelings. Excitement, exhaustion, anticipation, disappointment, and even depression are all parts of the emotional reality of holidays. Acknowledging and accepting the appearance of these feelings within yourself and among your students may ease the transition between regular school days and days off. The more you involve your students in the planning for special holiday activities, the more smoothly the holidays will go.

Suggestions

1. Everyone has a different idea of how the holidays should be celebrated. Share your picture, and be curious about how others celebrate instead of insisting that there is only one right way. During a class meeting, give every student a chance to share which holidays his or her family celebrates and how.

2. When you have students from different cultures, invite willing parents to visit the class and share food, traditional clothing, information about customs, and so on, with all your students.

3. Use limited choices around the planning: "Our room parents have said that they can be available at either eleven o'clock or at one o'clock next Friday. Will our party be in the morning or in the afternoon?" This gives students an opportunity to have a say in the scheduling and also increases their awareness of the needs and schedules of other people involved.

4. Explain to your students that there is a curriculum as well as certain responsibilities that can't be ignored during holiday times. To avoid nagging, write up your regular class schedule, show this to your students, and post it in the classroom. Let the schedule become the boss.

5. Use "as soon as," as in, "As soon as we finish math and science, we'll have time for holiday art," and "As soon as the literature assignments are turned in, we'll have time for holiday costumes."

6. Combine classrooms to enhance the air of celebration. Having sixth graders carve pumpkins with kindergartners is a way to create special bonds among students.

Planning Ahead to Prevent Future Problems

1. Take care of yourself. Think about your personal desires for a specific holiday. Then make sure that responsibilities at school don't overshadow your own observance or wishes for that holiday.

2. Some schools prohibit celebrations of religious holidays in an effort to be sensitive to different cultures and beliefs. Recognize that the holiday is happening outside the classroom, however, and will have an impact on your students. Elementary school children benefit from planning special events—anything out of the ordinary—that channel their surging excitement and energy.

3. Use the class meeting to get your students' input on holiday routines. Ask for ideas about parties, projects, and vacations. Involve them in creating a sense of closure for the holiday break. Before the vacation begins, have them envision some of the typical problems that occur during holidays and then brainstorm for solutions.

4. Let go of your need for perfection, and concentrate on having fun together instead of producing fabulous decorations, gifts, and cards. Holiday projects are great opportunities for all members of the class to contribute.

Inspirational Story

Thanksgiving was just around the corner. With the help of two room parents, Mrs. Heath had traditionally planned a special feast for the day before Thanksgiving. This year she had started holding class meetings with her fourth graders. With some apprehension, she decided to put the planning of this feast on the class meeting agenda. To her surprise, the topic yielded much discussion and many creative suggestions, which continued through several class meetings.

Mrs. Heath and her students decided to create committees to handle different parts of the planning. Because she was used to handling all necessary planning herself, Mrs. Heath felt overwhelmed by having a new system and was concerned about the students' ability to follow through. At the same time, she was excited to see the students work together toward a common goal. Mrs. Heath's image of the Thanksgiving feast began to change through this process.

When the day arrived and the feast began, Mrs. Heath was pleasantly surprised. She noticed the beautiful decorations, the personalized place settings, the abundance of food, and the students' excitement about the entertainment they had planned. She also noticed that the traditional apple cider was missing and became concerned about what they were going to drink. Her first impulse was to send a room parent to the grocery store, but she stopped herself and gave her students a chance to solve the problem. They decided together that water would suffice.

At the next class meeting, the students had an opportunity to appreciate themselves. They reviewed their successes and also their mistakes. Mrs. Heath was thrilled with the new skills she had seen her class develop and with her own ability to let go. She found herself looking forward to next year's celebration and feeling curious about how the next class would create its feast.

Homework, Nontraditional

Discussion

Thousands of students, parents, and teachers have suffered over the issue of traditional homework. The following approach may appeal to many of those who seek to eliminate homework frustration.

Suggestions, Planning Ahead to Prevent Future Problems, and Inspirational Story All Rolled into One

Cindy White is the owner and director of Granite Bay Schoolhouse, a private school in Granite Bay, California. Cindy doesn't believe in traditional homework. The only homework assigned to each student is to plan some time for his or her family to be together.

Cindy has taken this revolutionary route because she believes that homework is often more detrimental than helpful. She sums up the reasons:

1. If students understand a concept, why should they do twenty almost identical problems? If they know something, why practice? (Consider how much joy would be taken out of bicycle riding if we had to ride around the block twenty times every night to practice instead of riding for pleasure or to accomplish a particular task.)

2. If children don't understand a concept or don't know what they are supposed to do, how can they convey what they don't know to their parents? This problem usually ends up ruining the family's evening, making everyone feel frustrated, and damaging the child's self-esteem.

3. If the parents do the homework, what has the child learned? For example, parents frequently take over their children's science fair projects. Hence a perfect project arrives at school, but the child has been left out. The experience makes him feel inadequate and unimportant. How can this child live up to the superior abilities of his parents? The only projects that get oohs and aahs are the ones done by parents. What feelings then arise in the rare child who did her own project, which pales in comparison?

The teachers at Granite Bay Schoolhouse do assign daily homework—in the best sense of both *home* and *work*. The homework, to plan some time for the family to be together, is given shape by the student. Each child is responsible for choosing a shared activity and making it happen. Through this homework, children learn to budget time, to design and carry out plans, and to value time with the whole family together.

Each day the students are asked what they did for homework the night before. They answer in journal writing, in a cooperative group, or one-on-one with a friend or a parent volunteer.

One child reported that his dad wanted to mow the lawn. The child decided to get his dad to let him make a map of how the lawn should be mowed. They worked together on the map, and then the child followed his dad around to make sure he followed the map. They both had a great time.

Some parents are so busy that they have trouble finding time to spend with their

children. (This brings up the issue of priorities, but that's not the point of this discussion.) Just think of how much quality time becomes available when there aren't pages of math problems to fuss through and fume over or yet another map to trace and fill in.

The homework can be as simple as the child choosing a book for one family member to read to the others, or saving time for family fun by deciding to have a bath before dinner instead of after, or helping fix dinner. The point is for the child to assume some of the responsibility for family togetherness.

After hearing about this exciting concept, a parent might object, "But homework helps the parent know what the child is learning and how the child is doing." Cindy's response is that if parents want to know what their child is doing, they can volunteer to be in the classroom. Children love to see their parents at school, even if it's just for fifteen minutes during a lunch break from work.

Traditional homework creates many pressures. How many parents push their children to achieve until the kids believe their value depends on achievement? How many parents are judging their children for not getting straight A's? What do these judgments do to children? How many parents feel inadequate if their child doesn't do as well as the child next door? Whatever happened to appreciating children for themselves? Transforming homework time into family time could eliminate many of these problems. However, when teachers decide to implement this style of homework, they should caution children and parents that their planned time together cannot be used for lectures; only pleasant time will meet the requirements for the homework.

This concept of homework raises interesting possibilities for high school students who are pulling away from their families. It could help balance their intense need for peer groups.

The greatest thing parents can do for their children is to spend quality time with them. Nothing can do more to satisfy children's greatest need—to feel belonging and significance. The homework assignment from Granite Bay Schoolhouse is a wonderful reminder of this truth for parents and instills this truth in children for life.

Homework, Traditional

(see also "Assignments, Not Turned In"; "Homework, Nontraditional"; and "Failing")

Discussion

Homework has many possible purposes. Students, teachers, and parents need to understand the purposes behind various assignments so that they are all trying to achieve the same goals. These purposes may include the following:

1. Homework allows students to practice the skills they are learning in class.

2. Homework teaches responsibility for choices about use of time and efforts to learn, as well as accountability for assignments.

3. Homework teaches perseverance, as students must learn to stick with a difficult or demanding task until it's finished.

4. Homework develops self-discipline, because students must choose to work on an assignment when more appealing options are available.

5. Homework develops personal study skills and habits.

6. Homework provides parents with a link to their children's school and academic life.

7. Homework teaches time management—how to organize personal time and complete assignments on schedule.

Whether these are the purposes behind the teacher's homework assignments or he has a different list, all the participants should know the reasons behind assignments. With this understanding as the starting point, the issues surrounding homework can be examined in relation to the list. Consider the following example:

John had a book report due in a month. What were the first steps he needed to take on this project? Get a book and read it, right? John failed to take these small details into account. Sitting down the night before the report was due, having only just chosen a book, John had a problem on his hands. He would probably show up at school the next day with no report. But when that happened, the real learning began.

"Why is there no report?" Ms. Smith asked John.

"I didn't have time to finish the book."

"Oh, why was that?"

"I just started reading it last night."

"Can you remember when you first knew about this assignment?"

"Last month, I think."

Through dialogue, Ms. Smith helped John explore what went wrong so that he began to identify the time management skills he needed to develop. She helped him take this information and apply it to the future: "What ideas do you have about what you might do the next time you are assigned a book report?"

Next time, John can look at the calendar and count the number of days until the report is due. By subtracting how many days he estimates it will take to write and polish his report, he can plan his reading. Once he knows how many days he has to read the book, he will look at how long it is. He can then either set a goal of reading a certain number of pages each day or decide to be halfway through the book by a certain date.

This process helps John feel in control of the situation and optimistic about his ability to handle future assignments. It also achieves three of the stated purposes in the previously given list: developing self-discipline, teaching study skills, and showing how to implement time management skills.

Contrast this approach to a punitive one: "John, you didn't turn in your book report, therefore, you'll have to go to detention after school today." Which of the stated purposes for homework does this approach satisfy? When put in the context of addressing a reasoned list of purposes, a teacher's approach to handling homework problems changes entirely.

Suggestions

1. Consider renaming homework. Calling it "investment time" promotes a positive attitude shift.

2. Never use homework as a punishment.

3. Have clear guidelines for how you will handle the situation when homework is not turned in or is turned in late. (Refer to "Assignments, Not Turned In.")

4. Consider alternatives to posting daily assignments. Homework can be assigned on Monday and turned in on Friday to honor the pace of individual students. You may choose to do this with specific subjects and add other subjects daily.

Planning Ahead to Prevent Future Problems

1. At the beginning of the school year, lead a discussion about homework. Agree on a list of purposes or goals for homework. Post this list in the classroom with a heading such as "Homework Helps. . . ."

2. Send copies of the purposes-of-homework list home with students, so they can share them with their parents.

3. Periodically review the list of homework goals, and check with students to see which goals are being met.

4. Periodically send students home with notes for their parents that give an overview of the material being covered in class and let them know about any special projects or assignments coming up: "In May we begin our study of the planets. On May 23 each student is expected to display a planet model that he or she has prepared at home. Guidelines for these models, with a list of materials needed, will be sent home next week. Please plan to help your child gather the needed supplies by the following week-

end so that work on this project can begin. If you have trouble obtaining any of the materials, please contact me." Notes such as this one give parents a sense of connection (one of the purposes of homework) and enlist their support for the assignment.

5. Send parents a list of suggestions about how to support their children's learning through homework. Here is a sample note to parents:

Homework Hints for Your Child's Success

A. Provide an uncluttered space where homework is to be done. It's best for this space to be apart from the main living area. A desk or table in the child's room is ideal.

B. Assist children with the actual content of homework in these ways:

Help them understand a concept or problem that has them stumped.

Review or proofread completed work (if asked).

Offer help in developing study plans or calendars or in arranging when and how to get needed supplies.

Respectfully stop and leave the room if complaining, arguing, or fighting begins.

C. Establish a routine for homework. Agree together when homework is to be done—immediately after school, at 4 o'clock every day, immediately after dinner cleanup, or whatever time works best for you and your child. (Such routines replace nagging on your part and frustration on everyone's part.)

D. Remember that this is your *child's* homework. It's more important to discover whether he or she understands the material than to determine whether you understand it. If your child runs into difficulty, encourage him or her to let the teacher know of the problem. This will help the teacher identify areas that may need to be retaught or worked on more in class.

6. Spend time problem solving with students who are having difficulty with homework. Focus on helping them develop plans for future success. Don't blame or punish them for past failures.

7. Periodically ask students which assignments or types of assignments they see as most helpful. (Even if they don't jump for joy at discussions of homework, they probably liked some assignments more than others.) If there's a type they particularly dislike, a discussion of the skills they might learn through such assignments may help students dread them less. The teacher may also discover that a different type of assignment might be more effective.

8. If problems with homework persist, the teacher can present the issue at a class meeting: "I have a problem with receiving homework assignments that are sloppily written, on crumpled paper, or smudged with lots of erasures. It's very difficult for me to read these papers. Can anyone think of a way we might solve this problem?" In addition to the suggestion that the teacher quit giving out homework,

students' suggestions might include returning hard-to-read papers to the individual to
be redone or reducing the length of assignments with more careful work being expected in return. The teacher may discover
that certain assignments are so tedious that
the students become discouraged, resulting
in sloppy work; in this case, he may choose
to change the type of assignment entirely.
The result of such a discussion, regardless
of the solution chosen, is likely to be more
carefully prepared homework papers.

9. Elicit students' suggestions about future
assignments. Homework and out-of-school
projects can be a source of excitement and
cooperative achievement. When students
are involved in the planning, they find their
work more meaningful and their enthusiasm rises. Homework can even be fun!

Inspirational Story

*A story from Kerri McCaul, sixth-grade
teacher, Everett, Washington*

Positive Discipline has shown me how
to let go of the "I don't have my homework" dilemma. This response works for
me 90 percent of the time, which is far better than threatening and pleading ever did,
and the looks I get from my students are
priceless every time. When an important
assignment is due, I like to walk around
the room and collect it, by hand, from each
student. This allows me to talk briefly with
each one about how things went, et cetera.
It also allows me to set up contracts with

those students who do not have the project
ready to hand in.

I think that, too often, teachers are
guilty of letting students off the hook by
accepting homework excuses and that students have their roles practiced to perfection—the hanging head, the mournful
voice, the sincere sad eyes. Kids are great at
convincing teachers! Positive Discipline
holds students accountable. When students do not have their papers ready, I listen and empathize with their explanations.
I then explain why I feel the work is important and still needs to be finished. I then
ask, "When do you think you can finish
it?" (and watch their mouths drop open). I
gently and firmly hold my ground until we
agree on a date (usually the next day) that
the student will get the work in. I shake
hands to seal our agreement and ask the
student to hand the assignment to me personally so that I am reminded of our bargain. I still charge a late penalty to the
item, but 90 percent of the time, even at a
reduced score, the student walks in the
next day and hands me the work tri-
umphantly, proudly—here it is just like we
agreed! Quite often, I get the work before
the contract deadline. Yes, it takes extra
time to walk around the room and collect
projects from every student. Yes, I make
lots of deals with the same students over
and over. But, it also gives me the opportunity to check in with each of my students,
show them I'm listening and show them I
care. I am also holding them accountable

in a respectful manner. And, I get the homework turned in!

Class Meeting Solution

At a class meeting during the first month of school, Mr. Seling and his students formulated a list of homework goals they wanted to pursue for the year. One student volunteered to type the list on the classroom computer, and another offered to make two copies for each student, plus an extra copy for the bulletin board. One of each student's copies was to go home to his or her parents, and the other copy was to be placed at the front of the student's notebook. The class decided that when students felt frustrated with homework, they would review the list of goals and see whether this encouraged them.

Mr. Seling also asked the class to help plan a system for collecting homework. The students decided to have a brightly colored box for homework, and each week a different student would be assigned to pass the box around to collect the previous night's assignments as soon as the morning bell rang. Decorating the box became an afternoon art project during the first week of school.

In addition, the class determined that all homework was to be returned to students on Friday mornings and arranged a system in which helpers would pass out the corrected papers. The class requested that Fridays be no-homework days, and Mr. Seling agreed. By the beginning of October, the homework process was managed entirely by the students. When the occasional problem arose, a student or Mr. Seling brought it to the class meeting, and the difficulty was ironed out. Homework became a smoothly operating routine in this classroom.

Interruptions

Discussion

Students who interrupt give everyone an opportunity to learn about mutual respect.

Children learn at an early age how good it feels to receive attention, but sometimes they have the mistaken belief that they don't count unless they are the center of attention at all times. They may then seek undue attention. (Remember the Hat Message for undue attention: "Notice me! Involve me.") Teachers can foster a sense of belonging and significance in the attention-hungry student by handling interruptions in ways that show respect for his needs as well as those of others.

Another type of interrupter lurks in most classrooms. A characteristic of children with attention deficit disorder (ADD) is impulsiveness. (Refer to "Attention Deficit Disorder and Attention Deficit Disorder with Hyperactivity.") As soon as a thought enters the head of a child with ADD, it pops out of her mouth. Sometimes the thought is pretty fragile: if it has to run in place while another person finishes talking, it may disappear entirely. Give this student some special tools. Talk over the problem with her, and come up with strategies to help her hold on to an elusive idea. Suggest that she hold up one or two fingers to remind herself that she has a comment to add, or teach her to jot down a key word or sentence to which she can refer when her turn to speak finally arrives.

Suggestions

1. Keep control of your schedule. For instance, let students know that you are available to go over homework from 8:00 to 8:30. Give them specific times when you will answer questions regarding certain activities.

2. Use nonverbal signals to show that you are aware of the desire for attention. Lightly touch the student's arm, reassuring him that he is important, without responding directly to the interruption. If necessary, once you have finished speaking, you may address his concerns. Some teachers hold up an index finger to acknowledge a student's request. The student learns to be patient because the teacher has taken notice of his needs.

3. Put interruptions on the class meeting agenda as your concern. Students enjoy role-playing these situations, with one of the students playing the teacher. Afterward, ask the students who played the roles what they were thinking, feeling, and deciding in their roles. Also, ask the other students for their observations. This increases everyone's awareness of how frustrating and disrespectful interruptions can be. Finally, have the class brainstorm for ways they can deal with this problem.

4. When the student interrupts, remind him that you have an agreement to spend some special time with him at 2:15 and tell him that you are looking forward to it.

5. When you tell a student you don't have time now, let her know when you will have time. If a time for sharing has already been

set up, ask the student, "What is our agreement about when we can talk?"

6. Do the unexpected: Act as though the interruption is extremely important. Stop class, and give interrupters time to finish what they are saying or doing. The tone you use is very important. Sarcasm will lead to additional power struggles or to revenge cycles. Assume a lighthearted manner as you say to the class, "Excuse me, everyone. Stan seems to have something to say that can't wait. Will you give us a few moments?" You may ask Stan whether he would like the whole class to hear what he has to say, or you may leave the room with him for a minute. If two students are talking, try saying, "Stan and Sally seem to have something very important to discuss. We will wait until they're finished." Remember, this is effective when you use a respectful tone of voice; don't try to humiliate. When interruptions are treated as a big deal, it often makes students think twice before interrupting.

7. Share what you see, and share your feelings about it: "Sheena, I notice that you're talking to other people. I'm standing here feeling discouraged. I would like your help in working this out."

8. Be aware of how you may become engaged by students' interruptions. Don't be sidetracked. Remind students that they can use the class meeting agenda for questions or concerns. When a student interrupts, say, "That sounds like something you might want to put on the agenda," and say no more.

Planning Ahead to Prevent Future Problems

1. Notice when the goal of interruptions seems to be advancing beyond a need for attention and developing into a quest for power or revenge. Use your feelings as a source of information: If you're simply annoyed by the interruptions, the student is probably vying for attention. But if you're starting to feel angry and challenged or hurt, take this as a clue that you're now dealing with someone who believes she needs to be in charge or who is feeling hurt because something is threatening her sense of belonging.

2. Invite students to write down things they would like to tell you (so they don't forget), and then share these things with you during the times when you aren't occupied with lessons or specific tasks. It's helpful to establish times during the day when you are available to anyone who needs assistance or has something they would like to discuss with you.

3. Provide training and encouragement to students for whom interrupting is an innate problem (those who have ADD or ADHD). Empathize with how difficult it sometimes is for them not to interrupt, and be sure to notice and appreciate times when they curb the impulse to interrupt.

Inspirational Stories

Carly and Mrs. Adams

Mrs. Adams walked into her classroom with a feeling of dread. She knew that twenty minutes into her sophomore English class, Carly would interrupt her by talking to others or asking questions. Mrs. Adams had tried to deal with the situation by ignoring the interruptions, by asking Carly not to speak to her friends during class time, and by asking Carly to share her conversations with the class. The tension was rising between the two of them.

One day Mrs. Adams spoke privately to Carly, saying, "I notice that regularly when I'm speaking you begin to speak to your classmates or choose to make comments. I feel hurt and discouraged, and I want to work on finding a solution that we both can live with. I was wondering if you could share your perception of what you see happening."

Carly was surprised by both Mrs. Adams's willingness to confront her and the fact that the teacher had done this by sharing how she felt. Still, Carly sounded defensive and challenging as she replied, "This is just the way I am. I have a lot to say, and I speak my mind."

Mrs. Adams let Carly know that she appreciated the feedback and also told Carly that she admired people who have the ability to express their thoughts and feelings. She then asked, "What ideas do you have to work this out so both of our styles can be respected?"

Carly's attitude seemed to shift dramatically as she said, "I really didn't mean to hurt your feelings. I'll be more careful."

Mrs. Adams felt closer to Carly and could feel the door to respect opening between them.

Bonnie and Mr. Vasquez

Bonnie had been told to quit interrupting so often that she no longer even heard the admonishment. One day her teacher, Mr. Vasquez, lost his patience and really barked at her. Bonnie felt terrible, and so did Mr. Vasquez.

Mr. Vasquez asked Bonnie whether she was willing to spend some time during recess talking over what had happened. Bonnie agreed but felt even worse. When they met, Mr. Vasquez began by saying that speaking as he had done was very disrespectful, and he apologized for yelling at her. Bonnie thanked him tearfully and admitted that she knew she interrupted a lot. Proceeding to the final of the Three R's of Recovery (Recognize, Reconcile, and Resolve), Mr. Vasquez asked Bonnie why she continued to interrupt if she knew it was a problem. Did she need some help with this? More tears fell as Bonnie faltered that she interrupted because otherwise she forgot what she had to say and that she felt embarrassed and stupid about being unable to remember what she wanted to contribute. Mr. Vasquez was surprised to learn that she had so much trouble remembering her ideas.

Recalling that Bonnie's parents had told him that she had ADD, Mr. Vasquez asked her what techniques she had previously tried to remember her thoughts. She looked up in surprise and said that she hadn't thought there was anything to try except stating the thought right away. Mr. Vasquez asked whether Bonnie was willing to experiment with a new approach. When she expressed eagerness to do so, he proposed that she write down a word or two to remind her of a thought and then refer to it when the time came for her to speak. If the thought was one she wanted to share with Mr. Vasquez specifically, they agreed that she could simply write him a note and hand it to him when he was less busy. They planned to meet again in a week to check on whether Bonnie was finding this technique helpful.

Bonnie gave Mr. Vasquez a hug and thanked him for listening to her and sharing his ideas with her. (Now the tears were in Mr. Vasquez's eyes.) The number of Bonnie's interruptions decreased immediately, and she even took to carrying a small notepad with her to use outside the classroom.

Intimidation

(see also "Bullying" and "Gangs")

Discussion

We all know when we feel intimidated, but it's difficult to pinpoint the specific behaviors that evoke this feeling. A person may feel intimidated when a stranger simply stands too close to him. Put-downs, threats, and malevolent looks from one person to another often evoke feelings of intimidation. Harassment and acts of violence are unmistakable cases of intimidation.

Another version of intimidation occurs when one person is especially successful or aggressive. In the school setting, this may be the student who scores 100 percent on every pop quiz or the athlete who challenges all the other students to compete against her. These students' classmates often feel intimidated because their own skills are inferior or because they have less confidence.

When intimidation is more of an internal struggle, examining the feelings involved can lead to solutions. The student feeling intimidated will benefit from considering why certain behaviors intimidate him. This can lead to his acquiring more assertiveness skills and learning to take more risks. For instance, Bob is the smallest boy in his freshman class and feels very intimidated in the locker room. Learning to accept his size and working hard at developing his own athletic skills, perhaps as a runner or lightweight wrestler, will help Bob develop inner confidence.

A student whose behavior intimidates others may not know what she's doing that makes her classmates wary. Helping her identify and analyze how she is making others feel uncomfortable will give her the information she needs to make changes in her conduct.

Certainly some students are aware of and deliberate in their intimidating behavior. But whether or not a student intimidates others on purpose, it's wise to consult the Mistaken Goal Chart (see pages 12–13). The student may be trying to get attention, stirring up a battle of wills, hurting others because she feels left out, or urging everyone to leave her alone. Identifying her goal will lead you to the most helpful solutions.

Suggestions

1. Clarify the problem. Whose problem is it? What are the behaviors involved? Give each person an opportunity to examine what's taking place. Is the intimidating student aware that he may be causing a problem? Is the problem rooted in the way a student sees himself in relation to his peers? Simply checking out these details often solves the problem by raising awareness.

2. Put the problem on the class meeting agenda for all the students to work on together.

3. Use the Mistaken Goal Chart. What feelings are being evoked? Is the intimi-

dated student feeling irritated, angry, hurt, or helpless? Identifying the feelings and behaviors provides clues that lead to a variety of solutions (listed on the chart).

4. If the intimidation takes the form of violence, enlist the help of other staff members. Some schools have designated members of the staff whom you may call upon when violence erupts.

5. When dealing with intimidation and violence, it's important to maintain the dignity of everyone involved while meeting the needs of the situation and following through. Adding to any student's humiliation is damaging and invites more violence. This is especially important to remember when you need to involve law enforcement officials.

Planning Ahead to Prevent Future Problems

1. Some schools have trained conflict managers who are available to deal with problems. On the other hand, many teachers have found that when they are holding regular class meetings, every student becomes trained in conflict management. The beauty of class meetings is that the process also teaches skills that prevent students from resorting to violence or intimidation.

2. Learn about intimidation in a more general way. Ask students to bring in sto-

ries from the newspaper that illustrate the use of intimidation. Suggest that students be alert for and then tell the class about examples of intimidating behavior they observe on television shows or in movies. This eye-opening assignment may lead to discussions of broader issues. Prejudice, whether in the form of sexism, racism, or another ism, is frequently evinced in intimidating behaviors toward those perceived as less worthy or as having undesirable characteristics.

3. Review the meaning of mutual respect. Ask students, "In what ways is intimidation disrespectful?" "Is it disrespectful to treat others in ways that frighten or alarm them?" "Is it disrespectful for an individual to allow himself to be intimidated by another person or another person's actions?" "How is assertive behavior mutually respectful?"

4. Identify the differences between assertive behavior and intimidation. Role-play to discover the ways that assertiveness and intimidation look and feel different.

5. When dealing with students who are engaging in acts of violence and harassment, look beyond the behavior. Try to find the person who is living behind the acts. Find one quality in that student that you can appreciate, and share it with him. Remember that these students are collecting evidence that they are not likable and that they don't fit into the system.

6. Use support systems within the school; talk to counselors and school psychologists. Also avail yourself of support services in the community.

Class Meeting Solutions

Overcoming Fear

A story from Scheryl Richards, third-grade teacher, Mountainview Elementary School, Morgantown, West Virginia

Some third-grade students were fearful of an older student's behavior on the playground. The students discussed the problem at a class meeting and were relieved to discover that they weren't alone in their feeling. Other students shared what had worked for them in dealing with their fear. Their solutions included walking away from the older student, getting a teacher's help, and asking a teacher to stand nearby to keep an eye on the student.

After this discussion, the students' fears were allayed, and no further problems were reported.

New to the Process

A story from Kert Lenseigne, seventh- and eighth-grade teacher, Canyon Park Junior High School, Bothell, Washington

It was the first trimester of the school year, and Kert had just initiated the use of class meetings with a group of seventh graders. He had decided to hold the class meetings only twice a week because his class time was limited.

At the third class meeting of the year, several children had put a classmate's name on the agenda. When asked to explain the problem, one girl described the child's actions as intimidating. It was hard for her to explain what she meant, but she described ways in which this boy frequently said unkind things about his classmates. She also said that she felt menaced by the way he deliberately stood too close. Another student described the boy's words as "not exactly put-downs" but things that "bugged" her and left her feeling "uncomfortable." The class discussed these feelings of discomfort, and the child who had been intimidating others clearly knew that the problem was going to be solved by the class. This fact alone was very important.

The students proceeded to come up with a list of solutions. Among the suggestions were when he acts out again, the teacher should be notified, he should have an immediate time-out, he should receive an automatic detention, and he should not participate in the next lab. These were rather punitive suggestions, but this group of children was new to the process of seeking win–win solutions and therefore used the only methods they knew. Kert wisely realized that the real key here was the message that the students were going to work this problem out together. Two more solu-tions emerged: (1) The students would tell him right now that they didn't like these behaviors; (2) this discussion would be his warning to stop behaving in ways that seemed intimidating.

When the student in question was given the opportunity to choose the solution that he thought would be most helpful, he chose the final one.

Guess what? The problem disappeared. If there were any reminders or promptings to this student about his behavior, they came from his classmates. There was never another complaint about the problem. When Kert checked in with some of the students a few weeks later, they assured him that things were going fine. Although the class didn't identify a mistaken goal as part of the problem-solving process, several students casually mentioned to Kert that this student had been seeking attention. Children often see situations very clearly on their own.

This turned out to be the best trimester Kert had experienced in his teaching career. Although the class meetings took small amounts of time away from lessons, the resultant increase in cooperation made lesson times more productive. Kert was able to relax and focus on teaching, letting the kids work out solutions to the problems that arose during the year.

Jealousy

Discussion

A story from Bill Monro, third-grade teacher, Caernarvon Elementary School, Edmonton, Alberta, Canada

When I shared information about the new Positive Discipline book with our teachers, I asked them to look at the list of topics and suggest any they felt had been left out. Lorna Henker, a sixth-grade teacher, suggested jealousy. We then planned a class meeting at which we would facilitate a discussion of jealousy.

I asked the students what problems developed as a result of jealous feelings. They identified the following: stealing, fighting, people being left out, name-calling, and put-downs ("burns"). Among the causes of jealousy were other people's popularity, appearance, clothing, intelligence, athletic ability, and achievement in sports. Many students accompanied their responses with personal examples.

We then asked them for suggestions on how to deal with both their own and fellow students' feelings of jealousy. The class came up with the following:

Suggestions

1. Use self-talk to encourage yourself.

2. Use empathy when you are listening to others.

3. Try not to compare yourself to others.

4. Help people to see their own strengths.

5. Accept who you are.

6. Respect your talents and abilities.

7. Offer this thought: Grant me the serenity to accept the things I cannot change, the courage to change the things I can, and the wisdom to know the difference. (This was a teacher's suggestion, which was discussed with the class. It's based on *The Serenity Prayer* by Reinhold Niebuhr.)

Inspirational Conclusion

The class separated into groups, and each was asked to construct a role play on jealousy in which at least two of the suggested strategies were demonstrated. The students put together role plays that dealt with real-life experiences.

As a class, we concluded that once a person realizes jealousy is causing her to put someone down or to be put down, she can let go and feel some peace. Also, the students determined, this understanding alone will likely change negative behavior and responses to it.

The students and teachers planned to pursue this topic further, for they all felt that they had just scratched the surface. In addition, the teachers and I realized that we have to help students become more sophisticated at identifying their own feelings.

Kissing and Other Public Displays of Affection

Discussion

Older students are at a time in their lives where they are starting to explore relationships. The dilemma for teachers is to be able to show understanding and maintain connections with their students while they are helping them be aware of what is an appropriate display of affection and when these displays are not respectful of other people and themselves. Often there are missed opportunities to guide when we lecture and punish, which encourage sneakiness and defiance. We can be most effective when communication is based on mutual respect.

Suggestions

1. Speak with students individually if their behavior is inappropriate. Show understanding of what it is like for them. Be curious and interested in what the students may be thinking, feeling, and deciding. Share the existing guidelines of your school, and invite a discussion with the students about the purpose of those guidelines.

2. Check your own biases. If you see this behavior as being bad or promiscuous and are unable to move from this thinking, get support from staff or administration in dealing with the students. Not everyone can deal with every situation.

3. Share your feelings honestly: "I feel uncomfortable when I see public displays of affection. I wish we could work out something that would show understanding and respect for everyone concerned." When you take responsibility for your feelings and wishes, instead of judging and blaming, students are usually quite willing to brainstorm for solutions that work for everyone.

Planning Ahead to Prevent Future Problems

1. At the beginning of the school year, discuss the established guidelines of your school. Check for understanding and invite

discussion. If any students disagree strongly with those guidelines and are complaining, encourage them to create a case to present to the appropriate authority.

2. Initiate discussions of changes in social conventions that occur from generation to generation. When talking about why they occur, be sure to include the influence of television, movies, and music.

3. Invite students to brainstorm for solutions that show respect for all.

4. At meetings of parents and teachers, particularly at the middle and high school levels, ask the adults to brainstorm to create a list of things that were important to them when they were the same age as the students. Then compare it with lists that students have compiled during class meetings. This provides the adults with a wonderful opportunity to remember what adolescence was like and to see the similarities between their concerns then and the present students' concerns. This is an effective activity to use when discussing policies on such subjects as public kissing and similar behaviors.

5. Don't exaggerate the situation and hence create a problem where none exists. (See the "Inspirational Story" for an example of this.)

Inspirational Story

Windgate Middle School had no rules concerning public displays of affection.

Midway through the school year, a few thirteen-year-olds were spotted kissing good-bye after lunch. A couple of other young teens were often seen holding hands when walking from class to class.

At an assembly, the principal made a brief announcement that students would no longer be allowed to kiss or display affection in other ways on school grounds. The students were shocked and silent. Most of them had no idea that this was even a problem. Some felt angry and were already making decisions about how they would handle the new rule.

Some decided to do as they were told and not to question the rule. For others, it became a challenge that previously didn't exist. They spoke among themselves about how they were going to meet this challenge. It became a game to see how far they could press the issue. The bolder students took bets on how often they would be able to get away with the behaviors in question. Other students, who had never before considered touching at school, now saw this as an adventure in which they wanted to participate.

June Davis, the physical education teacher, spoke at a faculty meeting. She expressed her concerns about what she was hearing and seeing among the students. "Perhaps we made a mistake and made a bigger problem by the way we delivered the policy on public displays of affection," she said.

After the discussion, the administration and the faculty agreed to announce that they had made a mistake in ignoring the students when seeking solutions to a problem that directly affected them. Furthermore, the teachers decided to discuss the issue in all of the homerooms during class meetings. A team of students, faculty members, and administrators would gather input from the homerooms and work together to create a new policy.

The teachers put this issue on their class meeting agendas. They were surprised at all the fun and lively discussions that resulted. When the results were brought to the team devising the policy, team members saw that the adults and the students weren't far apart in their perceptions and suggestions.

Before including the students in finding a solution, the administration had addressed public displays of affection in broad terms. After gathering the students' opinions and ideas, administrators learned that most students and teachers were uncomfortable with kissing within the school environment but had no problems with holding hands or hugging. Thus the team concluded that it would be reasonable to create guidelines that allowed students to engage in displays of affection other than kissing. Rather than setting consequences for students who ignored the guidelines, the team decided to deal with any situation that arose on an individual basis or to ask the students to look for solutions. Team members wanted to avoid presenting a consequence that might be interpreted as a punishment.

The new policy transformed public displays of affection into a nonissue at Windgate Middle School. An unexpected development of having students and teachers work on the policy together was that they decided to plan and participate in a Teen–Adult Dialogue Night, to which they invited parents as well. This special event allowed students and adults to take a look into each other's worlds.

L

Lines

Discussion

What's the purpose of having students line up? When teachers ask students to form a line, their purpose is to ensure safe travel from point A to point B, especially when there are hundreds of students who need to leave their classrooms to get to cafeterias, buses, and assemblies. Older students seem to know how to travel within the schools without structure. However, younger students want to leap, jump, and run down the hallways. Often, their response to a request to line up creates problems such as power struggles, control issues, complaints about fairness, hitting, shoving, and name-calling. Line problems can present many opportunities for training in life skills.

Suggestions

1. In situations in which small groups of students can get to and from destinations quickly, quietly, and safely, there may be no need to require those students to travel in a line. Whenever problems arise, let the students find solutions during class meetings.

2. When students are having a difficult time in line, stop and, without words, wait until the behavior changes. This is most effective when students have prior knowledge of your unwillingness to proceed when their behavior is inappropriate.

3. Ask students who are complaining or having trouble in line to put the problem on the class meeting agenda. This usually satisfies them temporarily and eliminates the problem for the time being.

4. When a problem in the line comes up, ask the whole group, "Who can tell me what line rule is being broken right now?" Then, "Who has a suggestion for what needs to be done?" This is often enough to stop the problem.

5. When a student is fighting for a place in line or causing a commotion, either quietly ask the student to come join you in front or drop back and walk alongside that student.

6. Ask a student who is having difficulty lining up whether she would find it helpful to sit on the positive time-out bench until she's ready to line up respectfully or wants to put the problem on the class meeting agenda so the whole class can work on a solution. (Of course, this is effective only if positive time-out has been established. Refer to "Positive Time-Out.")

7. When a student is continually having problems in line, take time to speak to that student individually. Together brainstorm for a solution that can be tried for a week. Let the student know that you will be checking back with him and share with him your appreciation for his willingness to work on this with you.

Planning Ahead to Prevent Future Problems

1. During a class meeting, facilitate a discussion of the purpose of lines. Make a list of all the ideas the students bring up.

2. If you are open to the possibility, allow students to come up with a plan for getting to and from destinations quickly, quietly, and safely without traveling in lines.

3. When lines are needed, have students brainstorm to create a list of rules. This would be the time to decide the class rules for taking cuts, getting your place back, holding a person's place, and possibly having a line order. Some teachers like the idea of having a rotating line order to eliminate the problems of who is first in line, who gets to be the last one out, and so forth. Ask your students for ideas.

4. Make a list of line jobs, such as head-of-the-line supervisor, middle-of-the-line supervisor, and end-of-the-line supervisor. Allow students to discuss and determine job descriptions for each position. Rotate jobs.

5. During a class meeting, discuss and role-play typical problems that arise when students are in line, and brainstorm for solutions.

Inspirational Story

A story from Barbara Evangelista, kindergarten paraprofessional, Rocky Mount Elementary School, Marietta, Georgia

Andy repeatedly hit or pushed other students in our kindergarten class whenever they had to line up. He often hurt his classmates to the point of provoking tears. Andy's name appeared frequently on the class meeting agenda, but the students' solutions weren't working.

Andy and I had a private "feel-better" chat. I asked him what we could do to help him remember our motto "Hands are for helping, not hurting." He and I came up with the solution that he would keep his hands in his pockets whenever he was in line. This solution helped Andy, and soon all the students were walking with their hands in their pockets or behind their backs.

Andy is in first grade now. Recently I saw him walking down the hall. We exchanged smiles, and guess what? He had his hands in his pockets.

Class Meeting Solution

A story from J. Michael Fike, counselor, Mountainview Elementary School, Morgantown, West Virginia

Many of the first graders cut in line at the water fountain. On hot, dry days, this was a real problem. One particular class had thoroughly absorbed the concept of respect and always sought relevant solutions to problems. Therefore, these students didn't even mention the usual solution—to make the cutting student wait at the end of the line.

After much brainstorming, a classmate suggested that the line jumper could "make a line by himself, and when the class line was finished getting drinks, his 'line' could get a drink." This simple, yet respectful, solution worked perfectly.

Listen, Failure to

Discussion

"No matter what I say or even how loudly I say it, Bill acts as though he doesn't hear a word."

First, consider the possibility that Bill really doesn't hear you. One teacher noticed that whenever she spoke with one of her students, he angled his head so that his right ear was toward her. She recommended a hearing evaluation, and the student was found to have significant hearing loss in one ear.

Very young children often have inter-mittent hearing loss. This is especially true of those who suffer from chronic ear infections. Certain ranges of sound are lost, so that some children hear a staticky stutter. For others, all sound comes through as a steady buzz or hum.

If you have determined that a true hearing loss is not present, you can assess the situation further. When adults talk to children incessantly, they learn to let the flow of instructions and reprimands wash over them without hearing a word.

Suggestions

1. Listen. Remember that children listen to you *after* they feel listened to.

2. Learn to say less so that what you say means more. This is powerful. Instead of telling Bill in great detail first to put his coat on, then where to find it, then how to fasten it, and even why he should put it on, try saying, "Bill," while pointing to his coat. Limit what you say to ten words; use one word whenever possible.

3. Use clear gestures or nonverbal signals with no accompanying words. Point to what needs to be done, giving a knowing smile or wink. Or, with the class, match specific messages with patterns of clapping.

4. Recommend a medical checkup to evaluate the student's hearing.

5. Look for areas in the classroom that have the least amount of distraction. Sometimes when a student is placed near a window, next to a class pet, or by the classroom door he may have more difficulty focusing on the instruction. Speak to the student about what you may be observing. "Sometimes sitting next to the window makes it hard for students to listen to what is going on. I'd like to try having you sit in another spot to see whether that makes a difference for you. Let's check back at the end of the week to see how it's going."

6. Put yourself at the student's level, and make eye contact before speaking. (For some cultures, eye contact is disrespectful, so predetermine a positive way to connect. Putting a hand on his shoulder or sitting side by side might be more appropriate.)

7. Ask the student to repeat his instructions or to share his understanding of what he is to do next or of what was just said.

8. If a student frequently asks what you just said, tell her that you don't want to repeat yourself but that she can get the information from another student. (If several students didn't understand, perhaps your instructions were unclear and you should rephrase them.)

9. Do the unexpected: Teachers usually speak loudly to get students' attention. Instead, use a soft tone of voice as you invite students to listen closely to what you are saying.

Planning Ahead to Prevent Future Problems

1. Use active listening activities with the whole class. One student tells a partner a

story, and the second student repeats what he heard. Do this regularly to improve the listening skills of all class members.

2. Develop signals for communicating regular events with the whole class or with individual students. A certain song may be played when it's time to clean up, the lights may go off when it's time for quiet, or you may wink at a child when it's time for him to collect the papers.

3. Have a class meeting discussion about the general problem of not listening (or about a specific student's difficulties, if you have prior agreement from that student).

4. Talk privately to the student who often doesn't appear to listen. Ask him "what," "why," and "how" questions: "Why do you think we are having a communication problem?" "What could I do differently?" "What could you do differently?" "How could we help each other?" (This is effective only if the atmosphere is nonthreatening and friendly, and you have a sincere desire to hear the student's point of view.) Ask the student whether he's willing to hear your point of view. If he says no, there is no point in proceeding; you may both need a positive time-out for cooling off. You might also ask whether the student would like to put the problem on the class meeting agenda so that you both can get ideas from the whole class.

5. Do a simple hearing test: stand behind the student and ring a small bell. If the student doesn't respond—not even flinching slightly—then she may have some form of hearing loss. Do this same test first from one side and then from the other, while still out of view. Hearing impairment may exist in only one ear.

Inspirational Story

Mrs. Vera was always complaining that many of her high school students wouldn't listen to directions during class. They seemed more interested in talking to one another. She tried speaking above the noise in order to be heard, but that didn't work. Next she tried discipline referrals, which meant sending the offending students to the principal's office. She was amazed when the discipline referrals didn't work, either. In fact, the incidence of students talking while she was talking appeared to be increasing.

Feeling discouraged, she shared her problem with a colleague who was using class meetings. This colleague suggested she learn about Positive Discipline in the classroom. Mrs. Vera read about these concepts and decided to try some class meeting activities.

She found the courage to share with her students that she had been using discipline referrals as a means of getting even with them. She explained that she felt they were disrespecting her by not listening in class. Her students were surprised by the sincerity of her confession. They began to open up and share with her how angry they felt when she yelled at them and sent them to the office. They, too, apologized for their part in the problem.

Mrs. Vera was amazed at the positive change in the classroom atmosphere after this one meeting. It seemed too simple!

She and her students continued to use class meetings and learned how to respect one another's needs. Problems became easier to resolve because of the entire class's commitment to looking for solutions instead of blame. Furthermore, the exchange of compliments and appreciations in class meetings reduced personal conflicts and encouraged cooperation.

Class Meeting Solution

A story from Kerri McCaul, sixth-grade teacher, Everett, Washington

Class meetings taught me to talk less and listen more. There were times I had to sit on my hands to keep from taking control and talking too much. I realized how controlling and stifling my classroom management techniques really were. During meetings, my students would avoid throwing me the koosh ball because they knew I was either going to talk too much or end the discussion—they were so good at reading my body language! I was amazed at how well they knew me and how little I knew them. If I forgot to schedule a weekly meeting, they adamantly reminded me. We once invited the principal to attend a meeting because my students were upset about faulty playground equipment. We debated sexual harassment when the school took the doors off the boys' bathrooms because of vandalism and fighting.

Little by little, week by week, the agenda grew shorter and shorter. Complaints and problems were solved before they were brought up at meetings. When their name appeared on the agenda, students were eager to solve the problem before it was addressed at the class meeting. One week, the only item on the agenda was "planning the events of a field trip." We even planned Secret Pals at class meetings.

Our year together came to a dramatic close. Through Positive Discipline and class meetings, we built a relationship of trust and concern. During one of our last class meetings, my students shared their concern that a student had threatened to "bring a gun to school and shoot [me] and another teacher." The class, whom I thought once hated my guts, showed deep concern and fear for my safety. I doubt any of them would've told me the same information the previous December. I was touched beyond words. The class I dreaded became the class I'll never forget. I have used class meetings and Positive Discipline ever since.

Loudness

Discussion

They're booming, boisterous, bigger than life! Powerful voices can be appreciated at times and redirected at other times. Often a teacher's reaction is to quash the behavior, but his power actually lies in determining when speaking loudly enhances a situation and when it detracts.

Because the teacher's goal is to help students appreciate themselves and see how they can belong in positive ways, his challenge is to discover how and when a loud voice can make a positive contribution. In addition, he must learn how to gain the student's cooperation when a loud voice is inappropriate.

Suggestions

1. The first step in dealing with a student who uses an unusually loud voice is to suggest a hearing test.

2. Speaking to the student more quietly, rather than trying to match her volume, creates an awareness of voice levels and also eliminates competition between teacher and student.

3. Avoid giving negative reminders, such as, "Please don't talk so loud." A positive reminder might be, "Sara, please use a softer voice."

4. Talk to the student about arranging a signal that you can use to remind her when it isn't a time for speaking loudly.

5. If you're feeling annoyed, angry, or upset, use the class meeting format to talk to your students about how loud, boisterous behavior impacts you and their learning.

Planning Ahead to Prevent Future Problems

1. Teach students about the four mistaken goals of behavior. (Refer to "Mistaken Goals [Hat Messages].") Together you may discuss the beliefs that lead students to use loud voices at inappropriate times. Brainstorm with them about other ways to get attention, to feel powerful, to deal with hurt feelings, and to get help when they feel like giving up.

2. Create opportunities to use loud voices, such as acting in a play, calling out the day's announcements, or cheerleading. Appreciate the use of loud voices at these times.

3. In a class meeting, take time to discuss appropriate voice levels. Have the students come up with a list of situations both in and out of school where loud voices are appropriate and appreciated. Have them make another list of places where a quieter tone is needed. A follow-up meeting could be used to practice, demonstrate, and discuss their solutions.

4. Create opportunities for students to learn in active ways that make good use of exuberance. Math teams or role plays in history class may help them channel their energy in a positive direction.

5. Avoid labeling a student or a class as boisterous or loud. This limits the students' view and your view of both individuals and the group. Keep in mind that a loud voice can be a gift as well as a liability.

6. Find an opportunity to familiarize yourself with the family style of the student who always speaks loudly. There is a wide variety of voice levels, and people have many ways of expressing themselves. By collecting this information, you can develop a better understanding of the student's behavior and become more encouraging.

Inspirational Stories

Lucy and Mrs. Cunningham

Mrs. Cunningham's class was about to get a new student. As this new girl, Lucy, approached the classroom door, the entire class could hear her talking to the principal in the hallway. She introduced herself in a loud, confident voice.

As the week wore on, Mrs. Cunningham found herself becoming more and more irritated by the sound of Lucy's voice. Her first response was to push Lucy away through repeated reminders of class rules about voice levels.

Finally, Mrs. Cunningham consulted with the other teachers. They helped her identify her feeling of irritation, which helped her understand that Lucy might be seeking "undue attention." They pointed out that Lucy needed to see that she could receive attention in positive ways, and suggested that Mrs. Cunningham assist Lucy in finding better ways to develop a sense of belonging in the classroom.

When Mrs. Cunningham set up a time to talk with her, Lucy was worried that she had done something wrong again. So she was surprised when Mrs. Cunningham said, "Lucy, I've noticed that you have a nice, loud voice, and I was wondering whether anyone had ever told you that before."

With her head down, Lucy replied, "People are always telling me to be quiet."

"Well, Lucy," said Mrs. Cunningham, "I'd like you to have an opportunity to use your voice at certain times of the day. I've been thinking of doing a daily bulletin, and I need someone with a strong voice to make the announcements. Would you be interested in doing that job?"

Lucy was excited and accepted the offer enthusiastically. Mrs. Cunningham continued, "Lucy, I have a wish. My hope is that you will use your strong voice during this announcement time and that during instruction time you can practice using a softer voice. I realize that you may find it difficult to remember to do this, so I was wondering if we could come up with a signal I could give you. That way I won't embarrass you in front of the other students."

Getting into the spirit of this request, Lucy suggested, "How about if you tug on your ear? That would remind me."

Mrs. Cunningham agreed. For the first week Lucy talked loudly even more often than she had before. She seemed to enjoy the attention she got by having Mrs. Cunningham pull on her ear. By the second week, however, Lucy seemed to be getting enough attention from her announcing job, because she was no longer talking loudly the rest of the time.

One day Mrs. Cunningham became exasperated with the whole class for being too noisy in the lunchroom. After lunch, she started scolding her students in a loud voice. Suddenly she noticed Lucy tugging on her ear. Mrs. Cunningham laughed and said, "Thank you, Lucy." Then she asked the class whether someone would be willing to put the problem on the class meeting agenda for discussion later. A student volunteered, and Mrs. Cunningham went on to the next lesson of the day.

New Acceptance

A story from Stephanie Corvese, second-grade teacher, St. Catherine of Sienna, Woodbridge (Toronto), Ontario, Canada

One of the things that used to drive me crazy was a noisy classroom. For some reason, I expected my classroom to be extremely quiet all the time. Screaming at them to be quiet would work for about fifteen seconds, and then the kids would be chatting away again. One of the positive things I do is note passing. During seat work time, the children are given a piece of paper and are allowed to write whatever they want on the paper. If they have to go to the bathroom, they write out the question. I also came to the understanding that there are times when a noisy classroom is okay. Many times, during my centers, children are reading around the room or reading aloud at our classroom library, and the classroom gets loud, but if there is a lot of learning going on then, I don't let that noise bother me.

Lunchroom Behavior

Discussion

Many students use lunchtime to let go of responsibilities, to forget routine, and to socialize intensively for a short period of time. The potential for chaos is great. It's important to acknowledge that students need a break from their routine, but it's

also important that they learn to relax in ways that respect others.

Behavior in the lunchroom is a good indicator of the school personnel's style of leadership. Misbehavior in the lunchroom could mean that the leadership style is too controlling or too permissive. An authoritarian leadership style invites rebellion and resistance while failing to develop self-discipline, responsibility, cooperation, or social interest. A permissive style invites chaos and fails to develop these same qualities. Respectful lunchroom behavior suggests that the leadership style of the school personnel is authoritative. An authoritative (democratic) leadership style fosters all the qualities and skills that authoritarian and permissive styles disregard.

Suggestions

1. Anytime you see a problem behavior, simply ask the students involved what they are supposed to be doing according to the rules they helped create. (See the first item under "Planning Ahead.") Often this is enough to motivate students to change their behavior.

2. Describe the behavior you see: "I notice that you're throwing food." "I notice that you're yelling." "I notice that you didn't pick up your trash." Then ask, "What do you need to do to correct this problem?" This friendly reminder is more effective than punishment and inspires future cooperation instead of rebellion.

3. When the lunchroom is very noisy, adults typically believe that they must speak in a voice that competes with that level of noise. Rather than yelling, lean close to the misbehaving student or group of students, and speak softly.

4. Put a group of students in the same boat. When one student at a table is throwing food, involve all the students at that table in the cleanup: "As soon as this table is cleaned up, you may leave."

5. Let the student table monitor handle the misbehavior. (Student table monitors should be trained in methods of gaining cooperation respectfully, such as those contained in the suggestions here. Otherwise they may invite resistance and rebellion by trying to dictate behavior.)

6. Hand a copy of the list of appropriate lunchroom behaviors to the group at a table, and quietly ask the students to locate the misbehavior that they need to work on. Thank them for their cooperation.

7. When you have tried all the suggestions listed so far and a student or class persists with behavior that is disrespectful, firmly and kindly implement the respectful consequences that have been established. See "Planning Ahead."

Planning Ahead to Prevent Future Problems

1. A general school policy regarding lunchroom behavior should be established.

This process is most effective when all people involved have a voice, such as lunchroom personnel, custodial staff, students, administration, and faculty. The policy should include clear descriptions of respectful behaviors and consequences. Possible consequences might include the temporary loss of the privilege of eating in the lunchroom or time spent after lunch to help the custodial staff.

2. During a class meeting, ask each class to brainstorm about typical lunchroom problems and then to create rules that will prevent or solve these problems. (The most powerful method of solving problems at school is always to invite students to do it. They will feel respected and be motivated to follow rules they have helped create.) Students may enjoy role-playing both disrespectful and respectful lunchroom behavior. Contrasts are powerful teaching tools.

3. Invite lunchroom personnel to attend class meetings, where they can share their concerns and ask for help and solutions. Many students are unaware of how their behavior causes problems for others.

4. To involve students in maintaining acceptable lunchroom behavior, introduce a system of rotating student monitors. The monitors should respectfully motivate their fellow students to behave appropriately and to clean up after themselves.

5. Have students from the upper grades sit with younger classes to help teach and monitor proper lunchroom behavior.

6. Acknowledge and validate your students' need to take a break from the classroom routine. Share your own need for a relaxing lunch break. Balance this with a discussion of behavior that respects others as well as school property.

7. Don't expect perfection, but keep working for improvement. Whenever a guideline doesn't work or works for only a short time, put it back on the class meeting agenda so the kids can discuss it and either renew their commitment to it or work on another solution.

Class Meeting Solutions

Raising Awareness

During a two-day Positive Discipline workshop at a Navajo reservation school, the cafeteria personnel complained about the students throwing their utensils in the garbage barrels when they scraped their food trays. When the personnel returned to school, a representative from the cafeteria staff came to a seventh-grade class meeting to talk about this problem. The students made several suggestions. The one they chose to implement was to take turns as utensil monitors at the garbage barrels. After about a month, they decided that they no longer needed utensil monitors because the students were being more respectful of school property and had stopped throwing utensils in the garbage.

Creating a System

Mrs. Trumble, an aide working in the lunchroom, put an item on the class meeting agenda for Mr. Wong's fifth graders. She explained that she was frustrated over having to spend a great deal of time in the fifth-grade lunch area because of the students' behavior and the messes they were making.

Mr. Wong offered to have the students in his class come up with a solution to the problem, and Mrs. Trumble accepted. The students brainstormed and produced many ideas; they then voted to try the one that would most involve them in the solution. They would initiate a system in which a student monitor at each table would help maintain order and ensure that students didn't leave the area until they had cleaned up any messes. They decided that this position would rotate among the students seated at a table.

They were excited about trying this system and agreed to report on how it was working at the class meeting the following week. Mrs. Trumble came to that meeting and was delighted to talk with the students about the changes she had seen. She told them that she wanted them to share their system with other classes in the school. They immediately started making plans about how they would spread the word.

Lying

Discussion

Students who lie or resort to fabrication are neither defective nor immoral. Lying is sometimes a defense mechanism for people who fear that the truth will be ridiculed or dismissed or will reflect badly on them. It is difficult to tell the truth if the result is punishment or disapproval.

Teachers need to discover the reasons students lie before they can help them give up their need to lie. Whenever possible, look behind the falsehood or fabrication to see its intent. Teachers can learn a lot about students by letting them talk instead of correcting them or ignoring them.

Young children typically lie or fabricate stories because the difference between real and unreal is hazy to them. Older children may lie to prevent parents or teachers from worrying about what their kids or students are doing or to avoid hurting the adults' feelings. Students who deceive may feel trapped or afraid of punishment. They may fear rejection or feel threatened. They may truly believe that lying will make a situation easier for everyone. They may be trying to make themselves look better in other people's eyes because they don't believe they're good enough as they are. They may want to impress or upset others. They may be trying to tell you something important, but they lack the words or skills to do it any other way.

Suggestions

1. Be aware of asking setup questions that may invite lying. Focus on solutions to the problem rather than blame. If you're certain that a student has stolen money from a class kitty, don't ask, "Did you take the money?" Say, "I know that you took the money, and I'd like to work on a plan for how it can be returned."

2. If your instinct tells you that a student is lying, you might say, "That doesn't sound like the truth to me. Most of us find it hard to tell the truth when we're feeling trapped or scared. Let's both think about how we can focus on solutions and then talk about this during lunch or after school. Which would work best for you?"

3. Address the student's feelings instead of his words: "As you're telling me this, you sound nervous. Let's talk about that."

4. Rather than saying, "That's not true," try saying, "Tell me more about that."

5. If you think students are playing games with you, let them know that it's okay to tell stories and you like hearing them. Share with them that it's respectful for people to let their listener know when they're telling tall tales.

6. Help the student who deceives see how his fabrications impact others. He is hoping that this behavior will attract people to him and may not realize that it's actually pushing them away.

7. To understand the purpose of the behavior and to discover ways that you can be encouraging to a student, use goal disclosure. (Refer to the last section of "Wandering" for an explanation of this process.)

Planning Ahead to Prevent Future Problems

1. Teach about mistakes at a class meeting. Help your students see mistakes as opportunities to learn, so they won't believe that they are bad for making mistakes or that mistakes should be covered up.

2. Create an atmosphere that assures students they will be treated respectfully. Let them know that they will have opportuni-

ties to learn from mistakes and to find solutions to problems with the help of the whole class, the teacher, or a small group of students.

3. An insecure student may lie to enhance her image. This student has found that she can win attention and recognition by embroidering on her experiences or fabricating tales. Help this student find other ways to earn recognition or attention.

4. Share the story of a time when you told a lie and it caused you trouble. Students often feel freer to admit their mistakes if they know you have also made some. You may even have a true story of a time when it was difficult for you to tell the truth about something you'd done, but you decided that it was more important to experience the consequences and keep your self-respect than to protect yourself. Be sure that this is an honest sharing instead of a lecture.

5. All the ways in which you show your students that you care about them will help reduce the incidence of lying. Knowing that your teacher sees you as a likable person enhances feelings of belonging and importance.

Inspirational Stories

Mistakes Are Okay

A story from Stephanie Corvese, second-grade teacher, St. Catherine of Sienna, Woodbridge (Toronto), Ontario, Canada

I have this student who, at the beginning of the year, was constantly lying to me. He would always be getting into trouble at recess or doing things to bother his classmates and of course it was never him who did it. "Who, *me*, Miss Corvese?" he would say in a very astonished, confused voice when I would catch him poking his classmate. I was frustrated with his lying, so I made sure that whenever any student in the class "goofed up," I didn't punish them. I would say instead, "Wow, you made a mistake! Welcome to real life. I make mistakes all the time. Let's see what we can do to solve this problem." And then the student would think of a positive solution to solve the problem. Many times, I, too, made mistakes. In fact, just last week, I'd had a very bad cold and the noise was bothering me. I kept yelling at them to be quiet. The day after I felt bad about yelling at them, so I apologized and told them that I'd made a mistake. I wasn't feeling well, and I just wanted quiet. The students said very sweetly, "That's okay, Miss Corvese. We make mistakes, too!" After a few months of this, this student must have realized that it's really okay to make mistakes, so he never lies to me anymore.

David and Mr. Ventana

Mr. Ventana saw David break a beaker in the chemistry laboratory. This student had lied to Mr. Ventana in the past. David had an ability to use his words in a disarming way to get himself out of uncomfortable or threatening situations.

Instead of asking David whether he broke the beaker, which would almost certainly lead to a lengthy story, Mr. Ventana walked up to him and said, "David, I no-ticed that you broke the beaker. We all have accidents, but it will need to be re-placed. How can I assist in making that happen?" By stating what he saw and fo-cusing on finding a solution rather than placing blame, Mr. Ventana helped David accept responsibility for his action.

M

Manipulation

Discussion

A manipulative student may be uncon-sciously seeking revenge for some real or perceived injustice. Another student may use manipulation to show others how pow-erful she is and that she can always have matters settled her way—or she may feel manipulated by the teacher and plays the game rather than giving in. Others may use manipulation as a stalling technique to avoid areas where they feel inadequate. Stu-dents who try to manipulate others are dis-couraged, and discouraged students need the kind of encouragement that motivates change.

Suggestions

1. Let the student know that you've ob-served his manipulative behavior: "I notice that you're trying to get me to do what you want." You may not need to say anything else. Sometimes awareness is enough to take the wind out of his sails.

2. Use humor. Give the student a "know-ing" look and say, "Nice try."

3. Acknowledge the student's feeling with-out wondering whether you should change your course of action. Tell the student how you feel when you're being manipulated.

4. Avoid labeling a student as a manipula-tor. Instead, deal with the behavior and the belief behind the behavior.

5. Let your students know that it's better to ask directly for what they want. You may present this message to individuals or to everyone at a class meeting.

Planning Ahead to Prevent Future Problems

1. Try to discover the purpose of the behavior; then look for alternative ways to encourage this discouraged student. (See the Mistaken Goal Chart on pages 12–13.)

2. Look at the part you may be playing in fostering manipulation. If you make a decision, stick to it.

3. Teach problem-solving skills through class meetings so students develop skills that are more constructive than manipulation. Remember that students who are involved in the problem-solving process are more likely to cooperate than to manipulate.

4. Use a class meeting to talk about manipulation and how it affects people. Ask open-ended questions, and use role playing to explore the purpose of manipulation and what people are thinking, feeling, and deciding when they are involved in it. Together the group may brainstorm for ways to handle manipulation.

5. Look for books and plays in which a character manipulates others. Involve the class in a discussion or project. (Students will have great fun playing Tom Sawyer.)

Inspirational Story

All of Mrs. Lewis's high school Spanish students were aware that she was going through a divorce because she made comments about the situation during her classes. One particular class began to realize that if one of the students asked Mrs. Lewis how she was feeling, she would go off on a tangent and the day's lesson would begin much later.

The whole class participated in this manipulation; some asked questions, some shared comments, and some said nothing while their classmates encouraged Mrs. Lewis to digress. The students were deciding that they could get her—and possibly others—to bypass the work at hand by feigning interest and concern. They were also deciding that getting through their Spanish studies wasn't important.

As Mrs. Lewis was putting together the midterm exam, she realized that she hadn't covered nearly the amount of information she had intended to cover in this particular class. She felt disappointed in herself and thought back on past weeks to evaluate her performance. She realized that in many of her classes she had spent more time talking with the students about her personal life than teaching Spanish. She also realized that the students in this one class had shown an inordinate interest in her personal life. As she recognized that they had made a conscious effort to engage her, she felt embarrassed and concerned.

The following day Mrs. Lewis found the courage to address the situation without blaming, shaming, or lecturing. At the beginning of the class, before reviewing for the upcoming midterm, she said, "I noticed when I was preparing the midterm that this class hadn't covered a large percentage of the material. I have some guesses about how this happened, and I would like to discuss them with everyone."

At this point, a student named Nadine said kindly, "Mrs. Lewis, you look very tired."

Mrs. Lewis detected this as a familiar hook to move her thoughts away from the job that needed to be done. She said, "Thank you for noticing, Nadine. How-ever, the issue is midterm review and the reasons we are behind schedule." She shared with the class her observations and feelings about what had been happening. She acknowledged her mistakes and apolo-gized. Nadine spoke up again and let Mrs. Lewis know that the class did have a pur-pose, which was to avoid studying Spanish by sidetracking her.

Mrs. Lewis told her students that she was aware of her own susceptibility to being sidetracked and that she planned to keep them on a tight schedule for the rest of the semester.

Motivation, Lack of

Discussion

A student who lacks motivation presents one of the most challenging and discourag-ing situations a teacher faces. Typical re-sponses to a student who is idle in the classroom are to do things for him, to push him harder, or to make him feel bad in the hope that he will change his ways. Other re-sponses are to try to embarrass him or sim-ply to avoid him. All these responses make the situation worse. The challenge for teachers is to stop doing things that don't work and take time to find ways to encour-age both themselves and their students.

Suggestions

1. Ask "what" and "how" questions: "How could this be useful to you?" "What are the benefits to you now or in the future if you do this?" "How will you be affected if you choose not to do this?" "How would you be contributing to others if you did this?" These curiosity questions are effective only if you truly are curious about what the stu-dent is thinking and feeling. If it sounds at all lecturing or threatening it will create de-fensiveness and discouragement.

2. Use one word to communicate what the student needs to do: "Math." "Cleanup." Make eye contact, and try to have a firm yet kind expression.

3. Offer your honest emotions: "I feel upset because you spend time on everything but your schoolwork, and I wish it was more of a priority for you."

4. Act. Take a young student by the hand and lead her kindly and firmly to the task that she needs to do.

5. Let respectful consequences be the teacher. If a student is doing nothing, this will be reflected in poor grades and in missed opportunities. Show empathy for the student when he experiences the consequences of his inactivity. Don't display an I-told-you-so attitude. Follow up with "what" and "how" questions to help him understand cause and effect, and use this information to form a plan for success.

6. Notice when a student who usually participates abruptly stops. This may be an indication that something is happening at home, such as a divorce or serious illness. Or she could be having problems with her peer relationships.

7. Engage in joint problem solving. Decide together what the problem is and what some possible solutions are. Begin by sharing your perspective: "I notice that you aren't contributing your ideas in class lately and that you don't seem interested in your assignments." Then invite the student to share her picture of what's happening. Ask whether she would like problem-solving help during a class meeting.

8. Another approach is to refrain from offering your opinions and to let the student give his perception of the problem. Students usually know what's going on and they feel more accountable when they tell instead of being told.

9. Sit down together to make a list of all the things that are going well for the student, giving her a chance to speak first.

10. Don't take the problem personally. If you find yourself working regularly with a student or constantly worrying about him, you may be telling yourself, "If only I could come up with a way to fix things for him." Let the solution be the student's choice. There's a difference between letting go and giving up. When you let go, you can stay connected while handing the responsibility for the problem back to the student. When you give up, you cut all ties and send the message that you are no longer available.

11. Assure the student that you know he's capable of doing a fine job on a particular assignment. The two of you can determine together that he has all the necessary materials and information; then you should confidently count on him to do his work.

Planning Ahead to Prevent Future Problems

1. Explore your student's lack of motivation through the four mistaken goals of

misbehavior. (Refer to "Mistaken Goals [Hat Messages]" for more information.) Find productive ways for the student to get attention, to feel like she's in charge, to deal with hurt feelings, or to get help when she feels like giving up.

2. Invite students to discuss lack of motivation during a class meeting. Keep two things in mind. First, when students are involved in making decisions, they are motivated to adhere to the decisions. Second, students participate more when they understand the relevance of what they're doing.

3. Consider different styles of dealing with stress. A student who is afraid may withdraw and do nothing. What you can do for this student is to honor his pace, help him identify what he fears, look for a small first step, and require movement—however gradual—toward a goal.

4. Build on strengths. If a student is doing well in any area, encourage her to spend more time in this area. (Don't forbid her to spend time on a subject in which she does well until she does better in another subject.) A student needs to feel encouraged in her areas of strength. Teach her to manage her weaknesses, and let her know that barely passing or dropping a class once in a while is okay as long as she is doing well in areas where she has strength.

5. Create a peer tutoring program for students who are able to help and students who need help with academics.

Inspirational Story

Mr. Ingler came to his first teaching position with a tremendous amount of excitement and enthusiasm as well as many innovative projects. He hoped to engage each and every student. He was confident that he could inspire a love of learning in the minds of his young charges.

When the semester began, he was faced with Craig, who perceived school as a waste of time and who chose to do little or nothing in his academic classes. Mr. Ingler felt scared and helpless. He found himself wondering whether he was capable of doing his job.

In hope of finding the magic ingredient to turn things around with Craig, he talked with a veteran teacher on the staff. This teacher suggested that Craig's idleness could be his way of getting attention, seeking power, hurting others, or coping with a lack of skill.

When Mr. Ingler appraised Craig's level of discouragement, he understood his own feelings of helplessness and fear—which indicated Craig could be acting from the goal of assumed inadequacy. He decided to work in small steps to encourage Craig. The first step was to show faith in Craig as a person, not simply as a student. Mr. Ingler looked for a way to help Craig feel important within the class. He made a list of three jobs that needed to be done daily and asked Craig to choose one that appealed to him. Craig chose to help the janitor clean the classroom for ten minutes every day after school.

As far as the academic work, Mr. Ingler didn't rescue Craig or give him special service. He let the consequences of Craig's actions speak. As this was happening, Mr. Ingler continued to show interest by remaining friendly and talking to Craig about his life and sharing some of his own experiences.

One day Mr. Ingler shared with the whole class that he had once thought he wasn't smart enough to do well in school. He explained that he behaved rebelliously to pretend he didn't care. Fortunately, one teacher saw through his act and got him into a peer tutoring program. Because of the faith of that teacher, he became a teacher.

After about three weeks, Craig approached Mr. Ingler and admitted that he felt he wasn't smart enough to do well in school and was just acting like he didn't care. He asked whether he could get into a peer tutoring program. Mr. Ingler quickly arranged this.

The teacher's small steps to encourage Craig had a powerful effect. He began to show more interest in his schoolwork, and in time his performance improved.

Moving Away

Discussion

When a student's family moves to a new place and the student must leave her school, both the student who departs and the students who remain experience change and loss. This is a chance for all students to learn that it's normal to feel sad about loss and change. The student who's moving away may also learn that change can bring opportunities to enhance life experiences. Help students through the transition by involving them in plans for coping with the change and encouraging them to communicate about their feelings.

Some schools experience a high rate of transience. Some students move every month or so. This can create a huge amount of disruption in the classrooms as well as in the students' lives.

Suggestions

1. Check out how the student feels about moving. Don't assume you know. Some families move frequently and enjoy the challenges and opportunities of settling in new places. Others approach moving with a sense of loss, responding to the move as to a death. As with any loss, grieving is an essential part of healing.

2. Involve the class whenever a student knows he or she is leaving. Give students opportunities to share their feelings and thoughts during a class meeting.

3. Set up a system for corresponding with the student who is leaving. Have your students brainstorm for ways to stay connected, such as planned return visits, the exchange of school photos, and trading self-addressed, stamped envelopes to encourage one another to write.

4. When a student leaves unexpectedly, make sure his classmates have time to share their reactions. Give them as much information as you can about the situation without violating anyone's privacy. It is possible that this was a very discouraged student whom was disliked by others. If this is the case, remind the students that "a misbehaving person is a discouraged person." If it is possible to find a forwarding address, ask the students whether they would be willing to send an encouragement card filled with every possible compliment they can think of.

5. As a group, when possible, make contact at least once with the student who left. Send pictures, a class mural, a group letter, or individual letters.

Planning Ahead to Prevent Future Problems

1. Large numbers of Americans are continually moving. Parents relocate their families because of military commitments, economic opportunities or difficulties, and cultural inclinations. Examine your own attitudes toward these different reasons. Guard against negative assumptions that may affect your treatment of a particular child.

2. Tell your students about some of the transitions you have experienced. Share with them that you faced fear and uncertainty but grew in the process. This is a time for personal sharing, not a lecture.

Inspirational Story

At 8:30 on Tuesday morning, it looked to be a typical day in Mrs. Ryder's fourth-grade classroom. Some children noticed that Amy's chair was empty and figured she was out with a cold. No one attributed anything unusual to her absence.

After the class had quieted, Mrs. Ryder stood up to make an announcement. She told her students that Amy wouldn't be in their class anymore because she had moved up north to live with her grandparents.

There was a short silence while the students struggled to make sense of Amy's abrupt departure. Then some of them began to grill Mrs. Ryder, asking why Amy had to leave, why she was going to live with her grandparents, why she didn't say good-bye, and who would do her part of their social studies project. One student pointed out that Amy hadn't even removed her things from her desk.

The students' questions added to Mrs. Ryder's own confusion, and she felt overwhelmed. She told the students that their questions were all good ones. She promised that the class would work on some of these concerns today and that others would be discussed after she got more information about Amy's disappearance.

Mrs. Ryder shared her own dismay and invited the students to voice their feelings, especially about not saying good-bye, and to discuss how they might adjust their plans for the class project. They set up a time to continue their discussion later and decided that during this time they would create a gift to send to Amy.

At lunchtime Mrs. Ryder spoke with Amy's mother and let her know that she and the students were concerned, would appreciate more information, and wanted to know how they could get a gift to Amy. Amy's mother thanked Mrs. Ryder for her concern and asked her to tell the students that there had been a disturbance in the family and that Amy's parents had decided it would be better for her to stay with her grandparents for the rest of the school year.

During the next class meeting, Mrs. Ryder shared with her students what Amy's mother had said. When they pressed her for details, she reminded them about the need to respect people's privacy. She then acknowledged that Amy's move was a loss to the whole class and continued the discussion by asking the students to describe other times when they had experienced loss. The discussion moved to what people can do when they suffer different types of loss.

Amy's classmates found emotional relief and a sense of resolution by expressing their feelings and working on plans to accommodate Amy's departure.

Noise

(see also "Loudness")

Discussion

Have you ever camped in the woods and listened to the noises of the wind, birds, and other animals? Do you remember a time when you lay on the beach and listened to the crashing of the waves? Can you feel the changing vibrations in your seat when you're at the symphony, and do you revel in the blaring trumpets, pounding percussion, and cry of the violins? Some people love these sounds, and others don't.

What kind of symphony does your classroom produce? Do you enjoy these sounds, or do they annoy you?

Like every situation discussed in this book, problems with noise present opportunities for learning. This section diverts from the usual format to present a wonderful story written by eleven second graders in a classroom of fifty at Lakewood Elementary School in Lakewood, Washington. Mrs. Mullen and Mrs. Larrick were their team teachers.

Too Much Noise in a Large Second Grade

A story from Andy Cox, Sam Houston, Milissa Huber, Daniel Kelly, Jacob Kon, Steven Lengenfelder, Shaina Mason, Jessica Melhart, Mariah Page, Jeatt Walker, and Sarah Wilms

Once upon a time there were two second-grade teachers named Mrs. Larrick and Mrs. Mullen. In their classroom were fifty students.

The chairs scraped the ground. Scrape. Scrape. Scrape.

The pencil sharpener sharpened. Grind. Grind. Grind.

The faucet dripped. Drip. Drip. Drip.

"Too noisy!" said Mrs. Larrick and Mrs. Mullen.

The teachers went to see the wise man who was named Andy Cox.

"What can we do?" the teachers asked the wise man Andy. "Our classroom makes too much noise.

"The chairs scrape the ground. Scrape. Scrape. Scrape.

"The pencil sharpener sharpens. Grind. Grind. Grind.

"The faucet drips. Drip. Drip. Drip."

"I can help you," said the wise Andy. "I know what you can do."

"What?" asked the teachers.

"Get Jeatt Walker to join your class," said the wise Andy.

"What good will Jeatt do?" asked the teachers. But they got Jeatt to join their class anyhow.

Jeatt dropped her pencil. Bang. Bang. Bang.

The chairs scraped the ground. Scrape. Scrape. Scrape.

The pencil sharpener sharpened. Grind. Grind. Grind.

The faucet dripped. Drip. Drip. Drip.

"Too noisy," said the teachers. And they went back to see Andy the Wise.

"Get Sam Houston to join your class," said Andy the Wise.

"What good will Sam do?" asked the teachers. But they got Sam to join their class anyway.

Sam laughed all of the time. Ha, ha, ha, ha, ha.

Jeatt dropped her pencil. Bang. Bang. Bang.

The chairs scraped the ground. Scrape. Scrape. Scrape.

The pencil sharpener sharpened. Grind. Grind. Grind.

The faucet dripped. Drip. Drip. Drip.

"Still too noisy," said the teachers. And they went back to see Andy the Wise.

"Get Mariah Page and Sarah Wilms to join your class," said Andy.

"What good will they do for our class?" asked the teachers. But they asked the girls to join their class anyway.

Mariah wrinkled her paper. Crunch. Crunch. Crunch.

Sarah tapped her pencil. Tap. Tap. Tap.

Sam laughed all of the time. Ha, ha, ha, ha.

Jeatt dropped her pencil. Bang. Bang. Bang.

The chairs scraped the ground. Scrape. Scrape. Scrape.

The pencil sharpener sharpened. Grind. Grind. Grind.

The faucet dripped. Drip. Drip. Drip.

"Still too noisy," said the teachers. And they went back to see Andy the Wise.

"Get Steven Lengenfelder and Daniel Kelly to join your class," said the wise man.

"What good will Steven and Daniel do for our class?" asked the teachers. But they asked Steven and Daniel to join their class anyway.

Steven rolled his pencil on the table. Tick-tack. Tick-tack. Tick-tack.

Daniel stomped around the room. Stomp. Stomp. Stomp.

Mariah wrinkled her paper. Crunch. Crunch. Crunch.

Sarah tapped her pencil. Tap. Tap. Tap.

Sam laughed all of the time. Ha, ha, ha, ha.

Jeatt dropped her pencil. Bang. Bang. Bang.

The chairs scraped the ground. Scrape. Scrape. Scrape.

The pencil sharpener sharpened. Grind. Grind. Grind.

The faucet dripped. Drip. Drip. Drip.

By this time, Mrs. Larrick's and Mrs. Mullen's ears hurt! "Still too noisy!" they cried. So the teachers went back to Andy the Wise.

"Get Jacob Kon and Shaina Mason to join your class," said Andy.

"What good can Jacob and Shaina do?" asked the tired teachers. But they asked Jacob and Shaina to join their class anyway.

Jacob cracked his knuckles. Pop. Pop. Pop.

Shaina drew pictures all day. Scribble. Scribble. Scribble.

Steven rolled his pencil on the table. Tick-tack. Tick-tack. Tick-tack.

Daniel stomped around the room. Stomp. Stomp. Stomp.

Mariah wrinkled her paper. Crunch. Crunch. Crunch.

Sarah tapped her pencil. Tap. Tap. Tap.

Sam laughed all of the time. Ha, ha, ha, ha, ha.

Jeatt dropped her pencil. Bang. Bang. Bang.

The chairs scraped the ground. Scrape. Scrape. Scrape.

The pencil sharpener sharpened. Grind. Grind. Grind.

The faucet dripped. Drip. Drip. Drip.

Mrs. Larrick and Mrs. Mullen were at the end of their ropes! "Still too noisy!" And off they went to see Andy the Wise. They were desperate. The children were not learning.

"Get Milissa Huber and Jessica Melhart to join your class," said Andy the Wise.

"What good will Milissa and Jessica do?" asked the teachers. But they asked Milissa and Jessica to join their class anyway.

Milissa and Jessica talked all day. Yack, yack, yack, yack, yack.

Jacob cracked his knuckles. Pop. Pop. Pop.

Shaina drew pictures all day. Scribble. Scribble. Scribble.

Steven rolled his pencil on the table. Tick-tack. Tick-tack. Tick-tack.

Daniel stomped around the room. Stomp. Stomp. Stomp.

Mariah wrinkled her paper. Crunch. Crunch. Crunch.

Sarah tapped her pencil. Tap. Tap. Tap.

Sam laughed all of the time. Ha, ha, ha, ha, ha.

Jeatt dropped her pencil. Bang. Bang. Bang.

The chairs scraped the ground. Scrape. Scrape. Scrape.

The pencil sharpener sharpened. Grind. Grind. Grind.

The faucet dripped. Drip. Drip. Drip.

"Andy the Wise, we have had it! All day long the noise rings in our ears!"

Milissa and Jessica talked all day. Yack, yack, yack, yack, yack.

Jacob cracked his knuckles. Pop. Pop. Pop.

Shaina drew pictures all day. Scribble. Scribble. Scribble.

Steven rolled his pencil on the table. Tick-tack. Tick-tack. Tick-tack.

Daniel stomped around the room. Stomp. Stomp. Stomp.

Mariah wrinkled her paper. Crunch. Crunch. Crunch.

Sarah tapped her pencil. Tap. Tap. Tap.

Sam laughed all of the time. Ha, ha, ha, ha.

Jeatt dropped her pencil. Bang. Bang. Bang.

The chairs scraped the ground. Scrape. Scrape. Scrape.

The pencil sharpener sharpened. Grind. Grind. Grind.

The faucet dripped. Drip. Drip. Drip.

"Get rid of all the children in your class," Andy the Wise said.

"But we love all of our students," cried Mrs. Larrick and Mrs. Mullen. "We will not let any of them leave our classroom. We will have to bring it up at class meeting! They will come up with a better idea. They have learned to solve their own problems."

The children suggested these things to keep the noise level down in the classroom:

1. Ask the talking students to be quiet.

2. Say, "Quiet please," in sign language.

3. Say, "Wait please," in sign language.

4. Be responsible for not talking yourself.

5. Write a plan about what to do differently.

6. Have talkers stay in from recess.

7. Use a whisper voice.

8. Talk loudly outside.

9. Ask Wise Andy.

10. Ask people to sit still.

11. Ask Enzo (the custodian) to fix the faucet.

12. Ask children to use the hand-operated pencil sharpener.

13. Remind them not to talk.

14. Tell them how you feel about loud talking.

15. Apologize for being noisy.

16. Keep to yourself.

17. Listen during direction times.

18. Pick up the chairs.

19. Think before you speak.

20. Keep your feet still.

Mrs. Larrick and Mrs. Mullen were proud of them for solving the problem by themselves!

Note Writing

Discussion

Isn't it funny that teachers spend copious amounts of time encouraging communication skills and written expression, but when a student writes a note to another student, the teacher's reaction is to discourage the behavior? Note writing is a normal form of communication. The key to dealing with it during class time is to help students respect others, the teaching and learning process, and the needs of the situation.

Suggestions

1. Maintain a sense of humor and perspective about note writing.

2. Don't humiliate anyone. Reading a note aloud or requiring a student to read a note aloud to the class is disrespectful and leads to a desire for revenge. When we hurt or humiliate others, we invite them to look for ways to get even.

3. Do the unexpected: If you see Sally writing a note, stop what you're doing and, without saying anything, write a note asking her to refrain from writing notes during class. Hand it to a student and whisper to that student to pass the note to Sally. In a light-handed way, you will demonstrate to all the students how note writing disrupts the classroom.

4. Provide a note deposit box. Place a sign on the box: "Please fold it, put your name on it, and finish it at break."

5. Decide what you will do, and follow through on your decision. Let your students know that you are aware that note writing is taking place and that it distracts you. Simply say, "I'll stop teaching until the distraction stops."

Planning Ahead to Prevent Future Problems

1. At the beginning of the school year, discuss note writing with your students: "Writing notes seems to be popular with seventh graders. What are your ideas on how we can handle this problem in our class?"

2. When note writing is a problem for you, put it on the agenda for a class meeting. You can explain how it affects you and how it interrupts the class. Invite your students to share their thoughts and feelings about note writing. Sometimes a discussion is enough. If it doesn't take care of the problem, put it on the agenda again and work on a class solution rather than focusing on specific offenders.

3. Consider the possibility of allowing note writing in your classroom as long as it is done respectfully and does not disturb others. (Haven't you ever written a note to another teacher during a faculty meeting to avoid whispering?)

Inspirational Story

A group of high school students regularly passed notes to one another during Mrs. Stamps's class. She noticed that when the note writing was going on she felt distracted, which interfered with her teaching. Her first attempts to deal with the situation consisted of continually reminding the students that if they had something to say to one another, they needed to wait until after class.

As time went on, the students continued to write notes in class, and Mrs. Stamps continued to remind them not to. Eventually, Mrs. Stamps realized that reminding and coaxing were not effective ways to deal with this behavior.

She decided to focus on her own actions and follow through respectfully on whatever she decided to do. The next morning, when the note writing started, Mrs. Stamps said, "I notice that note writing continues to take place regularly in our class. I find it difficult to concentrate on my job when I see students composing, reading, and responding to one another's notes. I have decided to stop teaching and wait until I have your full attention before continuing."

Later that morning, when Mrs. Stamps stopped talking in midsentence, the students looked around in confusion. Several students, busily dashing off messages, nervously looked up toward the front of the room and saw Mrs. Stamps quietly pick up a novel and begin reading. It took only a moment for them to realize that she was waiting for extraneous activity to cease and attention to refocus on her. The offending students stealthily slipped their notes out of sight and looked toward the teacher. When she was sure all the students were paying attention, Mrs. Stamps put down her book and resumed the lesson. She never made it through as much as a paragraph of her novel before note writing had ceased in her classroom.

P

Parent Communication

Discussion

Are parents the enemy or the ally? That question has hovered in the back of every teacher's mind at one time or another. When you feel frustrated dealing with certain children's behavior and their parents seem to be making things worse, it's easy to focus on placing blame. Instead, see the situation as an opportunity for both you and the mother or father to grow and learn together. When you are on the same team, everyone wins.

Discouragement affects parents and teachers as well as students. When parents feel discouraged they can become entrenched in the four mistaken goals, just as children do. Listen for these clues:

1. "What you're doing isn't working. You need to try something else to help my kid!" The parent pesters the school nonstop for help with her child. The teacher groans to see yet another message on her desk from

this parent. (The parent is seeking undue attention.)

2. "I'm in charge! You can't tell me what to do with my child! Nobody knows what's needed better than I do. I have more degrees than you, teacher!" (The parent is seeking power.)

3. "I'll get even." The parent vows to sue the school district, to go to the principal about something a teacher did, or to go to central administration about something the principal did. (The parent is seeking revenge.)

4. "I give up. There's nothing I can do. You have the degrees and education, so you take care of it." (The parent has given up and is seeking to be left alone.)

Parents are pursuing these four goals because they're discouraged. Teachers and administrators can encourage parents by supporting their efforts to help their children and by giving them a sense of belonging—showing them that parents are an integral part of the workings of the educational system. Communication is essential to build trust between parents and schools. When trust is established, parents and schools will work cooperatively for the good of students.

Suggestions

1. If you are having difficulty with a parent, as in the examples given in "Discus-

sion," recognize that you are dealing with a discouraged parent. (Refer to the Mistaken Goal Chart [see pages 12–13] for ideas on how to be encouraging.)

2. Listen and respond to parents' requests and concerns. When the attitude is that the parent and the teacher are learning together, both feel less defensive and more open to possible solutions to a problem.

3. See problems as opportunities to involve parents. Finding a win–win solution can be a learning opportunity for all involved. Begin with the attitude of "We're in this together with the same goal of encouraging your child."

4. Document problems as they occur, so that you can clearly convey the nature of a problem and its frequency: "Juan hit Margo three times before lunch." Contrast that to telling a parent, "Juan's behavior is out of control!" Which message is more likely to make the parent want to work on a solution? Which message is more likely to make the parent feel discouraged and defensive? (It's important to inform parents of misbehavior without expecting them to solve problems that occur at school. Assure parents that you are teaching students to solve problems and to help each other through class meetings.)

5. Try to look at a problem from the parent's perspective. How would it feel to be a parent in this situation? What might you feel? Cultural differences sometimes affect this answer. One school discovered that its

policy of sending parents notes detailing problems as they occurred was doing considerable harm in one home. This Asian family's cultural belief was that a child's behavior reflects upon his mother. Both parents were suffering and humiliated. When the teacher instead began to send home information about their son's successes, the parents were encouraged.

Planning Ahead to Prevent Future Problems

1. Provide clear guidelines for how parents can contact you. Give them phone numbers and times when you are most accessible. Respond to parents' messages promptly.

2. Provide parents with information. Periodically send home overviews of upcoming study plans and advance notices of special assignment due dates. This allows parents to feel involved and to support both your efforts and those of their children. In response to a notice, a parent may schedule a timely trip to the library or enter the due date of a report on the family calendar.

3. Invite parents to participate in class meetings. When a problem occurs, welcome a parent to join the students in seeking a solution. Suggest to students that they offer to teach their families how to hold family meetings based on the class meeting process.

4. Help parents make connections with their children and with other parents by

sending home articles on child development or notices of special children's events taking place in the community. Periodically issue invitations to speakers who can share parenting information with your students' parents.

5. Provide schoolwide and classroom information on a weekly or biweekly basis. Some schools and some individual teachers send each parent a large envelope filled with schedules, sign-up forms, and notices; there is a lined page in front that parents sign and return. This is a means of regular two-way communication. If a particular family never returns its signed sheet, an effort to discover the problem may result in the school or the teacher reaching a family effectively for the first time.

6. Offer parent–teacher–student conferences. (Refer to "Conferences.") One or two parents, a teacher, and a student can become a team that works toward encouragement and improvement.

7. Remember that a child may have more than one household. Be sure to send home copies of information to both parents or guardians.

8. Help set up parenting classes at your school with child care provided. Strive to make these family times with special activities for all the children, such as pizza nights or group art projects.

9. Meet families in their own settings through home visits. Offer parents this

option, so that you and the family can spend some relaxed time getting to know each other.

Inspirational Story

A special education teacher was assigned to a group of children who were hearing impaired. Some of the children had emotional problems and severe behavioral disturbances. The administration told this teacher that she would get no support from these children's parents. Refusing to accept this, she began a campaign to involve the families of her students through encouragement.

The first contact the teacher made with her students' families was by making home visits. In some cases she traveled fifty miles to visit a student's family. Many of these houses had no phones, so calling wasn't a possibility.

During each home visit, she shared with the parents all the positive qualities and abilities she had seen in their child. She also asked whether they had any special concerns they wished to share with her regarding their child. The visits inspired trust and respect.

After this, when the teacher sent home notes, responses arrived quickly. The parents began to show up for meetings that they had never before attended (not an easy task for most of them due to the distance and the cost of gasoline).

Because the students knew the teacher had been to their homes and had met their parents, brothers, and sisters, they were more willing to cooperate with her. It made them feel special to know she had gone out of her way to make a connection with their families. This initial act opened the door to communication, which in turn led to improvement both in the children's efforts at school and in the parents' attitude toward the program.

Parent Involvement

Discussion

Involving parents makes a difference. Research shows that when parents are involved, test scores improve, incidents of violence decrease, and vulnerability to drug or alcohol abuse lessens. Involvement is the key to creating a sense of belonging. When parents feel that they're participants in their children's school programs, they don't seek to achieve that sense of belonging in inappropriate ways. (See "Parent Communication" for a discussion of parents' mistaken goals.)

The truth is that teachers and schools need parents very much. Parents are their children's first teachers. A full, rich education is best achieved when the child *and* his family participate in the school's programs.

Parents will participate when they are welcomed and encouraged to do so. But schools must invite them to take part in meaningful ways, not just to do the tasks teachers hate. If the only involvement offered consists of single-handedly patrolling three hundred students on the playground at recess or mopping up lunch leftovers, volunteers won't flock to sign up.

It's important to have fun together. Too often parent meetings and school events are neither fun nor well attended. Imagine a parent night at which all of the dads go up on stage and perform a rap song together while gyrating around in outlandish clothes. Visualize the glee of their sixth-grade children as they look on.

If parent involvement is low to nonexistent, figure out the reasons. Change what the school is offering, and the results will change, too.

Suggestions

1. Ask each of your students to think of something unique and special about one or both of his parents (a job, a hobby, or the family heritage), and invite the parents to demonstrate skills or talk about culture and family history to the whole class.

2. At class meeting time, elicit suggestions from the students on what the class could do to help parents feel welcomed and special at the school.

3. If you are having tremendous difficulty involving a parent, make a phone call or pay a home visit. Going the extra mile usually has a big payoff.

4. Brainstorm with other staff members about ways to involve parents.

5. Plan fun activities for families. Involve the children in the planning, and their enthusiasm will infect others.

6. Recognize that when you ask parents to become involved in your class, you need to take time for training. Parents sometimes need to be reminded of the particular responsibilities connected with a job. For example, when going on a field trip, perhaps the school requires that you go directly from the school to the destination, without any stops. (Refer to "Take Time for Training.")

7. You may need to set limits with some parents about their degree of involvement. With a parent who is overly involved, be sure to clarify guidelines for the job to be done. Point out the beginning, middle, and end of the task. Don't hesitate to mention the needs of the entire class as opposed to interests of a parent and his or her child.

Planning Ahead to Prevent Future Problems

1. Have students write and publish a weekly or monthly newsletter for parents. Students can design regular columns. Newsletters find their way home when students have been involved in their preparation.

2. Invite parents to visit the classroom at a variety of times and days of the week.

3. Give parents their own place in the school building. This "parent support center" can be a room, or even corner of a room, with a coffeepot, a few chairs, and a table. Here parents may visit together, work on materials needed for different classrooms (wouldn't it be great to have extra hands to cut out shapes for your students' collages?), and plan future events.

4. During the first week of the school year, mail a letter to each parent in which you share your curriculum plans, and provide a list of ways in which he or she might join in activities. Include some tasks that parents can do at home if their work schedules or physical limitations preclude coming to the school.

5. Whenever a parent helps or participates, take time to send them a written thank-you or some recognition of their service. Better yet, allow students to be in charge of drafting these. Be as specific as possible about how a parent's actions benefited you, the students, and/or the school.

6. Examine your feelings and beliefs about parent involvement. Do you really want it? Are you willing to look for and then accept what each parent is able to offer? When parents show up in your class uninvited, do they sense that you consider their presence a burden or a nuisance? Unannounced visits may be all the involvement some parents can offer. See such visits as opportunities, and make the most of them by having a special place in your room (perhaps an honored parent chair) to make the parent feel welcome. If unscheduled visits are a problem for you, speak with the parent and decide together what will work best for both of you.

Inspirational Stories

A Key to Success

At one school, students had the lowest achievement scores of all elementary schools in New York City. The incoming elementary school principal believed that parent involvement was the key to students' success. When she took over, she was told that getting these parents involved would be impossible. She didn't believe it.

Before her first PTA meeting, she designed a campaign to entice parents to attend. She had the children go home every day and tell their parents that they were expected at the PTA meeting. After work each day, the principal drove through the neighborhood and called out to the people sitting on their porches that she was looking forward to seeing them at the PTA meeting. If nothing else, she piqued their curiosity about this strange new lady at the school.

Her tactics paid off. On the night of the PTA meeting, so many parents and even grandparents showed up that there wasn't even standing room available. She explained to the families that this was *their* school and that she needed their help. She elicited the adults' help in the form of doing carpentry work, painting, repairing windows, helping in the office and the classrooms, monitoring the halls, and much more. Parents volunteered, and a new sense of pride was kindled. The school became everybody's concern.

Two stories from Michael Babb, principal, Flowery Elementary School, Sonoma, California

Second Cup of Coffee

Here's a quick and easy idea that we've used at our school to stimulate the dialogue between school and home. Each month our Flowery Family Support Team stages a simple and informal "Second Cup of Coffee." Members of the team (the school principal, the counselor, teachers, and the school–community liaison) serve coffee and pastries to parents as they drop off their children at school. Weather permitting, the event is held outside in a corridor where there's a heavy flow of traffic. Parents and staff drop by and chat, creating a natural venue where school program information can be shared, and parents can ask questions, give suggestions, and simply get

to know other members of the Flowery School community. Parents and staff look forward to this monthly get-together!

Getting to Know You

Like many schools with bilingual programs, ours offers regular parent language classes. At the request of parents in our Two-Way Immersion Program, we organized English and Spanish language lessons for parents in the evenings. We then took it one step further by organizing an Intercambio/Interchange segment. After class, parents go to a common area where they practice what they've learned with a partner from the other language class. Besides the practical advantage of providing the modeling of a native speaker of the language being learned, the interchange has been a real barrier breaker. Parents have developed relationships with other parents with whom they formerly had little contact. One mother explained, "I used to see parents, and the most we would do was nod hello when we dropped off our kids; now I feel like I know them."

Pestering

Discussion

Students who demand constant attention are discouraged. They may have decided that they need this attention to prove that they're likable or that pestering is a good

way to feel powerful. It could be that they feel certain they can't be a "good" student, but at least they can be "good pests."

Students can learn about respect and courtesy as well as how to earn attention and use power in positive ways. It's important for children to feel satisfied when they take care of themselves rather than needing nonstop service and attention from others to feel belonging and significance.

Suggestions

1. Give the student a limited choice when he's pestering somebody: "Peter, do you want to talk to Sally at morning recess or at lunchtime?"

2. When pestering takes the form of tattling on classmates and appears to be an attempt to get attention, you might say, "I'm sure you can work this out." Another possibility is to say, "Why don't you put that on the class meeting agenda?" (Refer to "Tattling.")

3. Remind a student who is being pestered about the four problem-solving suggestions:
    A. Ignore it.
    B. Talk it over respectfully with the other student.
    C. Work on a win–win solution.
    D. Put it on the class meeting agenda.

4. Avoid labeling a student as a pest. Separate the deed from the doer.

Planning Ahead to Prevent Future Problems

1. During a class meeting, have students role-play pestering. First process the reactions of those who took active parts in the role play. Ask each of them what they were feeling, what they were thinking, and what they were deciding. Then ask the rest of the class what they noticed and felt. Have the class brainstorm to find new options for the person who is being pestered and the one who is pestering. Ask each student to pick one idea to try for a week anytime he or she feels pestered or starts to pester someone. Find out how the solutions worked by having the students report on their experiences the following week.

2. If you find yourself feeling irritated by a student's pestering, the feeling may be a clue that your student thinks she matters only when she is noticed. (Refer to "Mistaken Goals [Hat Messages]" for tips on encouraging your student as well as yourself.)

3. If you are feeling challenged, angry, or threatened, the student may be pestering you to secure power. (Again, refer to "Mistaken Goals [Hat Messages].")

4. Sometimes students work as a team to keep teachers busy with them. They have learned the skill of group pestering. This classroom version of sibling fighting is a bid to get the adult to take sides and become inappropriately involved. Take the issue to the class by putting it on the class meeting agenda for group problem solving. Help them become part of a team that works together constructively instead of destructively.

Inspirational Story

Ms. Altman was approached one morning by one of her second graders. Luisa complained that Nathan, her table partner, was continually whispering to her. Ms. Altman reminded Luisa about the four problem-solving suggestions that all the students had learned together and that were posted in the classroom. When Luisa said that she had tried everything, Ms. Altman pointed out that the final suggestion was to put the problem on the class meeting agenda.

During the class meeting, after appreciations were exchanged, the first agenda item was Luisa's concern about Nathan. She asked for help in solving the problem, and Ms. Altman suggested that a role play might be useful. After the role play and after asking each role player how he or she felt, Ms. Altman said that sometimes simply bringing up a problem and watching a role play about it will lead to improvement. The students decided to check with Luisa in one week to see whether the situation had improved. In the meantime, Ms. Altman created a new job for Nathan to help him feel that he belonged in the class and was significant. It was never clear whether this job or the class meeting discussion caused the change, but Nathan stopped his constant whispering to Luisa.

Playground Behavior

Discussion

A playground is more than a place where students release energy or challenge themselves physically. It is also a laboratory for learning about respect of property, conflict management, and personal responsibility.

Involve students in setting up some of the playground rules and procedures. Some rules, especially those related to safety, will be carried over from year to year and should have clear consequences. However, in some areas student input should be encouraged. Students are more motivated to follow rules they have helped create. If a rule doesn't work, the students can discuss the problem and work on a modification or a new rule that might solve the problem. Every problem can be an opportunity for continued learning and growth.

Suggestions

1. Let the rules or guidelines be the boss. Refer students to the rules by asking

"what" and "how" questions: "What is the rule?" "How are you breaking that rule?" "How can you change your behavior to comply with the rule?" "What ideas do you have to solve this problem?" "What did you learn from this experience?" "What issues may need further discussion during class meetings?" You don't have to ask all of these questions. Sometimes just one is enough to invite the student to think and to stop the misbehavior.

2. Follow through firmly and kindly when a student or a group of students need to stop an activity. Remind them that they can try again the next day, week, or at an appropriate time.

3. Use a whistle or another means to get the attention of a student. Then, rather than shouting out instructions, quickly walk to that student and tend to the needs of the situation.

4. Sometimes allow a student involved in a playground problem to choose the solution he or she thinks will be most helpful: going to the positive time-out bench to cool off, giving up the use of the playground for a specified time, using the problem-solving wheel, or putting the problem on the class meeting agenda.

5. Direct students to their peers to seek suggestions and help. (See "Planning Ahead.")

6. Involve students in any problems that involve loss or damage to equipment. If a ball is punctured, the class can brainstorm for ideas about how to repair or replace it. When students take responsibility for small problems, they learn skills that prevent big problems.

Planning Ahead to Prevent Future Problems

1. Help students see the connection among privilege, responsibility, and consequences. Consider the following:

For every privilege children have, there is a responsibility. The obvious consequence for not accepting the responsibility is to lose the privilege. . . . Children have the privilege of using the school playground during recess. The responsibility is to treat the equipment and other people with respect. When people or things are treated disrespectfully, it would be a respectful consequence for that child to lose the privilege of using the playground until he or she is ready to be respectful again. These consequences will be effective only if children have another chance to have the privilege as soon as they are ready for the responsibility.[24]

2. Educate your class on existing safety guidelines and regulations. This informa-

---

24. Jane Nelsen, Lynn Lott, and H. Stephen Glenn, *Positive Discipline in the Classroom,* third revised edition (Roseville, CA: Prima Publishing, 2000), 126–127.

tion may be provided by your principal or by the local playground equipment manufacturer.

3. Take time for training. Demonstrate and role-play acceptable behavior for the use of equipment and interaction with other students. This can be done either in the classroom or on the playground.

4. Involve all the students in brainstorming for some rules regarding use of the playground, its equipment, and its physical boundaries. Some schools form a student council consisting of two students from every room. Before the council meets, each classroom's students brainstorm to create a list of playground rules. Then the student council members take their class's list to the student council meeting, where they narrow down the suggestions (by combining similar ones) until they have as few rules as possible. They take the condensed list back to their rooms to present to their classmates. Through this process, all students feel included in the development of the rules and motivated to follow them.

5. Establish several procedures so students can make choices when rules aren't followed. One choice is for the students involved to put the problem on their class meeting agendas to get suggestions from their classmates. Another choice is for students to go to a positive time-out bench where they can cool off. (Students must first be taught the concepts of positive time-out and be involved in the creation of

a positive time-out area.) A third choice might be a problem-solving bench where students can choose to work together on a solution. It's helpful to have the four problem-solving steps or the problem-solving wheel (Refer to "Problem Solving") painted on the bench or written and posted nearby. An alternative is to hand copies of the steps or the wheel to students when they choose to use the problem-solving bench.

6. Consider implementing a schoolwide program in which students are trained to help their peers with problems on the playground.

7. Notice when students act with respect for others and for equipment. Encourage them by sharing your observations informally or at a class meeting. Also remember to pass along compliments you hear about your students' behavior on the playground.

Inspirational Story

A story from Loretta Sedran, French teacher for grades 1 to 8, Holy Jubilee Catholic School, Toronto, Ontario, Canada

A stitch in time saves letters going home. During my second year using Positive Discipline in the classroom, I found that I used many of the strategies and principles of the program outside my French class. Our school only had 245 students and therefore was not big enough to have a vice principal. When the principal was not available, he asked or appointed someone to be what is called the "principal designate." This person's job was to "be principal" during his absence from the school. I found that I used many of the strategies during these situations with students. Here is one of the ones I valued most.

Two fourth-grade students, Paul and Cindy (not their real names), were playing tag outside with some of their other classmates. At some point during the game, Cindy grabbed onto the neckline of Paul's T-shirt and tore it a couple inches. When I saw the students sitting in the office after lunch recess, the little girl was crying uncontrollably because she was afraid of what might happen. The three of us talked about what had happened and how it happened. Cindy realized that she should have been more careful and there was no need for having grabbed onto the shirt. Paul said that he should have played fair and stopped when she had tagged him. However, I reminded them that we still had a torn T-shirt. I suggested that we could try and sew it. They were both surprised at my suggestion, probably because no one ever suggested that. We had a policy that a letter would go home to the parents and that the item would have to be replaced. I asked whether they wanted to bring in a radio to keep them company as they sewed, and Paul said he could do that.

At last recess the two showed up with the radio and the T-shirt, (Paul had put on his gym shirt for the rest of the day), and I had set up the sewing kit—something no

school should be without. We turned on the radio, and I started them off and taught them how to pull the needle and thread. Paul discovered that he liked sewing and that Cindy had been taught how to sew by her grandmother. They chatted away and took turns until it was done. The funny thing was that I just had to pop my head in now and then to see how things were going or to tie a knot. By the end of recess, the shirt was fixed and the two had actually had fun.

The next day I asked Paul about the shirt and whether his mom had said anything. He told me that she had said it was a job well done, and he had asked his mom whether she had any socks for him to fix. Cindy told her mom, but no comment was made. All is well that ends well.

Class Meeting Solutions

Second Grade Versus Third Grade

At Pinetree Elementary, the second and third graders often squabbled over use of the four-square court, each class complaining of the other's interference in its games. When this problem appeared on the class meeting agenda in the second grade, Mrs. Trainer pointed out that when the others involved in a problem are unavailable to work on a solution, those who are available can focus on solutions that are based on changing their own behavior. The second graders then chose to stay away from the third graders' games.

After a week, several class members reported that there had been no change in the situation. Mrs. Trainer suggested that they put the problem back on the agenda for the next class meeting. During the subsequent discussion, Nancie, who had been particularly vocal about the situation, said, "I think that we fight with them because we don't know them very well. I think that we should do something together." Mrs. Trainer asked for a show of hands to see whether others agreed with Nancie's thoughts and with her suggestion. Most of the class nodded and raised their hands. Mrs. Trainer asked the students to brainstorm for ways to spend time with the third grade. After listing all the ideas, the class decided to invite the third graders to participate in some art activities during class time. The second graders were excited and eager to invite the other class to spend time with them.

A week after the joint activity, Mrs. Trainer checked in with her students about how things were going on the playground. The students reported that the situation seemed to be better and that they were satisfied.

Playing Tag

A story from Peggy Payne, first-grade teacher, St. Eugene's Elementary School, Santa Rosa, California

One of our school rules is that games of tag are not allowed during recess time. This is presented at the beginning of the year as being a safety rule because of crowded conditions on the playground. This is a change for the first graders because when they are in kindergarten, their recess is at a different time and they have the playground to themselves. One year, my class was having difficulty following this rule. We had a class meeting at which we reviewed the policy. They did understand that this was a safety rule and that they could not be running wildly through games such as basketball, dodgeball, and jump rope. But they felt that they didn't have very many options for types of games to play, because games such as basketball were reserved for older students. When we talked about a solution to the problem, one student pointed out that in their rotation of assigned areas during the week, there are two days when they are assigned to an area where no other organized games are played and only the first grade is present. He wondered whether on those days and in that area they could play tag.

We invited our principal to attend our next class meeting to present our idea to her. She did come to the meeting and reviewed the safety policy with the students. She listened to their proposal and agreed that because of the less crowded conditions and the fact that there were not organized games in that area, playing tag would be within the safety guidelines. She congratulated them on their problem-solving abilities and diligence in coming up with a solution that met the needs of the situation.

Pouting

Discussion

Some students pout because they are accustomed to getting their way and don't know how to handle it when this doesn't happen. Students who feel overcontrolled may pout as a mild protest (instead of more blatant forms of rebellion) when a teacher requires them to do something.

If you scold, threaten, or humiliate a pouting student, you address only his behavior and fail to deal with the belief behind the behavior. It is more effective to use nonpunitive methods that allow students to experience their feelings while still responding to the situation. Students can learn that their feelings are acceptable but don't need to dictate their actions. They can learn to express their feelings in healthy, respectful ways without resorting to pouting. When students participate in making decisions and feel that they're part of the solution, they rarely pout.

Suggestions

1. Don't scold or humiliate a pouting student.

2. Take responsibility for what you may have done to invite pouting. Are you being too controlling? Is your tone of voice inviting resistance instead of cooperation? Do your students feel that you listen to them and take them seriously? Do you validate their thoughts and ideas?

3. If your student pouts as a manipulative technique, tell him, "I know you're disappointed, but I have faith in you to work it out." Or you might say, "I sense your resistance. Is this something we need to talk about together or with everyone's help during a class meeting?" When you approach the situation with dignity and respect, he may quickly conclude that pouting isn't effective.

4. Verbalize the feelings that led to the behavior: "I know you're disappointed and upset. I feel that way, too, when things don't work out the way I want them to." A student's behavior often changes just because his feelings were validated.

5. Offer a limited choice: "I know that you're feeling upset, but we still need to put away our supplies. What would work best for you: to begin picking up these papers by yourself or to choose a buddy to help you?"

Planning Ahead to Prevent Future Problems

1. During a class meeting, discuss the disappointment we feel when things don't turn out how we had hoped they would. Invite everyone to discuss ways to deal with

this and ways to support classmates when they're disappointed.

2. Invite the students to brainstorm about other things that they can do or tell themselves when their wishes go unfulfilled. If some of the following ideas aren't suggested, you can join the brainstorming: try breathing deeply for a few minutes, share feelings with a buddy, or try to look at the situation from another point of view. Set up a role play in which a student can experience a new way to cope with disappointment. She will see that although she may still feel let down, she can take a few minutes to adjust and then can verbalize her feelings respectfully. Tell the students that you know this can be hard and that it may take practice.

3. Tell the pouting student in private that you don't want to embarrass him with verbal reminders, so you would like to set up a signal (e.g., a double wink) that you can give him when he needs to find another way to communicate.

Inspirational Story

Mr. Mike was supervising students on a playground. Jorge was sitting on a bench by himself with his shoulders down, his lower lip sticking out, and his brow knitted. This was a familiar scene to Mr. Mike. He was worried about Jorge, and once again felt the urge to give Jorge some special attention and to coax him back into playing with the other children.

This time, however, Mr. Mike looked at the boy's behavior and his own reactions and feelings. He realized that Jorge was feeling discouraged, and he wanted to find a better way to increase Jorge's feelings of belonging and significance in the group. Mr. Mike sat down next to Jorge and said, "I can see that you're disappointed. I feel that way, too, when things don't work out the way I wish they would." Mr. Mike had to hold himself back from saying more.

They sat next to each other quietly for another five minutes. Mr. Mike felt uneasy and wanted to do something, but eventually Jorge got up, his shoulders still slumped, and walked toward the swings. Soon he was playing with the other students. Over time he learned that Mr. Mike cared about him but wasn't going to give him special attention and service.

Procrastination

Discussion

Procrastination is a socially acceptable, nonverbal way of saying, "I don't want to, and you can't make me." When students are slow or forgetful, they don't get in as much trouble as they would if they said honestly, "I don't think I'll do my homework," or, "I don't really want to do this project."

Another name for *procrastination* is *passive power*. If left unchecked, procrastination can become a lifelong habit. It can also be an unconscious way of getting undue attention, seeking revenge, or avoiding tasks that seem too difficult. Students are usually unaware of the goals behind their behavior. Your awareness (Refer to "Mistaken Goals [Hat Messages]") can help them find more productive ways to have their needs met.

Suggestions

1. Allow the student to experience the consequences of her procrastination. Don't remind her that her work is due soon; don't bail her out with excuses or extensions. Show empathy without pity if she gets upset when experiencing the consequences of a poor grade.

2. Ask the student whether he would like help. (Don't try to help if he doesn't want it.)

3. Avoid lectures. Instead, ask "what" and "how" questions: "What happened as a result of your procrastination?" "How do you feel about the consequences?" "What did you learn from this?" "How would you feel about getting different results?" "What could you do to get different results?" These questions help students think for themselves whereas lectures make them stop listening. They often feel motivated to change after examining the long-range ef-

fect of their behavior and coming to their own conclusions.

4. Without shifting into a lecture, share stories of times when you have procrastinated with the student. Tell him about the impact your delaying had on the project and on your feelings of self-worth. Ask whether he has experienced similar situations or feelings.

Planning Ahead to Prevent Future Problems

1. Ask your student whether procrastination is a problem for her and whether she would like help with it. If she would, assist her in setting mini-deadlines and check-in points when she is working on a long-term project. Help her think through a project, starting from the deadline and moving backward toward the present. She can create a time line for all the steps that need to be done.

2. Take time for training. Help a student learn to take small steps. Schedule a time to check in with him, such as eight in the morning on Mondays and Fridays. At this time, give feedback on his progress and make suggestions for the next step. Be sure to give the student an opportunity to evaluate his own progress.

3. Establish clear expectations for the completion of assignments. Involve all your students in a brainstorming session about how

to meet deadlines. Let them devise a plan that will help them be successful.

4. Be flexible. If a student really needs extra time to complete her work, listen respectfully as she presents her needs and act accordingly. A "free pass" for one or two late assignments, built into your grading system from the start, might help a student who is feeling overwhelmed. (Keep in mind that procrastination is sometimes a sign of giving up. A rigid classroom serves to further discourage a child who feels inadequate.)

5. Discuss procrastination during a class meeting. Help students understand the possible hidden goals: attention, power, revenge, and giving up. Allow the whole class to respond to questions about long-range consequences of procrastination and to brainstorm for solutions. Suggestions gathered this way are often more effective than the same suggestions when they come from teachers in the form of lectures.

Inspirational Story

Paula created a reputation for herself as a procrastinator. Everyone expected her to leave everything until the last minute and then work everyone around her into a frenzy. With her adorable ways, she had no trouble enlisting last-minute help.

In the past, her teachers had always rescued her by making excuses for her and by giving her extensions on homework and projects. They found themselves working overtime as they continually checked back with Paula on her progress and kept track of her unfinished work.

Ms. Taylor had a different philosophy. She decided to help Paula by being firm and kind. She was clear about her expectations as well as Paula's abilities. Her class was working on nutrition reports that were due at the end of the month. She told the students that they would receive credit only for work that was turned in on the due date.

Ms. Taylor noticed that Paula was missing work at the checkpoints that had been established. But Paula assured her that it would all be ready on the scheduled day.

When that day arrived, Paula had a note from her parents explaining the reasons that she was unable to complete the report but assuring Ms. Taylor that she would have it on the following Monday. In response, Ms. Taylor said that she was sorry but wouldn't accept any reports after the deadline. She suggested that Paula turn in any work she did have to receive partial credit.

When Paula objected, Ms. Taylor reminded her of the deadline for the report and adhered to her decision not to accept late work. Paula wasn't happy, but she never again tried to give Ms. Taylor excuses when her work wasn't finished. She either got her work in on time or accepted the consequences of her procrastination.

Put-Downs, General

(see also "Put-Downs, Older Students")

Discussion

Sometimes students dispense their put-downs to classmates they actually admire: "That girl can eat everything in sight but stays skinny as a rail." This is likely intended as a compliment. But the fine line between funny and painful is easily crossed, leading to hurt feelings and even despair. Neither children nor adults do a very good job of recognizing the boundary. Of course, some put-downs are intentionally mean: "Bill couldn't fit in the van for the field trip even if we gave him two seats!" This may bring tears from Bill, who knows he is overweight.

Children can be extremely cruel to each other, and they often believe the insults they hear, even when adults try to assure them otherwise. Shaun once told Mary her hair was so frizzy it looked like she had stuck her finger in an electric outlet. Ever since, Mary has hated her tresses no matter how many times her parents and peers have exclaimed over her good fortune at having naturally curly hair.

Suggestions

1. Invite the students who have been insulting one another to collect data on the number of times they give or receive put-downs. By objectively gathering information, the children can gain perspective. If a student claims, "Jack always puts me down," the teacher may ask, "How often is always? Once a day, once an hour, once a minute?" By learning the facts, both students may realize that the problem is smaller than they had supposed or bigger.

2. Facilitate a problem-solving meeting with the students involved. Ask each child whether she is hurt by the other person's insults. Are put-downs being used to gain attention, to show power, or to intimidate a weaker classmate? Using this information, brainstorm for possible solutions.

3. Encourage students to express their feelings and to let other people know when they feel hurt or embarrassed by a comment.

Planning Ahead to Prevent Future Problems

1. Teach that words can hurt. When someone makes a comment that feels mean or hurtful to the person being addressed, then it isn't humorous. True humor doesn't cause pain.

2. Invite the class to look for examples of put-downs in movies, TV shows, books, and magazines and to share and discuss them with the class. Ask students, "Is this funny or hurtful? Why?" "What makes the difference?"

3. Discussing put-downs during class meetings is often enough to help students

become aware of how much they can hurt others. They often don't intend to hurt—they just want to get attention or to look powerful and smart.

4. When put-downs are a general problem in the classroom, place the topic on the class meeting agenda. The group can share individual interpretations of put-downs, why they put each other down, and whether the put-downs are perceived as funny or hurtful. Then brainstorm together for an agreement on the use of disparaging statements. This agreement might include the suggestion that anyone who starts to formulate a put-down should try to change the remark into a compliment.

Class Meeting Solution

A story from Suzanne Smitha, school psychologist, Sharon School, Charlotte, North Carolina

A child in the first grade had terrible body odor. Some children made disparaging remarks about how he smelled. Those who sat near him would occasionally ask the teacher whether they could move away because he smelled so bad.

Then one day a child put the problem on the class meeting agenda. The teacher was concerned about the boy's feelings and hesitated to let the class discuss the problem with him there. Rather than singling him out, she posed a question to the class, asking them why someone might come to school some days not smelling his or her best. The children offered many suggestions: maybe the washing machine broke and the family couldn't wash their clothes; maybe a child slept with a younger brother or sister who had an accident in the bed that night; maybe the parents had to work late and didn't have a chance to wash the clothes.

The teacher then asked how someone might feel coming to school without being clean. The children used a variety of words to describe their possible feelings. "What might a student do in such circumstances?" the teacher asked. Many helpful ideas emerged. One boy offered to let a child come to his house anytime to shower. The teacher informed the class that there was a shower at the school and arrangements could be made for anyone to use it. Clean clothes were also available from the school.

Opening this sensitive issue up with this age group made it a problem that could happen to anyone and that had practical solutions. Children were less inclined to complain about body odor after that, and the child with the problem occasionally asked to use the shower at school.

Inspirational Story

A story from Bob Huppe, fourth-grade teacher, Shorewood Elementary School, Seattle, Washington

Two boys in a class were frequently putting one another down. The problem began to escalate into other issues between them. At that point, the boys brought the topic of put-downs to their teacher for a problem-solving session.

At the teacher's suggestion, the boys agreed to keep a record of this problem for a period of time. Together they developed a chart with four categories for data collection. The first column read "Win–Win." To have a check mark in this column, the comment (made by either boy) had to be positive—a nice thing to say and to hear. The next column was headed "Win–Lose." This was for a put-down that one child enjoyed giving but that was at the other child's expense. The third column was "Lose–Lose." This was for any time both boys got in trouble for and felt badly about a put-down. The final column was "Lose–Win." The flip side of the second column, this was for the child who had been on the receiving end of the hurtful put-down. Another feature of this system was that, even though each boy kept a chart, they had to agree on where they would place each mark.

They followed this plan for a week and almost always agreed about where the marks should go. Each boy became aware of how often he was using put-downs.

At the end of the week, the boys checked back in with the teacher. He asked them what they had learned by gathering the data. As they discussed their observations, both boys noted that they preferred win–win remarks to any other kind. They also discovered that they were now exchanging fewer put-downs. However, one of the boys clearly felt more disparaged and much worse about the put-downs than the other boy. This was an important realization for both of them.

After becoming more aware of their own behavior and its consequences, these two students chose to stop using put-downs. In fact, they became friends, and for the rest of the year they frequently gave each other compliments in class meetings.

Put-Downs, Older Students

(see also "Put-Downs, General")

Discussion

Whether it's known as name-calling, putting people down, mouthing off, or "dissing" (a teen neologism meaning to show disrespect), this skill is practiced and honed by students at middle schools and high schools across the country. These students don't need knives to slash each other to ribbons; they do it with their tongues.

For some students, disparaging others is a social survival skill. It is a misguided way to fit in and find belonging and significance. Students may use put-downs to receive attention. They may put people down to experience power or to get revenge. In some cases, mouthing off is a form of protection, keeping people at a distance.

Our society has a tremendous need for leaders who know how to find the best in others, who don't try to tear people down. Many individuals are losing their jobs today not because they don't have the skills for the position itself but because they don't have the skills for working cooperatively with others. People will work together well only if they feel a sense of connection and involvement. When an individual's choice is to disparage coworkers rather than to support them, no sense of connection will develop and functioning smoothly together becomes nearly impossible. The ability to identify other people's strengths and to name those strengths is a valuable one. Students who develop this skill have a real advantage. With training (primarily through class meetings) students learn to be good encouragers, instead of using put-downs.

Suggestions

Most put-downs can soon be prevented by following the suggestions in "Planning Ahead." However, until then, try the following suggestions:

1. Ask students involved (both the "putdowner" and the "put-downee") if one of them would be willing to put the problem on the class meeting agenda for later discussion and problem solving.

2. Ask both students whether some positive time-out would help them calm down until they feel better and can work on doing better.

3. Suggest that the student who has been put down use "emotional honesty" to tell the other person how the put-down made her feel—without a return put-down.

Planning Ahead to Prevent Future Problems

1. Begin to hold regular class meetings with time for appreciations. Activities for teaching this skill are in the book *Positive Discipline in the Classroom.*[25]

2. Ask your students to do a research project on how many put-downs they hear in a typical school day. They can share the results at a class meeting.

3. Ask the students their opinions on why they hear so many put-downs. Record their answers where everyone can see them. Information gathering, without trying to fix the problem or lecture about it, often produces a heightened awareness that lessens the problem.

---

25. Jane Nelsen, Lynn Lott, and H. Stephen Glenn, *Positive Discipline in the Classroom,* third revised edition (Roseville, CA: Prima Publishing, 2000).

4. Discuss the long-range value of becoming good at cutting others down. Ask the students whether any of them plan to have a job, a marriage, or children someday. How likely is it that their future coworkers, spouses, or children will say, "Gee, I just can't wait for you to put me down today"? If the students recognize that they may need to replace their skill at disparaging others with another skill, ask them whether they are willing to devote thirty minutes a week to practicing the skills of appreciation and encouragement. This can be an effective introduction to class meetings for students in middle school and high school.

5. Make time daily for students to practice appreciating one another. Some teachers have an appreciation box; students drop written appreciations into it, and the teacher reads them aloud each day.

6. Demonstrate being an encourager by giving your students encouragement and appreciations. If you have thirty-five students per period, single out seven students per period to receive encouragement or appreciations from you and their peers. Keep a pad of paper handy, and write down your discoveries about students to share them later. Teachers who do this are amazed at how much more respectful and cooperative their students become.

7. Make sure your own actions aren't modeling put-downs. Imitating students' behavior to increase rapport doesn't set the example that students need.

Class Meeting Solution

A story from Carolyn Carr, sixth-grade teacher, Mountainview Elementary School, Morgantown, West Virginia

A sixth-grade boy was routinely making fun of others, verbally harassing them. After the issue of his put-downs had appeared many times on the class meeting agenda, one member of the class again raised the question of why the boy was behaving this way. A student who had been an object of this boy's derision suggested that maybe he didn't receive much attention at home and maybe he didn't feel loved.

Although this was a very sensitive question, the boy was visibly moved by the caring way his classmates addressed it. Many of the class members—not to mention the teacher and counselor who had been called in to help—shed tears during the discussion. The boy's behavior changed markedly afterward.

Inspirational Story

A teacher decided to use class meetings at an alternative high school. Many of her students were in gangs, and several were involved with the juvenile authorities for vandalism and stealing. These students were experts at putting people down.

For four weeks, the teacher worked diligently on getting the students to buy into the class meeting process and form a circle. At the end of that time, she proceeded to the second Building Block for effective class meetings: exchanging compliments, appreciations, and encouragement. In preparation for this step, the teacher wanted to model these skills to the students. She needed one person to sit in the center of the circle. Attending the class meeting was a school counselor whom all the students liked and admired, so the teacher asked the counselor to be the first person to sit in their "encouragement chair."

This all-male class included two rival gang leaders who were constantly competing to be head honcho. The teacher wanted to start off slowly to keep this situation from breaking down into a fight.

Each of the class members in turn gave the counselor a sincere appreciation. When they had finished, one of the gang leaders called out, "Next!"

The teacher's heart skipped a beat, fearing that the students would succumb to the temptation to use put-downs when a fellow student sat in the chair. Instead, each student who took his place in the encouragement chair received sincere expressions of appreciation from his classmates. For the rest of the year, name-calling and put-downs all but disappeared from this class, and cooperative behavior became the norm rather than the exception.

S

Scapegoats

Discussion

Every classroom seems to have a student who assumes the role of scapegoat. (An interesting phenomenon is that if the student moves to a different school, another student will take over the scapegoat role.) Sometimes this student is admired by other students. More often he becomes the target of blame, anger, and snide remarks from other students or from teachers and admin-istrators. Often students take their cue from the adults around them as to whom they can use as a scapegoat.

The scapegoat may have decided to avoid competing with the high-achievers or to avoid taking risks; thus, he portrays himself as a failure. Scapegoats find belonging and significance by earning negative attention. They may look sullen or defiant; they may appear not to care about what's happening. The student who is saddled with the blame for all sorts of problems is regularly found in the principal's office. Adults typically respond to this child with punishment and humiliation, feeding his belief that he isn't likable.

It's truly a challenge to look beyond a scapegoat's behavior. But if you decipher the message the student is sending, you will be in a better position to work toward positive change. Use the Mistaken Goal Chart (see pages 12–13) to identify the probable goal of a student who plays the part of class scapegoat. When you understand the goal that underlies the behavior and focus on the student's beliefs about herself and others, your responses to the behavior change.

Suggestions

1. When students focus on blame, redirect them by asking the whole group, "Are we looking for blame, or are we looking for solutions?" Of course, this works only when you have taught this concept to the students and possibly had them create a poster to hang in the classroom that reads, "We are looking for solutions instead of blame."

2. When a student has experienced blame, take a moment to listen to that student express his feelings. Offer empathy and validation: "I can tell that you're feeling hurt by the expression on your face and by your words. It's okay to feel that way. I bet I'd

feel hurt, too, if that happened to me." Let him know that his feelings are always appropriate, but he is responsible for the actions he chooses: "It's okay to be angry, but it's not okay to punch someone." Help the student come up with some alternatives to punching or whatever disruptive outlet he chose.

3. Separate the deed from the doer. It's crucial to let the student know that you like her and value the person she is, even when you don't like what she is doing.

4. Notice whether you are focusing on the behavior of one particular student. Rather than singling out that student, put all the students in the same boat. You might say, "Students, we agreed that there would be no throwing papers in the classroom," as opposed to, "Larry, stop throwing the papers."

Planning Ahead to Prevent Future Problems

1. Avoid using labels such as "culprit," "troublemaker," and "ringleader." Such labels help keep students in those roles.

2. Build a friendship with any student who has the potential to become a scapegoat. Spending a few minutes after school once a week to talk about special interests helps a child experience belonging and significance and thus reduces misbehavior.

3. Hold regular class meetings. When students are participating in class meetings, their tendency to target a scapegoat

changes. Both students and teachers look for solutions instead of blame. One student's name may appear on the agenda over and over, but the class will sincerely try to help that student instead of hurting her.

4. Encourage other students to develop friendships with the student who frequently takes the role of scapegoat. (See the "Class Meeting Solution" in the entry on "Bothering Others" for an excellent example of how this may be done.)

5. Notice the number of times other students or staff members blame a certain student for starting trouble. If everyone believes that this student causes most problems, everyone immediately assumes he is guilty whenever difficulties arise. Help students and staff members make the shift from finger pointing to finding solutions.

6. Help the student shift his perception of himself. Encourage the development of social interest by inviting him to engage in tasks that help others. He could learn to be a tutor to younger children, a peer counselor, or a buddy to a new student.

7. Examine your own biases toward particular students. Discover whether those biases are encouraging the development of a scapegoat in your classroom.

Class Meeting Solution

During a second-grade class meeting at a school in San Bernardino, California, a visitor observed students working on solutions to four problems, three of which centered on a student named Phillip. The students' attitude was respectful and their suggestions were helpful, but the visitor wanted to check out Phillip's perceptions. She asked, "How do you feel about this, Phillip? Do you think that the students are helping you or ganging up on you?" Phillip grinned and said, "They're helping me!"

After school the teacher told the visitor, "Phillip used to be the scapegoat. All the students were angry at him and wanted him to be punished. Phillip is still the student who is most involved in problem situations, but now the kids really work hard to help him. The atmosphere in our classroom is totally different. Phillip is improving a little, but the other students have turned around completely in their attitude toward him."

Inspirational Story

Larson Elementary School's new principal, Mrs. Lopez, believed in giving people opportunities to change. Scott was a frequent visitor to her office. He was regularly reported for disrupting class, for spitting, for causing trouble in the lunchroom, and for taking other students' supplies.

Scott would shuffle into the same chair and scowl at the office clock on each visit to Mrs. Lopez's office. Mrs. Lopez recognized that punishing, threatening, and yelling at Scott hadn't changed his behavior.

During one of her talks with Scott, Mrs. Lopez told him that she had decided not to lecture him anymore and that she knew he was capable of dealing with the consequences of his choices. She expressed confidence that he would use his mistakes as a means to discover new options. She created a friendlier relationship with Scott by asking "what" and "how" questions: "What happened?" "What caused it to happen?" "How do you feel about what happened?" "What did you learn?" "How could you use what you learned in the future?" Mrs. Lopez listened carefully to his answers, giving Scott the experience of having his thoughts and ideas taken seriously. As often happens, she was surprised that he decided on some solutions that he had ignored when they came from her in the form of a lecture—and that he followed the solutions much more consistently when "he decided."

Mrs. Lopez also told Scott that she liked him. She laughed often when his marvelous sense of humor manifested itself. Recognizing Scott's creative ability, she enlisted him to work with her on the upcoming talent show and made it clear that she valued his help in coming up with ideas for the program. Whenever she saw Scott around school, her eyes twinkled as she greeted him. Gradually Scott started to see himself as a worthwhile part of the group rather than an outsider. He misbehaved less often and cooperated more.

Sex

Discussion

"It must be springtime," Alice sighs. Alice has taught school for six years, and as surely as the daffodils burst into color, her class of five- and six-year-olds heralds the season with playground games of boys-chase-girls or girls-chase-boys.

Mrs. Jones notices more of her high school students walking around holding hands and girls dissolving into tears because they've been rejected by the loves of their lives. She wonders how students can learn when they seem so preoccupied with sexual issues.

Long ago children who lived on farms learned about sex from raising animals and helping in the birthing process. Although little was said about sex, it was considered a natural part of life. Today a great deal of controversy exists in this country regarding sex education and its place in schools' curricula. Advocates say that teaching children about sex will help reduce the number of unwanted pregnancies, encourage abstinence, prevent sexually transmitted diseases (particularly AIDS), and curtail promiscuity. Those who believe that schools should not teach children about sex say that this subject is the responsibility of parents and not of the educational system. The ideal solution would be one that is respectful to those on both sides of this issue and that has the welfare of children as its main objective.

No matter how much adults wish to protect them, students are exposed to sexuality through magazine ads, billboards, television shows, and movies, as well as through the talk and behavior of fellow students. A parent may place her child in a private school known for its strictness and adherence to her personal value system. But what will happen when the student leaves the protected environment and enters the world (perhaps by going to college) without the skills to deal with the onslaught of different value systems and behaviors?

Through class meetings, students can experience the sense of belonging and contribution, learn the basic life skills for good character, and develop the skills necessary to deal respectfully with different value systems, while maintaining the integrity of what they believe or were taught in their homes. This can be done without ever

mentioning the word *sex* if your school isn't permitted to offer sex education.

Developing students' sense that they belong and can contribute is important in helping prevent teen pregnancy. The Children's Defense Fund, in its study of the influences that lead to teens getting pregnant, found that girls were having babies to feel a sense of belonging and importance in society.[26] Too often a girl decides that a baby will give her a person to love and a way to feel like an adult who has some control over her life.

In class meetings, students are given a chance to have power (through making decisions) and thus to have meaningful control over what happens to them. They are also given a chance to experience a healthy sense of belonging in the classroom system. During class meetings, students are taught mutual respect, which includes respect for themselves. When a student has developed strong self-respect, it's very difficult for other students to lead her into doing anything that could hurt her or go against her belief system.

During the class meeting process, students also learn decision-making and critical-thinking skills that equip them to deal with the many enticements of the media and peer pressure. In the teen years, students are in the process of forming their own moral codes. Without the aforementioned

---

26. Children's Defense Fund, *The State of America's Children Yearbook* (Washington, D.C., 1995), (800) CDF-1200.

skills, they may follow the promptings of others without considering the long-range consequences of their choices.

Suggestions

1. When a student's behavior is objectionable, talk with the student in private. Share your perceptions without lectures or humiliation. Simply state which actions were objectionable and why. Follow up on individual problems with appropriate classroom discussions to provide training for all students.

2. If a student complains to you about a sexual problem, use your own wisdom to decide whether the problem should be referred to a school counselor, whether the student should be given a choice about putting the problem on the class meeting agenda, or whether the student would like to use the Four Problem-Solving Steps (pages 44–45) to work on the problem with whomever else is involved.

Planning Ahead to Prevent Future Problems

1. Always address issues of gender discrimination. A chant of "No girls allowed" on the playground needs to elicit more than a tolerant smile from a teacher. Use individual conversations, class meetings, and group discussions to help students understand that exclusion is disrespectful, demeaning, and hurtful.

2. Learn about the normal sexual development of children as they grow. Use this knowledge to evaluate the appropriateness of interactions between students.

3. Involve parents, community groups, the medical community, and other educators in planning any course of study for sex education.

4. If parents and the teaching curriculum allow, actively teach (or invite a counselor or psychologist to teach) about sexual issues. The topics should include human reproduction, inappropriate touching, and sexual harassment. The latter topic is especially important for junior high and high school adolescents whose sensitivity and interest in sex are at an apex.

5. During class meetings, invite students to discuss ways to treat one another appropriately.

6. Use role play to allow students to experience the exclusion of a no-boys-allowed rule or related types of sexual discrimination. You may also want to explore the definition of sexual harassment through role playing.

7. Don't portray sex as bad. Explore the issues about inappropriate use of sex and sex roles in a way that allows students to draw their own conclusions. Look at TV commercials or magazine ads with upper elementary, middle, and high school students, and challenge them to discover whether sponsors are trying to manipulate viewers. This practice arms students to withstand

other manipulative pressures, such as peer pressure.

8. Initiate discussions on how sexuality is portrayed in the media. When a sexually charged movie is popular, ask students what they noticed in the movie and how they felt about these things. What messages about sexual behavior did this movie give them? Ask the same questions about TV shows. Conversations of this type give students an opportunity to thoughtfully evaluate what they've seen and to ask questions in a safe environment, while providing you with an opportunity to dispel misconceptions.

9. If you've been asked to teach a class or lead a student discussion on sex, practice talking about the topics involved with your peers to expand your own comfort zone. You want to be at ease when you engage in conversations about sex with your students.

Class Meeting Solutions

Boyfriends and Girlfriends

An item that came up on the class meeting agenda in Mr. Halston's sixth-grade class was "teasing about girlfriends and boyfriends." The boy who had put the problem on the agenda said that he would like to have a female friend who is really just a friend without being teased that anything else was involved other than just friendship. As the talking stick went around the circle, most of the students said they felt the same way. This class decided that they would en-

courage opposite-sex friendships and that they would stop teasing each other for it.

Peer Pressure

A class meeting was taking place in a Lifeskills Class at a public high school whose students came from homes with a range of value systems regarding sexual behavior. One of the girls in the class, Yvonne, had put on the agenda that her friends were pressuring her to lose her virginity. Both her female and male friends had been making fun of her. If she told her friends that she was having a bad day, they would reply that all she needed to do was get laid and she would feel better. Yvonne shared with the teacher and her classmates that it was getting harder not to give in to the pressure to be "like everybody else."

The teacher asked the students whether any of them had ever allowed themselves to be pressured into doing something they didn't really want to do. All of the students said that they had. Then the teacher shared a story about a butterfly in a cocoon. If anyone opened the cocoon before the butterfly forming inside was ready, it would die and never get to fly. The teacher used this example to illustrate how important it is for an individual to do things only when he or she is ready. The teacher went on to say that if outside pressure leads people to do things that they believe are wrong or that they don't want to do, then those individuals have hindered their own growth.

The students sat quietly for a while after the teacher finished speaking. Yvonne had tears in her eyes.

Nothing more was said on this subject until a few weeks later during appreciation time in this Lifeskills Class. Yvonne thanked the teacher for the butterfly illustration because it had given her courage to withstand the outside pressures. She also thanked her classmates for backing off from the topic of her virginity.

Shyness

Discussion

There is a difference between having a quiet, introverted manner and being shy. *Shyness* means a fear of behaving improperly or an uncertainty about how to express oneself, while *introversion* is a preference for inner reflection while processing information. Societies often try to dictate how a person should be. In the United States, outgoing behavior is valued over a reserved, reflective personality. By labeling students as shy, teachers limit the students' choices and often fail to value their uniqueness.

Some students will adopt the "shy" label and unconsciously use it to attain a goal. They may find a sense of belonging and significance by being "the shy one." Shy behavior may serve to bring them attention (even if they seem to retreat from it) or special service. Some students use shyness as a way to be left alone because they feel inadequate and want to avoid participation.

Suggestions

1. Accept that some students have soft voices, are less aggressive, and prefer small groups to large ones. If teachers believe that these qualities are less desirable, they are failing to respect different styles.

2. Don't speak for a student or try to coax him to contribute to a discussion. Have faith that he will enter in if and when he is ready. A child will usually give up a behavior when it no longer serves a purpose.

3. Avoid calling attention to self-conscious behavior. A common mistake is to believe

that you are being helpful by saying, "You're so quiet." This gives reinforcement to the student who wants undue attention and discourages the student who feels inadequate.

4. Let your student have his own relationships without you getting in the middle. As long as a student has established some friendships, don't create a problem where none exists. (For more ideas, refer to "Friendship Problems.")

5. Don't force a student into situations; allow him to take the lead. Be alert to subtle messages he may be sending you. His hesitant comments about an upcoming class play may indicate a readiness to be given a line or a small part.

Planning Ahead to Prevent Future Problems

1. Avoid telling students, parents, and other teachers that a certain student is shy. When you use labels, you reinforce the child's mistaken belief and discount her choice to make changes. (Refer to "Mistaken Goals [Hat Messages].")

2. Find out whether a student perceives her shy behavior as a problem. If she doesn't, accept her introverted style. If she does, ask how you might help her feel more comfortable around others. Create a list together of ideas and small steps for her to try. More and better skills will boost her confidence.

3. Don't let a student's shyness excuse her from participating in class projects. If a student is part of a group that must present its work to the entire class, encourage her by saying, "It's okay to feel uneasy, but you still have to explain a part of the project. Are there some ways I could help you feel more comfortable?"

4. Be sure that an item—such as a talking stick—that confers the opportunity to speak is passed around the circle during class meetings; all students should have a chance either to talk or to pass. A student who is less assertive about offering her comments will often speak up when the item is in her hands.

5. Provide nonthreatening opportunities for children to stand in front of the group and share information. Show-and-tell in the younger grades gives students comfortable access to the whole group. Older students may enjoy demonstrating a skill that doesn't require them to say much. Watching a classmate stir up a batch of brownies or show how to tie a fly for trout fishing is interesting to students and increases their esteem for the individual's talents. The familiarity of the task reduces the self-conscious student's anxiety in front of a large group.

Inspirational Story

Although his students held regular class meetings, Mr. Sheppard noticed that one student, James, never spoke during the compliments and appreciation time. The teacher was also aware that James was reluctant to speak, to ask questions, or to raise his hand during lessons.

One morning Mr. Sheppard spoke with James before the rest of the students arrived. He said, "I notice that you pass during compliments and appreciation time in our class meetings." He deliberately focused on this particular behavior, rather than overwhelming James with the numerous times he didn't contribute to discussions. Mr. Sheppard engaged James in a conversation and learned that he didn't speak up because he was afraid he wouldn't say things right or that people would laugh at him.

Mr. Sheppard had a couple of ideas that he thought might help James. One idea was for James to sit next to him during the meeting. Another was that James could practice giving a compliment right then.

James was willing to do both. He suggested a compliment and rehearsed it several times with Mr. Sheppard's encouragement. By taking one small step and experiencing success, James gained courage.

Later that day James offered an observation during the class science experiment. The next day he gave a student the compliment he had practiced with Mr. Sheppard. James's participation expanded through the rest of the semester.

Sickness and Feigned Sickness

Discussion

Most of us can remember at least one time when we were sick at school and felt too embarrassed to tell the teacher or feared he wouldn't believe us. Most of us can also remember a time when we claimed to be sick to avoid something or to get special attention.

Sometimes students claim illness because of fears or discouragement. They may be afraid of a bully or teasing or may be experiencing discouragement about their school progress.

Regardless of which scenario is being played out, don't dismiss the student's comments. If he isn't truly sick, you may find clues in what he says that lead you to the real problem and hence allow you to help him.

Suggestions

1. If a student says she doesn't feel well, take her seriously instead of assuming that she's trying to trick you. Listen to her, and validate her feelings. It is okay to make guesses about what you think might be going on. (See the "Inspirational Story.")

2. Whether a student is truly sick or not, trust your own feelings of concern. Get help from the school nurse, or talk directly to the parents.

3. If a student has a chronic illness or an allergy, take this as an opportunity to teach the whole class about the condition. In the process you will be developing the students' compassion.

4. If a student needs to take medication regularly, work with him so that he can take responsibility for the timing, dosage, and availability of his medicine.

5. If you suspect that your student is saying he's sick to avoid a class activity, explore the possibility in a nonthreatening way: "I don't know for sure, but I was wondering whether you're saying that you're sick so you won't have to do your oral presentation."

Planning Ahead to Prevent Future Problems

1. Invite your students to discuss the issue of feigned illness during a class meeting. Lead them into discussing why students do this and what they could do instead. Students often find courage through talking with other students who have felt the same way and who can brainstorm together about ways to solve the problem.

2. Be open to the idea of students occasionally needing "mental health days." Stresses at school or at home can overwhelm children. Allowing a student to take a day off will bring him relief and eliminate the need for him to pretend he's sick.

3. Encourage your students to say how they feel, and then take their feelings seriously. Teach them to say, "I'm feeling worried," instead of having to say, "I'm sick," to get help.

4. Let the class know that you don't make exceptions for students when work is due unless they explain the circumstances that made finishing their assignments impossible. Let your students know that they don't need to fear blame or shame when they talk with you. On the other hand, let them know that you're pretty clever about catching on to manipulation.

Inspirational Story

Ken, a sixth grader, was a regular visitor to the nurse's office on Tuesdays and Thursdays. He complained of stomachaches and headaches that occurred at eleven o'clock and were usually much better by the time lunch was over.

Miss Swingle, the school nurse, noticed the pattern quickly and decided to talk with Ken about what she was seeing. She was confident that he would arrive at her office on schedule the following week.

When he came in complaining of a severe headache, she treated him as she would normally. Then she sat down and said she had some ideas to share with him. "I don't know for sure," she said, "but I was wondering whether your headaches and stomachaches might be related to your band practice." Ken sat up and denied that there was any connection. Miss Swingle continued to express her curiosity as to how he felt about playing the trombone and being in the band. She also shared the story of a recent time when she had to give a presentation to the school district and felt sick to her stomach. She tried to call the superintendent to let him know that she couldn't be at the meeting. When she couldn't get through to him, she realized that she should say she was scared and overwhelmed rather than saying she was sick. This gave Ken food for thought. He wasn't used to hearing adults share their fears.

Ken was back in Miss Swingle's office the following week. He asked her some questions about how she knew the difference between when she was scared and when she was sick. As time went on, Miss Swingle was able to teach Ken to say how he felt instead of feigning sickness. Ken learned that acknowledging his emotions gave him the courage to feel his feelings and carry on. He stopped coming to Miss Swingle's office but would grin and hold his stomach whenever he saw her on the school grounds.

Skipping School/ Cutting

Discussion

Skipping classes is hardly a new phenomenon. As long as there have been teachers teaching, there have been students skipping classes. A student may skip school to stretch her wings, to avoid a peer with whom she's having problems, to join in the fun with schoolmates, or to avoid facing the consequences of not having prepared for a lesson or test. Often there are serious problems at home that a student has to deal with (e.g., chemically dependent parents, abuse, or money problems) but doesn't want others to know about. Rather than dismissing skipping school as typical student behavior, teachers should examine the belief behind the behavior as a basis for finding solutions (refer to "Mistaken Goals [Hat Messages]") or get help from a social worker or school counselor if you suspect there are home problems.

Suggestions

1. Don't take it personally. Remember that there are a multitude of reasons that stu-

dents skip classes. The part of this situation that you have control over is your own response. Avoid sarcasm, humiliation, and threats. Follow through with dignity and respect.

2. Find time to discuss the problem with the student who cuts your class. Ask "what" and "how" questions: "What were you trying to accomplish by skipping?" "What influenced you to cut?" "How do you feel about the consequences?" "What did you learn?" "How can I help?" "How can you use what you learned in the future?"

3. Consider whether the goal behind a student's cutting might be attention. If the behavior annoys you and the student stops temporarily when reminded of the school policy, the mistaken goal is probably undue attention. Let the school policy be the boss, and back away from additional involvement.

4. Consider whether the goal behind a student's cutting might be power. If you feel challenged or angered and the frequency of the behavior seems to be increasing, the mistaken goal is probably power. The student is saying, "You can't make me." Don't try to solve the problem at the moment the student reappears in your class. Let him know that you both need to cool off before talking about it. When you address the issue with him later, redirect his efforts so he can use his power constructively. Ask for his help and ideas. If he isn't ready to work with you, present him with a limited choice that fits within the boundaries of the school policy. Acknowledge the student's power and his right to make choices: "Won't it be interesting to see which choice you make about this?"

5. Consider whether the goal behind a student's cutting might be revenge. In this case you may feel hurt because you've tried so hard to encourage the student, or you may feel disgust and disbelief that the student seems to be hurting herself or others. Dealing with revenge calls for a challenging shift in attitude—moving from your own hurt feelings or disgust to empathy. Understand that you are dealing with someone who is hurt for some reason you may not understand. Maintain respect for her, and let her know that you like her. Share your concern that she may feel hurt, and ask whether she would like to talk about it. If she can't or doesn't want to discuss her feelings, ask whether she will listen while you make some guesses. If she agrees, mention anything you've done that may have offended her as well as any occurrence you observed in which her peers may have hurt her feelings. You might ask whether something going on at home is bothering her. (If she does talk about this and mentions some kind of abuse, tell her that you will need to report this to people who can help her.) Just knowing that you care may heal some hurt feelings, encourage her, and lead to a change in behavior. Another way to initiate a dialogue is to recount a personal story of a time when you felt hurt

and what you did as a result. This shows your empathy and helps the student feel less isolated.

6. Consider whether the goal behind a student's cutting might be to make you leave him alone. If you feel helpless and find yourself avoiding the student who cuts, the mistaken goal is probably assumed inadequacy. Look for one small enticement that might get him back on campus. Allow him to experience meaningful involvement by sharing one of his skills with classmates or by learning to tutor younger students. You may need to arrange for testing to detect learning problems that require special intervention. Take small steps that show your faith in him and offer encouragement.

Planning Ahead to Prevent Future Problems

1. Talk to your students about the most recent school policies on skipping classes. Involve them in a discussion of these policies. Let them present their ideas about the reasons for the school's rules and procedures as well as about how they can succeed in following the rules.

2. Implement the school policy with dignity and respect for all. Follow through consistently. Don't overlook infractions by "good" students, and don't pounce on those you think of as troublemakers.

Inspirational Story

Ms. Ventnor, a history teacher, had explained her own policy as well as the school policy on cutting classes to her incoming students. Because a large part of her class involved experiential activities, she made it clear that class participation and attendance were the keys to success.

Adam, a bright, charismatic, popular student, was used to being casual about his class attendance. Especially since turning eighteen, he had figured that he could do what he wanted to do. He listened to Ms. Ventnor's speech and decided that it didn't apply to him.

Adam skipped one class with no consequences. This gave him a feeling of power and freedom. He decided that it would work out for him not to attend class on Fridays, so he could get an early start on his weekends. The second time Adam cut her class, Ms. Ventnor asked to speak with him privately. Her concern was that Adam was unaware of her policy. She asked him to explain his understanding of the consequences of cutting. He acknowledged that, in addition to the school's enforcement of detention for skipping class, he knew that his grade in her class would be affected after the next cut.

Adam nonchalantly chose to cut class the next two Friday afternoons. Ms. Ventnor followed through by lowering his grade for the quarter. He was surprised and came to her, hoping for a chance to do some extra-credit work to make up for the skips.

Ms. Ventnor stuck to her policy. She told him that she was aware that he did exceptional work when he was in class and that he knew what the consequences were for cutting. In a kind tone, she added that it would be interesting to see how he decided to handle this next quarter.

Because Ms. Ventnor was kind and straightforward, Adam couldn't justify being mad at her. He realized that she meant what she said and that he couldn't con her into letting him break the rules. He wanted a better grade, so he stopped skipping Ms. Ventnor's class.

Sloppiness

Discussion

What seems sloppy to one person may seem perfectly acceptable to another. Looking at teachers' desks, you'll see that some are neat and some are messy. People have different styles.

It doesn't help for teachers to become angry or frustrated when a student's appearance, schoolwork (including handwriting), or work space is below their standards. It also doesn't help for teachers to punish the student or be permissive and tidy up after her. It does help when teachers avoid humiliation, take time for training, and teach

the skills each student needs. Find ways to encourage the student's efforts. Rejoice over improvement rather than bemoaning anything less than perfection.

Suggestions

1. Speak with the student about your concerns and how his messiness is a problem for you. You might say, "I'm having trouble reading this paper. When a student gives me a paper that's difficult to read because of erasures, ripped edges, and illegible writing, I feel discouraged because I can't correct it or help you with your work."

2. Discuss with the student how messiness may be a problem for him. If he has difficulty recognizing the problem, ask questions such as, "What happens when you try to reread your papers?" and "How do you feel when you can't find something in your desk or your notebook?" The idea is to help the student reach conclusions that have meaning for him instead of giving him a lecture.

3. Notice improvement and comment on it. Let the student know that you appreciate her efforts and that it was much easier for you to read her last assignment.

4. Be open to other ways to master a task. Modern technology makes it possible to succeed in a variety of ways. A student with poor and labored handwriting needs to learn computer keyboarding. This skill is just as valuable for long-range success as precise penmanship.

Planning Ahead to Prevent Future Problems

1. Don't tell other teachers, students, or parents that a student is sloppy. Using labels reinforces an image and limits the person's ability to make changes.

2. Help your students create a list of qualities that both you and they think are important in work that will be read by others. Post this list of classroom standards as a reminder to students, and then let the list become the boss. When a student falls short of a standard, refer to the list, asking, "What was our agreement?" and "What do you need to do to meet the standard?"

3. Establish regular times for the entire class to clean up. Ask a student who has trouble keeping her things in order whether she would like help from you or from another classmate. (Refer to "Cleanup.")

4. If your school has a dress code, make sure that all students and their families are clear about its provisions. Allow time for students to ask questions and express dissent. Even if the code cannot be changed, a chance to voice their opinions will make adhering to the policy less distasteful. Discuss why a dress code might be important, and invite them to discuss what they can do to cooperate.

5. When a problem occurs, use it as an opportunity for more learning. Have a class meeting in which students can discuss the problem and work on solutions.

Class Meeting Solution

Every time Martha opened her desk, papers fell out onto the floor. She was constantly losing her compositions and notes on lessons.

She asked for help in a class meeting. She was encouraged to learn that she wasn't the only one who lost papers. After a discussion and brainstorming to produce a list of suggestions, Martha selected the idea that she believed would help her most: she would choose a buddy, and the two of them would take turns cleaning out each other's desks twice a week.

The teacher checked in with Martha during the next class meeting. Martha reported that she felt happier with how her desk was organized and less nervous about losing things.

Cautionary Story

A high school in south Texas instituted a strict dress code without involving any of the students in the decision-making process. The administrators and the rest of the staff felt the students had become sloppy about their appearance. The adults saw sloppiness as disrespect. They also felt that, despite the heat and the fact that the students walked outside on breezeways to reach their classes, the wearing of shorts should be prohibited. Until this decision was made, students had been allowed to wear knee-length shorts.

During the summer, students from other high schools had attended summer school at this particular high school. These students had worn torn and sloppy clothes, and the girls had worn very short shorts.

The year-round students felt it was unfair of the administration to penalize them with a dress code that they believed was a reaction to students from other schools.

Students in a history class at this school discussed the dress code in a class meeting. The students expressed frustration, anger, and even a desire for revenge. One of their suggestions for bringing about a change was for the students to picket and invite the attention of the news media. However, after further discussion, the students decided that the administration might feel threatened by this and consequently dig in its heels. One student pointed out that the new dress code didn't prohibit miniskirts, which were less modest than the shorts they were previously allowed to wear.

The history teacher suggested that the students look at what people had done in the past when trying to amend a law that they found unfair. Petitions were suggested, as well as presenting a proposal verbally and in writing to the administration and staff to request that they and an elected group of students review the new dress code. Some students suggested that they role-play different ways to present this proposal, so that they could practice and experience what it might be like to hear this request as adults.

The students decided to try all the suggestions except for the picketing, which they would save for possible use at a later date. When the students and teacher evaluated the session, they were amazed at how working on a goal together had eliminated their frustration. They felt hopeful and capable of making a positive difference. The anger and revenge had been replaced by constructive action.

This story doesn't have a happy ending. The administration was unwilling to give the students a voice and refused to listen to their suggestions. These administrators were poor role models for their students. The adults didn't perceive the disrespect they were modeling in trying to control the students, nor did the adults realize that the students *were* behaving respectfully.

Special Needs/ Inclusion

(see also "Abuse," "Discouraged [Dysfunctional] Families," and "Attention Deficit Disorder [ADD] and Attention Deficit with Hyperactivity Disorder [ADHD]")

Discussion

"Alice needs her asthma treatment after lunch." "Be sure to pack the antihistamine when taking Jane on a field trip. She's severely allergic to bee stings." The details of students' health problems can take up much of a teacher's time. A student whose behavior continually impedes lessons may turn out to have a hearing problem or a condition such as attention deficit disorder.

Other special needs include problems that aren't related to health. Difficulties may be primarily emotional or academic: Sam's parents separated last night, and he is feeling very scared. Evan cannot sit still or concentrate even for short periods.

Matthew has a bruise on his cheek from a beating his dad gave him over the weekend.

Teachers have to deal with many problems for which they received no training in college. With the mainstreaming of students who have special needs into regular school classes, teachers now have students in their classrooms who used to be in resource or special education classes. Teachers are burning out from all the extra demands.

Of course, it would be lots easier to have a class filled with calm, even-tempered, thriving students. In today's world, however, that possibility is less likely than ever before. The beauty of using class meetings is that the teacher isn't alone in dealing with all the problems. The class meeting process involves the whole class in awareness of and respect for differences. Students can develop empathy and tolerance, and they can learn what it takes to help everyone feel included.

Suggestions

1. Give up the vision of the perfect class. It doesn't exist. There will always be some

students who need extra help. Helping a student with special needs of any kind is an opportunity for you and your students to grow personally and to affect another life positively. Classmates of students with special needs learn compassion and have many chances to practice social interest.

2. If teasing is a problem, ask those involved to put this problem on the agenda at the time of conflict. This is enough to interrupt the immediate conflict. It is usually best to wait until tempers have cooled and feelings have calmed before addressing the issue. During the class meeting, have students role-play teasing with many of them taking a turn playing the person being teased. After processing the role play by asking the players to share their feelings, invite all the students to discuss what they learned from being in the role play or from watching. Then ask for their suggestions about what to do to solve this problem in the future.

3. Most problems can be avoided through planning ahead to prevent future problems.

Planning Ahead to Prevent Future Problems

1. Educate students about all kinds of special needs. What is understood is no longer feared.

2. Welcome all students into the classroom, whatever their needs. Classroom jobs can include a committee of two (rotating every week) who stand at the door to greet every student who enters the room before each class.

3. Meet with a student privately to ask whether she is finding something particularly difficult about being in school. One fourth-grade student, who had undergone surgery that resulted in her needing to use a colostomy bag, simply wanted permission to use the faculty bathroom for privacy. Once she was reassured on this point, she happily returned to school.

4. After obtaining the student's permission, discuss her special needs with the class and ask how her classmates can offer her their support and encouragement.

5. Sometimes it's appropriate to involve the class in a discussion about a student who isn't present. When a student is absent due to surgery, for example, the discussion is likely to take place in his absence. Remember, one of the purposes of class meetings is to help one another. The students can create a plan for helping the student who returns to class with special needs.

6. A student behaves the way he does for a reason. It's very important to keep this in mind. You can sometimes discover the reason for the behavior by using the Mistaken Goal Chart (pages 12–13). Other times you can learn the reason by getting more information from parents or through careful classroom observation and

documentation. Special needs can also be identified through the use of referrals to specialized professionals or by inviting the school nurse into your class to observe a student.

7. Use role plays and special activities to help students understand the experiences of a person with a particular need. For example, a teacher wanted to help the students in his classroom respond more thoughtfully to a boy's mother who used a cane because she had lost her vision. The teacher set up an activity in which students paired up and then one student put on a blindfold and his partner guided him around the classroom. In another setting, to simulate the experience of a person who has no use of her hands, students taped a pencil onto a tongue depressor and attempted to write while holding the tongue depressor in their mouths. Such activities increase understanding and empathy, eliciting more considerate responses to others.

8. Have all students make a list of things they are good at doing. Then have them all make a list of things that they find difficult. Point out that everyone has strengths and weaknesses. Students with special needs simply need help in ways that other students don't. They can also benefit from learning the skill of being able to advocate for themselves.

9. Demonstrate compassion by creating an atmosphere of respect for each student's needs. Don't label students as bad, sickly, or problem kids. Each student simply has a different set of needs.

10. Be sure that each student is offered what he needs. Sometimes identifying a student's special needs takes considerable effort on the teacher's part. This effort includes receiving additional training to understand a variety of special needs, using the resources available within the school and through community or private agencies and individuals, as well as maintaining an attitude of flexibility. Moreover, don't underestimate the excellent resources you have in your classroom—your students. The help they give each other can be more effective than help from any adult or agency.

Inspirational Story

From the time Maria entered kindergarten at Calk Elementary, she was the butt of other students' jokes and put-downs. They shunned her because she had no hygiene skills, was infested with lice, and wore the same clothes every day. Periodically sent home because of the lice, she would be absent for a week and come back with a shaved head. This produced more cruel teasing and isolation.

Maria would remain in school until she got lice again (which was about every three weeks), and then she would have to go home. Everyone could hear her screaming as she was dragged to the principal's office to be sent home. Maria missed a great deal of school this way and was miserable while she was there because none of the students or teachers wanted to be around her. As if grubbiness and parasites weren't enough, Maria also had poor social skills and was often disruptive.

Then Maria entered Ms. Owen's class. The first thing this teacher did was visit Maria's home. The school personnel had told Ms. Owen that Maria's parents didn't care about the problem, but this turned out not to be the case.

Maria's family was living in a small house with no hot water. They had very little money. There were five kids, and Maria's mother wasn't a United States citizen, so she didn't know how to get financial help. The family barely had enough food and certainly didn't have the money to buy the lice shampoo or to do what was necessary to delouse the entire house. Clothes were rarely washed because there was little money for soap and the laundromat. Maria's mom was overwhelmed and lacked the resources to overcome her situation.

Ms. Owen received Maria's and her family's permission to talk to the class about Maria's situation during a class meeting. Maria wasn't there. She was absent again because of the lice.

Ms. Owen told the class that she had saved some money to buy Maria some new clothes and lice shampoo. The teacher had also secured permission for Maria to wash every day at school and put on clean clothes. Ms. Owen asked the students what they could do to help. The children had many suggestions: some said they would include her more in their games, others would invite her to sit with them at lunch, and some of the girls offered to bring extra hair ribbons and clothes they didn't need. Soon, instead of being the class outcast, Maria was its Cinderella.

Maria was now hearing warm compliments and encouragements at class meetings. As she felt more accepted and developed a sense of belonging, her behavior improved, and her classmates found even more things to encourage her about. When she entered the room each morning, the whole class would ooh and aah at how nice she looked, which encouraged her to continue attending to her personal hygiene. In addition, the word spread through the school, and children from other classes began to offer clothes they had outgrown. Some of the older girls came to school early to fix Maria's hair in pretty styles.

Helping Maria had become the common goal of Ms. Owen's class. The students were treating one another more thoughtfully as a result, and behavior problems began to disappear. The amount of time spent on learning increased.

Dealing with Maria's special needs thus developed social interest in all the children. They learned that giving encouragement to others is encouraging to the giver.

Spitting

Discussion

When someone starts to yell angrily, responses vary: one child bristles; another cowers; a third yells back. But when someone spits, the instinctive response is to recoil. There is something more primitive about spitting. In many cultures, spitting at someone is a sign of mortal enmity. Given our strong feelings about spitting, dealing with it in the school setting is especially difficult.

It's important to keep in mind, however, that spitting was an acceptable habit in American society for a long time, especially during the period when gentlemen commonly chewed tobacco. Many homes and places of business provided a cuspidor or spittoon. The key here was that people who needed or wanted to spit had appropriate places to do so, making the situation respectful to the needs of all.

These days, as in years past, boys may try to outspit each other. They may spit on the ground as if it were a rite of passage into manhood or a way to mark their territory. Furthermore, spitting can be simply a bad habit that a child acquired by imitating someone he admires—a father, an older brother, a friend, or a hero.

The practice of spitting frequently, which annoys some teachers, usually starts off innocently and gradually becomes an irresistible impulse as the student is reminded a thousand times not to do it. Students don't plan bad habits to keep adults busy with them, but they are willing to play that game when an adult starts it. If a student likes the powerful feeling she gets from the adult's reaction, the student is more likely to continue her behavior. The more we remind, nag, and suggest, the worse the habit gets.

Although spitting may be a habit, it can also be a way for a student to show that he is in control and doesn't have to follow rules. A student who feels hurt may use spitting as a way to show disrespect and thus hurt others. A student who wants to be left alone may use spitting to keep others away from her. Whatever the individual's purpose, the problem provides students and teachers with an opportunity to learn and seek solutions.

Suggestions

1. Recognize your own deep-seated reaction to spitting, and make a conscious attempt to look at the situation from either a historical or a psychological perspective. When third grader Mary spits at fifth graders, she is probably just trying to make them pay attention to her. (It is unlikely that she is declaring them to be her tribe's most despised adversaries.) Remember that overreacting to spitting may only increase its incidence, while discovering the underlying problem creates opportunities to get students involved in problem solving and to teach important life skills.

2. Spitting could be related to physical problems. Ask the student's parents whether

there is a physical reason their child needs to spit.

3. Don't get hooked by the repulsiveness of the behavior, and don't draw undue attention to it. Hand the student a tissue, and say kindly and firmly, "I would appreciate it if you would use this. If you need more, they are on my desk."

4. Respectfully ask a student who has spit on the playground blacktop or sidewalk to get a hose or bucket of water and rinse the spit from the area.

5. Let students know that some behaviors are appropriate in certain settings and not in others. Spitting into a toilet is appropriate. Spitting on floors or grounds where people walk is not appropriate.

6. Let the consequences of a student's behavior among his peers take effect. Often students will let a classmate know that spitting bothers them by saying, "That's gross!" and walking away or by avoiding the student who spits.

Planning Ahead to Prevent Future Problems

1. Young children have fairly primitive responses and behaviors. If they spit, try not to take it personally. Remember, you are the adult and have supposedly outgrown your need to engage in tribal warfare. Model self-control.

2. Use the Mistaken Goal Chart (see pages 12–13) to identify the student's reason for

spitting. Encourage your student by helping him develop a plan that involves stopping himself when he wants to spit, thinking about what he could do instead to express his feelings, and then acting with respect.

3. Talk about spitting in a class meeting. You might want to bring in a real spittoon for students to see or show a movie in which the characters use spittoons. Let the students have fun with the topic; invite them to talk about situations in which spitting is part of the scene. Have them discuss how spitting affects other people.

4. Have your students brainstorm for solutions that are respectful to people and property. During the cold season, many children are coughing up phlegm and may need to spit into tissues. Suggestions for dealing with this might include providing a covered trash container for disposing of tissues, attaching a small plastic bag inside a child's desk to gather used tissues, or authorizing all students to get up and take a tissue from the box at any time without asking permission.

Class Meeting Solution

A group of third-grade girls put the subject of spitting on their class meeting agenda. They thought spitting was gross and wanted to let several boys in their class know how disgusted they were. Their teacher, Mrs. Sanchez, said that a first step in solving a problem might be to discuss people's thoughts and feelings about it. The girls agreed. Mrs. Sanchez guided the discussion by asking questions that helped draw out the students' attitudes about spitting.

After a general discussion and lots of laughter, it became clear that while the students thought that spitting might be appropriate in some situations, they did not think it was acceptable in the schoolyard. The students decided to check back with one another in a week to see whether simply discussing spitting had solved the problem.

During a class meeting the following week, the girls who had put the problem on the agenda admitted they had not witnessed any spitting since their discussion. They decided they didn't need to brainstorm for solutions because spitting was no longer an issue in their class.

Sportsmanship

Discussion

"Who cares about some stupid ball game, anyway?" "You're all a bunch of cheaters!" Students who feel unimportant often display poor sportsmanship. All children want to be included, but discouraged children may deal with their feelings in ways that push others away and eventually lead to exclusion from group activities. It may be-

come a vicious cycle. The student wants to belong, acts obnoxious, is excluded, and acts more obnoxious. However, this isn't the only reason for poor sportsmanship.

Oldest children may be poor sports because they have difficulty not being the first or the best in a group. Middle children may be poor sports because they feel others treat them unfairly. Youngest children may be poor sports because their fellow students don't pamper them.

Some students simply haven't learned social interest or the skills of good sportsmanship. This could be because adults emphasize competition instead of teaching students to do their best and enjoy the game.

Rather than labeling a student as a poor sport, focus on his poor sportsmanship as a behavior that can change. Scolding, threatening, and punishing deal only with the problem's symptoms and are disrespectful to the person with the problem. It's far more helpful to use nonpunitive methods that teach the attitudes and skills of good sportsmanship and that allow the student to develop a sense of belonging that doesn't depend on winning or performance.

Suggestions

1. When a student complains that the teams weren't fair or that her team shouldn't have lost, listen and validate her feelings without fixing the situation: "You sound really disappointed that you lost the game."

2. Don't overprotect students by trying to make everything fair. Allow them to experience disappointment without interference.

3. Show faith that a student will learn how to experience disappointment with grace. Don't demand immediate change, but encourage improvement.

4. Tell your students about times when you handled disappointment successfully and unsuccessfully. This shows empathy and gives them a role model.

5. Part of good sportsmanship is being a gracious winner. Model and teach how to celebrate good fortune without putting others down.

Planning Ahead to Prevent Future Problems

1. Some students believe that they belong and are important only if they are the best and the first. This belief is confirmed in a competitive atmosphere where prizes and praise go to the winner. Teachers can create a cooperative atmosphere where effort and enjoyment are more important than winning.

2. Use the class meeting as a forum for the students' discussion of good sportsmanship. Encourage a thoughtful dialogue by asking such questions as these: "How do you feel about participating in games?" "How do you think others would feel about playing if they always lost?" "What can you do to enjoy a game whether you lose or win?" "What do you think it means to be a good sport?" "How do you feel about unsportsmanlike behavior?" "What are you deciding about yourself when you lose a game?"

3. Have fun playing cooperative games with your students. Cooperative games have no winners or losers. (Check your library and bookstores for resources on cooperative games.)

4. Watch the Olympic Games and other sporting events with your students. Pay special attention to the attitudes of competitors who don't win. Acknowledge the athlete's disappointment; then invite students to discuss whether she lost graciously, with respect for her opponent and without anger for herself or teammates.

Class Meeting Solution

A story from Bill Scott, principal, Birney Elementary School, Marietta, Georgia

Jimmy was making rude comments and taunting other students when they made mistakes while playing four-square. Someone put the problem on the class meeting agenda.

The students told Jimmy that his comments hurt their feelings and made them not want to play with him. They suggested things he could say to encourage people instead of hurting them.

Jimmy agreed to try this new skill and eventually stopped his offensive behavior. In later class meetings, his classmates began to give him compliments for his good sportsmanship.

Cautionary Story

Many years ago *Reader's Digest* published an article about a very encouraging Little League coach. He didn't stress winning but encouraged his players to do their best and to enjoy the game. He made sure every child had an opportunity to play in every game. They lost every game, but they had a good time. The parents appreciated the coach's efforts to help their children feel good about themselves and the game, and they often went together for pizza or ice cream after the games. Everyone felt good.

However, the coach's encouragement started to pay off. The kids gained confidence and skills and started to win games. The parents started yelling from the sidelines—encouragement when things went well and disappointment when mistakes were made. The kids started feeling good only when they won and would complain when the coach put the less skilled players into the game.

The coach finished out the season, but then he quit. He did not enjoy the poor sportsmanship that evolved when competition became more important than cooperation and encouragement.

Stealing

Discussion

One of the main reasons children steal is because they feel hurt. If a child takes something of yours, he may be feeling hurt because he thinks he doesn't get enough of your attention—which makes him want *something* from you. If a child feels hurt because she doesn't have friends, she may try to fill that void by stealing things. If a child feels hurt from financial deprivation, he may steal in response to society's materialistic message that people shouldn't have to wait for the things they want, regardless of other people's feelings. Or children who steal may simply not have developed the social interest, communication skills, and problem-solving skills that would prevent them from resorting to theft.

The type of stealing engaged in by kindergarten children is another matter. Stealing at this age is often part of a developmental transition. As a child loses her ego-centric outlook, she learns that not everything belongs to her. She is also trying to make sense of what she observes. If it's okay to eat the food samples in the grocery store, what's wrong with helping yourself to other things in stores? Adults need to respond with clear messages about property ownership. When the child takes something, they need to help her find ways to make recompense. If they do this with kindness rather than blame, the child learns important new skills without feeling ashamed.

Suggestions

1. When something is stolen, share with the class how this makes you feel.

2. Give students opportunities to share their feelings about the theft—emphasizing that this is not a time for blame but simply a discussion about how it makes you feel.

3. Give the student a chance to return what she took by saying, "We aren't interested in blame; we just want the item to be replaced. We trust that this will be done before the end of the day."

4. Invite students to brainstorm about how they can encourage someone who is discouraged enough to steal. Does this person need friends? Does he need opportunities to contribute? Does he need help figuring out how to get what he wants without stealing? This kind of discussion can be enlightening to children who steal. The students can follow up by finding ways to implement their ideas; for example, they can discuss how to be a helpful friend to someone in need of encouragement.

5. Don't ask setup questions. "Did you steal this?" invites a lie or some other defensive behavior. If you're positive you know who stole something, you might say, "I know you took a wristwatch that didn't belong to you, and I would like to work respectfully on some solutions with you." Another possibility is to say, "This doesn't belong to you. Would you like to put it where it belongs, or would you like me to?" (Putting it this way is especially helpful with young children.)

6. Ask "what" and "how" questions either of the student who stole something or of the whole class: "What happened?" "What do you think caused that to happen?" "How do you feel about it?" "What did you learn from it?" "How can you use what you learned in the future?" "What can you do now to solve the problem?"

7. Invite the student who stole something to figure out a way to make restitution that is respectful to himself and to the person from whom he stole.

Planning Ahead to Prevent Future Problems

1. Remember that a misbehaving child is a discouraged child. Dealing with a student's hurt feelings will help prevent future problems more than any kind of punishment.

2. Focus on helping and solutions instead of blame, shame, and pain.

3. You can prevent many problems through a class discussion of stealing as well as by teaching students to ask for what they want, to express their feelings, and to help one another.

4. Remember that stealing doesn't define a person, turning her into "a thief." Stealing is something a person does. And behavior can be changed.

Class Meeting Solutions

A Lasting Solution

A lot of thefts were taking place in a third-grade classroom. The problem was discussed during a class meeting. Prompted by the teacher, the students decided to forget about trying to find out who was stealing and to focus instead on how they could discourage stealing. They brainstormed to produce the following ideas: (1) Don't bring valuables to school. (2) Lock the classroom door during recess and lunch. (3) Take turns being a security monitor for a day.

The students tried the first and second suggestions, and the thievery stopped. They didn't know whether the problem was solved by the solutions they chose or simply because their discussion had made the person who was stealing more aware of how his behavior affected others.

A Speedy Solution

During a class meeting, the first graders discussed the problem of an item that had been stolen from the teacher's desk. A little girl made the following suggestion: Why don't we all leave the room? Then we can go back in and out one at a time. The person who stole the item can put it back, and no one has to know who did it." The class decided to try this, and it worked. The item was replaced. The problem was solved with dignity and respect for all concerned—and nothing else was stolen that year.

Substitute Teachers

Discussion

An outsider taking over a class can bring out the worst in students. They forget or don't consider the fact that substitute teachers are people with feelings. Students often treat substitutes as fair game to tease, trick, and torment. Even elementary school

students, following the example of older students, will drop their books again and again, switch names and seats, and make rude comments.

However, when students are challenged to think of substitutes as people with feelings and asked to treat them as such, the students will usually behave respectfully, helpfully, and kindly. By doing some advance planning with students and inviting them to exercise their power in positive ways, misbehavior ceases and chaos diminishes. In the process, students strengthen their interpersonal skills, practice taking leadership roles, and develop their social interest.

Suggestions

1. Most problems can be eliminated if you follow the steps outlined in "Planning Ahead."

2. Once students have participated in the role playing and problem solving discussed in "Planning Ahead," assign a student to explain the process to the substitute and then facilitate the meeting. (If they are familiar with the class meeting process, this is extremely effective.)

3. When a substitute lets you know that she enjoyed your class, make sure you share the specific compliment or appreciative remark with your students.

4. Ask for your students' feedback on the substitute. Spend some time listening to

their experiences, and be ready to assist with solving any problems that occurred. This keeps them involved in the process of working cooperatively with substitutes.

5. Make time during a class meeting for students to give each other compliments or appreciations about specific things they did to help the substitute.

6. If you have to deal with a student who has been discourteous to a substitute, share your own feelings respectfully, and ask for help in rectifying the situation.

Planning Ahead to Prevent Future Problems

1. Use class meetings to discuss what happens when a substitute teacher comes into a classroom. Ask, "What do students like to do to annoy a sub?" List students' ideas on the blackboard. Then ask, "How do you think substitutes feel when students do these things?" Again, record their ideas.

2. Role-play some of the ways students annoy and deceive substitute teachers, allowing students to take turns playing the substitute. They can also role-play solutions to the problems that are created. Doing this gives them a vivid picture of what is going on.

3. Now ask students how they think the substitute feels when being treated this way. Usually, students have simply not thought about the substitute's feelings.

4. Ask students how many of them are willing to be helpful instead of hurtful when they have a substitute. Have them brainstorm to make a list of ways to help. Write all their ideas down, and ask for volunteers to make a chart of these ideas that can be posted in the classroom. They might want to title the chart "How to Encourage Our Substitute."

5. Appoint student assistants for each academic subject as well as for lunch, recesses, and any assemblies. Let the students brainstorm to create a list of things the assistants could do to be helpful to the substitute. Provide the substitute with a list of the student helpers and a copy of the class's list of suggestions.

6. Try to let your students know when you aren't going to be in class. This gives them a chance to ask questions about where you'll be and to make constructive plans for how they will behave, work, and organize themselves while you're gone.

7. Invite your students to look at having a substitute as an opportunity to work together in a new situation. Tell them you have faith that they will handle the event respectfully.

8. When a long-term substitute is scheduled, arrange time for students to get to know the substitute and to interact with him in positive ways. Involve your students in planning the substitute's preliminary visit. They can write interview questions, plan a group activity, or prepare a list of some special features about the classroom.

9. Involve your long-term substitute in the class meeting process. Share information with him about how you use class meetings to enhance the atmosphere in your classroom.

10. Be aware that substitutes often feel left out and isolated from other teachers and members of the school staff. During a faculty meeting, discuss the problem and get everyone involved in finding solutions.

Inspirational Stories

A Quick Fix

Mrs. Julian was substituting in a fourth-grade class. She was writing an assignment on the board with her back to the room when she suddenly heard a loud bang. Startled, she turned around to see grinning faces and lots of books on the floor. The students had participated in an organized "book drop."

Mrs. Julian was a quick thinker. She hurriedly grabbed a book from her desk, dropped it, and said, "Sorry I'm late." The students laughed, and they treated Mrs. Julian with respect from that moment on.

A Long-Term Change

A kindergarten teacher was soon to go on maternity leave. She had been preparing her students in many ways for her three-month absence. She invited the substitute to come into the classroom for a getting-to-know-you session. The students planned and prepared for this encounter during their class meetings. They came up with a list of questions to ask the substitute and planned a game to play when she came to visit.

One of their concerns was that she wouldn't know their names. They decided to make a book for her with their pictures and names in it so that she could get to know their faces. When the time came for her to take over, she was part of their world and they were part of hers.

Taking Turns

Discussion

"Who gets to be first in line?" "How long before I get a turn on the computer?" "She's hogging the swing!" "I had my hand up. How come I didn't get called on?"

King Solomon himself would cringe at all the situations in which teachers are asked to make fair decisions. The logistics of having a group of children doing things together involves apportioning limited resources. From time, space, and classroom materials to privileges, special tasks, and attention, resources must be shared by many users. To cope with this situation, most teachers have children take turns.

The practice of taking turns teaches students about fairness, mutual respect, co-operation, impulse control, and the everyday realities of group dynamics. There are countless strategies for managing turn taking, but the most important point to remember is that children will cooperate when they have participated in determining the rules about when and how they will take turns.

Suggestions

1. Get rid of your "fair button." Kids seems to know when they can push this button, and they will work it for all it is worth.

2. Use reflective listening. "You don't think this is fair? You are upset." After you have listened, you might ask, "What ideas do you have about how to solve this?" If the student doesn't have a clue, you might suggest, "How about putting this on the class meeting agenda?"

3. Taking turns is an ongoing process. Discuss problems as they arise. Place a new problem on the class agenda, and work out a solution together.

4. Don't take sides in a dispute. When two children argue over materials or a privilege, treat them the same way. Send both to the end of the line rather than trying to determine who got to the front of the line first. Even better, invite the children involved to work out a solution that they both find acceptable.

Planning Ahead to Prevent Future Problems

1. Help your students identify situations in which they will need to take turns. What does your class particularly prize? If getting to sit next to the teacher during class meetings is the Holy Grail of seating locations in your room, the class might come up with a rotation that allots these seats to two different children each meeting. If another group of children feels that staying in to help the teacher during recess is better than winning the lottery, a sign-up sheet may be the best way to ensure that each child who wants to help gets his or her turn.

2. With your students, agree on expectations for the use of certain high-demand items. The classroom with only one computer might decide to establish a time limit of twenty minutes per person.

3. Consider using a deck of playing cards on which students' names have been written. These cards can be used to randomly pick students for activities until the entire deck has been used.

4. Consider providing a limited number of certain desirable items, so that children have to learn to use them cooperatively. Place only three puzzles on the "free time" shelf, and your students will either work together in small groups or devise a way to take turns.

5. Teach children that the quantity of any resource is limited. Through this discussion, you can introduce topics such as crop rotation, soil depletion, water conservation, and recycling, or the effects of famine on the world or discrete populations.

6. Congratulate children when they are taking turns peacefully. Be sure to recognize the types of behavior that you want to encourage. (See the discussion of encouragement vs. praise in "Encouragement.")

7. On the list of classroom jobs, include that of monitoring turn taking. The child who has this job may be responsible for keeping track of who gets to put the number for the day's date onto the calendar each morning, which reading group presents stories first, or whose day it is to carry the attendance report to the office.

8. Encourage impulse control by explaining that you will not call on children who leap out of their seats to volunteer first, who yell, "Me! Me! Me!" or who wave their hands wildly.

9. Don't forget the power of discussion to increase awareness and cooperation. During class meetings, discuss issues of space (some people need a lot; some prefer less,

and others don't care); how people feel when they aren't chosen for a special project; or how people react when time runs out before everyone gets a turn. Awareness solves many problems.

Class Meeting Solution

A story from Trilby Cohen, second-grade teacher, Syre Elementary School, Shoreline, Washington

My second graders spent lots of time working on disagreements about taking turns. Worn out by the daily squabbles, I presented the basic problem in their class meeting. The children discussed the issue and came up with the idea of the "fair shake" can.

They would write each child's name on a slip of paper and place it in the can. Whenever they had to make a decision about who would get a turn, a child would draw the name of a classmate from the can. The child whose name was drawn would get a turn. The frenzy over turns quieted with the advent of this system.

Later in the year, daily disputes over where children got to stand in line began erupting into crises. Again, the agenda filled with variations on this difficulty.

It soon became clear that the children didn't care about the position they held in line so much as they cared about standing near their friends. One child wanted to stand next to her best friend, who wanted to stand beside another child, who wanted to stand next to someone else, and so on.

With a better understanding of the real issue, the class proposed lining up in two parallel lines instead of a single line. This plan doubled the number of friends near whom each child might stand.

The next day, the children formed two lines. The agitation, ruckus, and place saving stopped immediately. I was delighted with the children's simple, creative, and effective solution.

Talking Too Much

Discussion

People who love to talk come in all age groups. Sometimes teachers find their chattering students delightful. Perhaps, for example, you know a Megan: *Effervescent, bubbly,* and *lively* are words written on Megan's report cards by teacher after teacher. Megan possesses an abundance of charm to divert her teachers from the fact she just plain talks all the time. She loves to talk and has lots to say about everything. Problems occur when this potentially delightful trait infringes on the needs of the situation, as when another person is speaking or schoolwork needs to be done.

When they are less adept at charming others, the Megans of this world are simply annoying. Teachers may become angry with them or feel shocked when they blurt out comments at inappropriate times.

Whether teachers see a particular chatterbox as entertaining, irritating, or rude, the "gift of gab" is a talent. Teachers can value this talent by guiding students to use it in ways that enhance learning in the classroom.

Suggestions

1. Give the student who loves to talk a speaking job in the classroom. Let him know that you recognize his gift and have faith that he will use it in constructive ways during class time. His job could be to introduce new students, make announcements, and draw out students who rarely talk.

2. Set up a signal with the student. You might agree to tug on your ear or put your hand over your heart when the student's talking begins to interfere with the needs of the situation. (This is effective only when the student agrees in advance that a signal will be helpful—and especially if he has suggested the signal that would work for him.)

3. If you notice the student talking at an inappropriate time, wait and watch before saying anything. Students will often stop talking when they notice that you are waiting patiently. This is even more effective if you explain to the class in advance that you intend to stop lessons if all the students aren't giving you their attention.

4. Talkative students miss instructions. Initiate a discussion with these students. Tell them that today you noticed at both spelling and math lessons that they didn't hear the instructions you gave. Ask "what" and "how" questions to help them recognize the way their talking interferes with their ability to follow along with the class: "What happens when you miss instructions?" "What causes this to happen?" "How does it affect the teacher and other students?" "What ideas do you have for solutions?" This exchange shifts the responsibility for the behavior to them.

5. Your own emotional honesty helps. Use this formula: "I feel _____ when _____, and I wish _____." In the case of a talkative student, your statement might sound like this: "I feel frustrated when I repeat directions several times, and I wish that I had to give them only once." Notice that this formula doesn't include a "you" statement. Keep the focus on your needs and observations; don't talk about how you would like to change or control the student's behavior. Students often feel more cooperative when they have heard your feelings respectfully stated.

Planning Ahead to Prevent Future Problems

1. Students prefer to cooperate and to do what is in their own best interests. But if you treat them disrespectfully, they will go to great lengths to show that you can't boss them around. Use the Mistaken Goal Chart (see pages 12–13) to decipher why a child chooses to talk incessantly. Is he seeking attention, displaying power, getting revenge, or covering up anxiety over feeling inadequate? Use the last column of the chart to find effective responses.

2. Rather than trying to control talkative students, teach them how to control themselves. Help them learn to make lists of what needs to be done before engaging in the fun of conversation. When talking interferes with class work, ask them to check their lists.

3. Take the student aside, and ask whether he or she would be willing to help you draw out the more introverted students who don't feel as secure about talking. Talkative students can be taught to look for signs (body language such as a timidly raised hand) that another student wants to talk. They can encourage this student by saying, "I'd like to hear what Ariel has to say."

4. Help those who talk inappropriately see the long-range results of their behavior. In a friendly manner, ask them what happens when they miss instructions, what happens when they don't finish their work, and how others probably feel when they don't get equal airtime. Students need information about the consequences of their actions and will listen when they are involved in the process of gathering this information. They will tune out lectures, however.

5. In a class meeting, set up a role play to explore what happens when someone continually talks during class time. Then invite the students to brainstorm for suggestions on solving the problem.

6. Develop a public speaking program, and offer talkative students frequent opportunities to address the group.

7. Encourage a loquacious student to run for an office in the student government, where oratorical skills and the willingness to speak before others are assets.

Class Meeting Solution

Mr. Lindberg was continually irritated by students talking during his lectures. He decided to put this problem on the class meeting agenda. During the next class meeting, he explained how he felt and then suggested that a role play might help everyone understand his situation. He asked for two volunteers to play students and one to play him. He handed the student playing him a book and asked this student to pretend that he was giving a lecture on nouns. The other students were asked to talk while the instruction was going on.

Afterward, Mr. Lindberg helped the students process the role play by asking the players what they were thinking, how they were feeling, and what they were deciding to do in the future. He felt hopeful that his class now understood his needs and would respond accordingly.

The students showed increased sensitivity by containing their chatter while Mr. Lindberg read his notes to them the next day. But the problem hadn't finished unfolding. A few days later, one intrepid student suggested to Mr. Lindberg that perhaps if he talked a bit less and allowed the kids to join in more, they would find it easier to sit quietly.

Mr. Lindberg's mouth opened in surprise, but he quickly realized that his lengthy lectures were contributing to his problem. He also appreciated the fact that class meetings could be eye-opening—and not just for the students.

Tantrums

Discussion

When a student has a temper tantrum, it helps to remember that his behavior may have a purpose. (Refer to "Mistaken Goals [Hat Messages].") A student may throw a tantrum to get a teacher's attention, to get his own way, to hurt somebody because he feels hurt, or to get a teacher to leave him alone. If the student has one of these goals, the teacher will be most effective by dealing with the tantrum first and dealing with the belief behind the tantrum later.

However, tantrums aren't always a result of seeking mistaken goals. Sometimes a child's system simply gets overloaded, and anything can trigger an explosion. This type of tantrum is comparable to a thunderstorm. It clears the air, leaving the child relieved, soothed, and refreshed. Unfortunately, the adults in his life are probably still recovering several hours later. The knowledge that this outburst is in some way healing for the child broadens the adults' perspective and lightens the emotional toll on them by alleviating the guilt, feelings of inadequacy, and misgivings that typically arise when they feel they should have prevented the behavior.

Some children may have tantrums simply because they haven't learned how to communicate in more effective ways and are feeling powerless. This situation presents teachers with an opportunity to teach invaluable life skills.

Suggestions

1. If your students have helped you create a positive time-out area, you might ask, "Would it help you to go to our 'cooling-off' place until you feel better?" After a cooling-off period, tell the child, "We need to find a way for you to let me know how you're feeling without hurting yourself or others."

2. If a student isn't hurting himself or others, quietly stand aside and approach the student when the tantrum is over.

3. You might want to show the student a copy of the Feeling Faces Chart on the next page and ask whether she can find a feeling face that expresses how she feels. Some students are open to this and it diffuses the tantrum. Others are too caught up in their tantrum to be distracted.

4. If possible, remove other students, who serve as an audience. Tantrums are less powerful when there's no audience.

5. You may notice that it's part of a student's style to have a small tantrum when asked to move on to another subject or activity. If this behavior doesn't hurt anyone and the student does what needs to be done after her fit of bad temper, you may decide to ignore it. With some students, handling the problem this way keeps a minitantrum from turning into a megatantrum.

6. Don't respond to a student's tantrum by throwing one of your own. Still your turbulent inner emotions so that you can approach the situation calmly.

Planning Ahead to Avoid Future Problems

1. Let students know that it is okay to feel what they feel and that they are responsible for their actions. Then take time for training. This could mean role-playing alternatives or teaching the child to express strong feelings using appropriate words. The Feeling Faces Chart may help them become more aware of appropriate ways to express their feelings by simply stating what they feel.

2. The more you involve your students in decisions that affect them, the less they will feel the need to use tantrums to gain control.

3. Talk to the student and her parents to find out whether she has tantrums at home and how her parents handle such outbursts. Ask for both the student's and the parents' suggestions for dealing with the situation, and share your ideas. Work together on a plan for responding to tantrums in a consistent manner.

4. Consult with your principal and school counselor. Tantrums may signal a more serious problem for which the child needs additional help.

5. Raise the general topic of tantrums during a class meeting. Explore the reasons

FEELING FACES CHART

people have tantrums, and invite students to suggest more effective ways for people to get what they want.

Inspirational Story

Five-year-old Hallie was on the playground at her school. She noticed that there was no line at the slide, so she ran over to go down it, but Kerri got there first. Hallie was so mad that she started screaming and stamping her feet; she turned red and threw herself on the ground. As she continued to kick and scream, Mr. Kempton came over and held her so that she wouldn't hurt herself or the other children. In that moment, he chose to act and not talk.

Mr. Kempton waited until Hallie had calmed down and then said softly, "It's okay to be mad. It's okay to be upset. We all get upset sometimes."

Later in the day, when he could see that Hallie was able to listen, he said, "We need to find some ways for you to let people know that you're upset without hurting yourself or anyone else." Hallie looked

confused and didn't have any suggestions. Mr. Kempton asked her how she would feel about putting the problem on the class meeting agenda instead of stamping and screaming the next time she felt upset. He added that she could either write her name herself or dictate the problem to him and he would write it on the agenda.

The next time Hallie had a problem, she flounced over to Mr. Kempton and said, "Sam won't give me a turn on the monkey bars. Will you put that on the agenda for me?" Mr. Kempton said, "Of course, and what a good job you did to control your temper! I'm sure the class will have lots of ideas to help you solve this problem." Hallie promptly forgot about the monkey bars and went to play with some other students.

Two days later, when her problem was discussed during a class meeting, Mr. Kempton complimented Hallie again for controlling her temper and asking for help. The students then discussed the problem, and they all learned some good ways to share and ask for help.

Tardiness

Discussion

School districts throughout the country have developed strict policies on tardiness without regard for the many purposes be-

hind the misbehavior. These policies typically do nothing to encourage responsible behavior in students.

Students are tardy for all sorts of reasons. One is simply that they don't understand the importance of promptness in everyday living. Another reason is that they like the attention they receive when they walk into class late. In addition, a student may enjoy a sense of power when her late arrival means the lesson stops so the teacher can give her a tardy slip to take to the office—which means another class interruption when she gets back.

Sometimes students use being tardy as a way to strike back at their parents or teachers for some real or imagined hurt. Some students who are chronically tardy may feel hopeless about school—and perhaps about their situation at home, too. In their discouragement, they just don't care whether they are on time or not.

Personal circumstances may also result in tardiness. A student whose mother or father works the night shift may have to stay at home with a young sibling until the parent gets back from work. A chaotic situation at home can result in all members of the family being tardy, which in effect creates a family habit that may be difficult to break.

In addition, school hours don't suit most adolescents, who have a different body clock. The majority are not morning people and would do much better if school hours were noon to six.

Finally, of course, many students are late because the curriculum or teaching methods don't engage them. Too often teachers and administrators blame students without taking a look at other possibilities, including failures of the system.

Most schools' systems for handling tardiness create rebellion or revenge because these are what punishment invites. And consider who is left with the responsibility for the problem: The parents must rearrange their schedules so they can drive their kids to detention or let them borrow the car. The teachers must keep up with the necessary paperwork as well as deal with interruptions during class. There are better ways.

Suggestions

1. First, find out why the student is late. He may have a good reason, such as the baby-sitter who cares for a younger sibling was late that morning and his mother was already at work. Teachers need to remember that at times there are mitigating circumstances.

2. Share your feelings. Discuss how tardies impact the classroom system and all its members. Tardies may not be a problem for your students, so accept ownership of the problem, explaining how late arrivals interfere with your teaching. Ask for their help in solving your problem.

3. If a particular student or group of students is consistently tardy, discuss the problem privately: "I've noticed that every Wednesday, Thursday, and Friday you walk into class five minutes late. I feel irritated when this happens. Please give me your picture of what's going on." After listening respectfully, ask them to join you in brainstorming for solutions, and then pick one they are willing to try. Be sure to follow

through on your part of the agreement. Check back with the students in a week.

4. Be willing to look at tardiness within the context of the families. You may find patterns or family situations that may require an intervention. Work with your administrators, counselors, and Family Support Teams to provide help to these families.

Planning Ahead to Prevent Future Problems

1. At the beginning of the year, have a class meeting in which you and your students brainstorm for reasons why students and teachers may be late. Then brainstorm to come up with ways to help one another be prompt. Remind yourself and the students that all suggestions are to help with learning and not to hurt anyone. Try the selected suggestion for at least two weeks. Then, during another class meeting, evaluate how it is working.

2. The beginning of the year is also a good time to mention and practice how one enters a classroom already in session. Explain that you will continue teaching and that there are particular procedures that you would like for students to follow—for example, enter quietly, and take their seats with a minimum amount of distraction to the rest of the class. This would be an excellent topic to role-play in a class meeting.

3. Involve the students in planning some of the curriculum, giving them guidelines

as to your content needs and state or school requirements. When students perceive that they are contributing to the class, they are motivated to be there on time; they certainly won't want to miss any activity that they helped plan.

4. If tardiness hasn't been a problem in your class, make sure that you share your appreciation with your students.

Inspirational Method

This note was posted on the door of a high school classroom in Charlotte, North Carolina: "Tardies, please come into the room quietly, find a seat, and look for your directions on the board. Learning begins as soon as the tardy bell rings."

Instead of humiliating or punishing latecomers, this teacher respectfully allows them to experience the consequences of their actions and to do what they need to do to catch up. Students can come in and start working right away instead of going to the teacher for tardy slips, going to the office, feeling like they're in trouble, and disturbing the class.

Inspirational Story

Mrs. Fernandez had many tardies among her ninth graders. She had been sending tardy students to the office, but the number of tardies simply increased. Making the situation worse was that when she sent students to the office, they were often gone fifteen to thirty minutes, because the office was dealing with large numbers of students who were there for the same reason.

A large number of Mrs. Fernandez's students were considered at risk for delinquency and dropping out. Hence she was concerned with the tardy students missing so much class time as well as frustrated by all the interruptions they caused.

She decided to try the Positive Discipline process. First she resolved not to assume that tardy students didn't care about being on time or wanted to cause her grief. She also started letting the students know that she was really glad when they showed up for class, even if they were late. (Many students drop out in ninth grade because they don't believe that anybody will miss them.)

Mrs. Fernandez realized that she and her colleagues were also late at times, usually because of teacher meetings before or after school, and she began asking her tardy students why they were late. She discovered that they generally had valid reasons, such as the need to take care of a young sibling until Mom got home from working the night shift. Mrs. Fernandez was amazed that, when she began to treat the students respectfully, they would answer honestly even if they didn't have good reasons for being late.

She stopped sending latecomers to the office, so they no longer lost valuable learning time walking to and from the office. During a class meeting, she and all the students brainstormed for ways to prevent and deal with tardiness. Mrs. Fernandez was delighted to discover that this approach to the problem began to pay off in a reduction of tardies.

Tattling

Discussion

"Teacher! Teacher! Tommy took my pencil." "Mr. Smith! Alice has the watercolors again."

Beleaguered elementary teachers often lament, "The students are constantly tattling. I feel like a referee instead of a teacher." On the other hand, by the time kids go to middle school, teachers often complain, "My students won't give me information I really need to help them because they don't want to be accused of 'ratting' on another person." It is interesting that class meetings can solve both problems when students learn to focus on solutions instead of "tattling" or "ratting."

Students tattle for a variety of reasons. Some need constant attention. Others seek a sense of power from knowing they can get another student into trouble. For still others, tattling is a way to get even with a peer who has done them a real or imagined wrong. Also, tattling may result from students' lack of faith in their abilities to work out their own solutions to problems. Class meetings give teachers an effective way to use tattling as a source of problems students can use to learn problem-solving skills and to acquire more effective social skills.

Suggestions

1. When a student comes to you to tattle on a classmate, ask, "How is that a problem for you?" Sometimes this is enough to help the student see that the problem isn't his concern.

2. Child psychiatrist Rudolf Dreikurs encouraged parents and teachers to "put kids in the same boat." For example, when your student Juanita complains to you about Selena, the girl who sits behind her, say, "Juanita, it sounds as if you and Selena have a problem. I'll look forward to hearing how the two of you plan to work it out." You might want to provide a quiet corner in your room where students can go to work out their differences. (See item 4 in "Planning Ahead" for a format they can use when working it out together.)

3. Let the student who tattles know that you care about her and that you have faith in her ability to work out a plan to solve her problem.

4. Devise a verbal or hand signal to remind your students to use the class meeting agenda for listing problems.

5. Don't forget to listen and use your common sense. It could be that a problem is serious enough that it requires adult intervention rather than class meeting problem solving.

Planning Ahead to Prevent Future Problems

1. At the beginning of the school year, invite the entire class to make a commitment to seeking solutions rather than affixing blame when problems occur. Hang a banner in your room that says, "Our class looks for solutions, not blame." Use the banner as a reminder of the class's objective when individual students bring problems before the group.

2. It is important to help your students recognize situations in which information needs to be shared with adults. Beginning with younger students, we can discuss the difference between tattling and sharing important information (usually involving some form of safety). With older students, who may have decided not to trust adults, it is particularly important to create an environment in which their opinions and experiences are appreciated and taken seriously. Brainstorm with your students situations that may put them in the position of deciding whether or not information needs to be reported. A discussion should follow regarding the consequences of withholding information.

3. Explain to your students that you won't be available to listen to problems between students during regular class time but that they may write situations with which they need assistance on the class meeting agenda, and their issues will be discussed during a class meeting. Let them know that if they think a problem is too serious for the class meeting agenda, that they can come to you between class time, or write you a personal note.

4. In an area where students can meet to work out solutions to problems, post a chart displaying the four problem-solving suggestions: (1) Ignore it. (2) Talk it over respectfully with the other student. (3) Work with the other student on a win–win solution. (4) Put it on the class meeting agenda. Help your students understand what each suggestion means, and practice the four methods through role play. When you're sure they understand how to use the suggestions, refer them to the chart whenever they have disputes.

5. Another tool which can be posted in the classroom or displayed on the schoolyard is the Problem-Solving Wheel of Choice. (See "Problem Solving.")

6. Work on building community spirit within your classroom. Take time to connect with each of your students, and give them structured opportunities to connect with one another in positive ways. Class meetings are excellent for this; the time spent on appreciations at the beginning of each meeting is especially valuable. Students who feel a sense of connection with each other will spend less time tattling and more time helping their classmates when problems occur.

Class Meeting Solution

Mrs. Castillo's third-grade students squabbled constantly. They wore a track in the rug running up to her desk to tattle on one another. She soon felt like a broken record, telling them repeatedly that problems should be placed on the class meeting agenda. Personally, she felt that many of their issues were petty and unimportant, but she kept these thoughts to herself.

In class meetings, each student's problem was read in sequence from the agenda, and the student was asked, "Is this still a problem for you?" If the student said no, the class would proceed to the next item.

One day during a class meeting, ten problems were read in sequence, with each student saying there was no longer a problem because he or she had already worked it out with the other person. At this point, a student asked to speak and commented that, if all the students had already worked out their problems, shouldn't they try doing this before putting their quarrels on the class meeting agenda? The other students agreed and discussed how little things can seem big at the time, but if you just wait a while they don't seem so important after all. This discussion gave Mrs. Castillo an opportunity to talk to her students about an important problem-solving tool: a cooling-off place. (See "Positive Time-Out.")

Mrs. Castillo marveled that, without her giving another lecture, the students had discovered on their own that they were making mountains out of molehills. Tattling items seldom appeared on the agenda after this, as the students began using the agenda only when they truly needed help.

Teasing

(see also "Put-Downs, General," "Put-Downs, Older Students," and "Bullying")

Discussion

Statement: "You can't catch us." Interpretation: "Come and play with us. Chase us."

Statement: "Here. Want this book? Try and get it!" First interpretation: "Pay some attention to me." Second interpretation: "I want to embarrass you and make you look silly." Third interpretation: "I'm going to get you in trouble!"

From elementary to high school, students tease each other. Many people think that teasing is harmless. How often have you heard someone say, "I was only teasing," while acting surprised that the object of her teasing feels hurt?

Some teasing is benign and actually meant to initiate social interaction: "Hey slowpoke, I'll bet you can't beat me to the swings." Some teasing is likely to cause pain, whatever the intention of the teaser: "Where did you get all those freckles? Got splashed with mud?" "What's the matter—your parents too poor to buy you some decent clothes?"

Sometimes teasing is a response to the unknown. Children may tease a classmate who stutters because they don't know how to react. They don't wonder why he talks that way; they just know that the way he talks is different and a little frightening. Also, some students tease because they believe they can build themselves up by tearing others down. (Refer to "Gossip" for a discussion of this belief.)

Teachers have three main ways to deal with teasing. The first is to sensitize students to the pain it causes. This means moving students from egocentric or insensitive points of view toward looking at others with empathy. The second is to educate students about people who have different needs or abilities; when students are aware of special challenges or disabilities, they won't find these differences disconcerting. The third is to invite students to find ways to stop hurting others and start helping them instead.

Suggestions

1. When you hear students teasing each other, put the problem on the class meeting agenda. If students complain to you

about teasing, ask them to put the problem on the agenda.

2. Share your feelings when you hear a student tease his classmate: "Teasing makes me feel sad and angry because I know how much it can hurt people." You might add, "I don't know for sure, but I'll bet you didn't intend to be hurtful. Am I correct?" (Much of the time students aren't trying to inflict pain. They think they are being funny, and they don't consider the effects of their words.)

3. Ask directly, "Are you willing to change that statement to something that's encouraging instead of hurtful?"

4. If you think the student is seeking revenge (refer to "Mistaken Goals [Hat Messages]"), you might say, "I suspect you wouldn't hurt others unless you were feeling hurt. Why don't we wait until we've had time to cool off, and then I'd like to hear what's going on for you." Recognizing and validating a student's feelings can greatly encourage him.

5. When a student is hurt by teasing, let her express her hurt feelings to you; follow up by brainstorming for ways she could handle the problem besides striking back. She could let the teaser know how and why she felt hurt. She could get her classmates' help with the problem during a class meeting. She could wait until her composure returns and then discuss solutions directly with the person who hurt her.

6. Be aware and help your students be aware of when teasing crosses the line and becomes bullying or harassment (see "Bullying").

Planning Ahead to Prevent Future Problems

1. Focus on respect. Teach children that everyone is worthy of respect and that their intentions don't excuse disrespect. It's not acceptable to say, "We didn't mean to hurt his feelings. We were only playing." If behavior is hurtful, it's not respectful, no matter how it's intended.

2. Model respectful behavior. A teacher's teasing of his students can be a sign of rapport. It can also be disrespectful and condescending. Take time to check out your students' perceptions. You may intend to communicate affection when you say, "Hey there, curly top," or "How are you doing, big fella?" but your student may feel embarrassed or even offended.

3. Discuss teasing, and offer examples from your childhood. Share things you were teased about that made you feel bad and things you were teased about that made you feel good.

4. Have students role-play incidents of teasing. Afterward, ask them to share how the comments affected them. Reverse the roles so that each student experiences both teasing and being teased.

5. Develop a list of alternatives to typical teasing comments. Instead of saying, "Hey, shrimp, I get to be first in line," a student could ask, "Want to stand by me in line?" Cooperation can start with words.

6. Educate children about differences. If a child with Down's syndrome attends weekly art classes with your students, help them discover this child's special needs and abilities as well as how they might best support and encourage him. Children respond to differences—from learning problems to physical characteristics—far more responsibly when they have learned to understand and appreciate one another as unique human beings.

7. Use literature to create awareness and understanding of differences among people. A rich supply of children's books is available on this topic. Build a classroom library whose books portray many types of families, situations, and abilities.

8. Teach, practice, and model effective communication skills, so that students don't resort to teasing to show how they feel or what they want.

9. Make sure that the pictures in your classroom portray children and families of many races and cultures. Also provide pictures of children in wheelchairs or with other visible disabilities and of children who have lost their hair through cancer therapy or who are coping with other serious illnesses. Such pictures make differences seem less frightening. Moreover, they are great jumping-off points for discussions that will uncover students' misconceptions and broaden their understanding.

Inspirational Story

Mrs. Downs found Mary, a fourth-grade student, crying in the hall after school. She invited Mary to come sit with her on a bench in the school yard. She asked, "Do you want to talk about it?" Mary said, "I hate my curly hair. All the kids tease me about it all the time. They call me frizz ball and lots worse." Mrs. Downs empathized, "I know how much that hurts. When I was your age, I was teased for being bow legged. Sometimes I didn't even want to go to school." Mary looked at her in surprise and said, "I had decided I was never coming back."

Mrs. Downs asked, "Are you the only one that gets teased?" Mary thought about that and then said with surprise, "No. Just about everyone gets teased—even the popular kids. Suzie is the most popular girl in school, and she gets teased for her 'bunny' teeth."

Mrs. Downs asked, "Why do you think kids tease each other?"

Mary said, "I don't know. If they get teased and it hurts their feelings, why would they do it to others?"

Mrs. Downs asked, "Do you think this would be a good thing to discuss during one of our class meetings, and would you be willing to put it on the agenda?"

Mary agreed. When the class talked about it, the students were surprisingly thoughtful about how silly it was to tease each other when they didn't like it. The students agreed that they would stop teasing—and they did.

Class Meeting Solution

An elementary school in Woodland, California, gave its teachers preservice training on how to use class meetings. A special education teacher brought up her concern about the way her students were teased. Other students called them "retards," "dummies," and other disrespectful names.

The teachers agreed to bring this problem up in their first class meetings. Through role plays, they helped their students become aware of how it felt to be teased. They then brainstormed to find ways they could include and encourage the special ed students.

During a follow-up training three months later, the special education teacher said, "My students have never been treated so respectfully. It's wonderful."

Toilet Accidents

Discussion

Imagine feeling a sudden rush of warm liquid run down your legs and soak into your socks. Within minutes, a definite odor emanates from you. Right now, what you need as much as dry clothes is compassion.

Bad days, stress, and unforeseen events happen to all of us. Toilet accidents have many causes, including physiological problems, and are embarrassing for students.

Consistent use of encouragement in the classroom maintains an atmosphere in which a person's mistakes and accidents don't diminish his sense of significance and belonging. Any personal revulsion a teacher feels is of no consequence when a child's need for dignity is considered. An accident is nothing but an accident when nobody induces additional embarrassment.

Suggestions

1. Maintain an attitude that protects a child's dignity and self-esteem.

2. In primary grades, have a set of clothes available for students who have accidents. Simply and respectfully let them know they can go to the "clothes closet" and choose something to change into.

3. Never use a censorious tone when talking about accidents. Speak matter-of-factly yet kindly: "Sometimes when people aren't feeling well, they may sneeze or cough, and urine leaks out. Or sometimes people are so involved or excited about something that they delay using the bathroom, and their bladder overflows."

4. If a child is gone an unusually long time in the bathroom, send an adult to check on him. He may have soiled his pants and could be trying to clean himself.

Planning Ahead to Prevent Future Problems

1. If a child has frequent accidents, consult with the school nurse and with the child's parents. Suggest a medical checkup to see whether the problem is physiological or developmental. By communicating with the parents, you may become aware of a source of stress in the student's life. A regression in bladder or bowel control can be a reaction to a divorce or to the birth of a sibling; it can be a sign of a more serious

problem, such as sexual abuse. Don't hesitate to seek the help of the school counselor or psychologist. You might want to provide a questionnaire for young students' parents to fill out. Ask about any special difficulties of which a teacher should be aware, such as a history of toilet accidents. Another question should be about current sources of stress in the child's family life, such as a new baby, a move, a divorce, or a new marriage.

2. Sometimes a student needs assistance in scheduling toilet breaks. Simply helping develop that schedule with her can be effective and encouraging.

3. At the beginning of the year, when setting up guidelines for use of the rest room, take the time to talk to your students about how accidents will be handled. Designate a place where extra clothes will be kept; all of the children should have easy access to this place.

Inspirational Story

A story from Betsy Licciardello in Positive Time-Out: And Over 50 Ways to Avoid Power Struggles in the Home and the Classroom.[27]

This year I have a little girl in class who comes from an abusive home. She suffers

---

27. Jane Nelson, *Positive Time-Out: And Over 50 Ways to Avoid Power Struggles in the Home and the Classroom* (Rocklin, CA: Prima Publishing, 1999, pp. 162–163).

from severe self-esteem problems. She was wetting and soiling her pants daily at school. My aide and I tried many solutions. We cleaned her up—she adored the attention. We had her clean herself up—no improvement. We tried hugs for dry pants every half hour and had very inconsistent results.

One day, as I was walking this girl to the office for dry socks (she had soaked herself all the way to her shoes), I decided just to tell her how I felt about her. I said, "Sally, I love you and will always love you, no matter what you do—good days or bad. I will love you even if you wet your pants every day or if you never wet your pants again. I like dry pants better, but I will love you no matter what you choose—wet pants or dry."

She hasn't wet her pants at school since we had this little talk. We have the talk every once in a while as a reminder, and we still have lots of hugs. We no longer have wet pants. Hooray!

Discussion

The most important part of this story is that Betsy meant it when she said she would love this little girl even if she continued to wet her pants. Betsy didn't pretend or use a declaration of love to manipulate the girl into changing her behavior. It's important to realize that children can almost always tell the difference.

V

Victims

Discussion

Do you have a victim in training? When adults step in and take responsibility every time problems arise, a child may begin to see himself as powerless. His thought process goes like this: "I don't have any responsibility for what happens to me. It's al-ways someone else's fault. And I can't do anything to solve the problem. I need to call in the big guns."

Continually rescuing students allows them to excuse themselves from accountability. Students who see themselves as victims learn quickly that grievances about the behavior of others are an excellent way to get attention and sympathy—and to get the heat off themselves. A victim decides that any problem she has with other students or with adults has nothing to do with her own behavior.

Victims don't learn how to solve problems or how to accept responsibility for the consequences of what they do. Instead, they learn how to get others to commiserate with them and solve their problems. As a consequence, their emotional development is hindered. This does not mean that there are never times when students are victims of circumstances beyond their control. (See "Bullying" and "Abuse.") It is important that teachers and students understand the difference between victim mentality and the times when they need to know how to ask for help.

Suggestions

1. Ask the student who sees himself as a victim to put his concerns on the class meeting agenda. This encourages personal responsibility. Just by doing something with his problem, the student experiences a feeling of control. This is effective even if the child is being victimized by others. (See the "Inspirational Story.")

2. Invite the student to fill out a "what/how" form so he or she can gain some perspective before you engage in a problem-solving session based on what the student learns from this journaling exercise.

What/How Form
What were you trying to do or accomplish?
What happened?
What caused it to happen?
How do you feel about what happened?
What did you learn from what happened?
What suggestions do you have for solving the problem?

How can you use what you learned in the future?

3. Notice the hoopla generated by the allegations of a student who plays the victim. A satisfying outcry usually follows his report that a student once again hit him or took away the swing he was using. Instead of fussing, listen and nod without saying anything, or simply reflect the facts from what you hear: "Tyrone took the swing away from you." "You feel very upset about that." After the student has vented and you have listened, ask whether he has ideas about how to solve the problem or if he would like to put the problem on the class meeting agenda so he can get ideas from the class.

Planning Ahead to Prevent Future Problems

1. Teach that each person has power over his or her actions. Even when we can't control what happens to us, we can control how we respond and what we do.

2. Actively teach assertiveness skills. With very young children, this means that when a classmate hits the child and he seeks assistance from an adult, he learns to go back to his classmate and state clearly, "No hitting. I don't want you to hit me." For older students, this involves making a similar statement: "Leave me alone. Listen to what I am saying." Teach students that another choice is to walk away from a situation with dignity.

3. Explain to your students that when someone treats them in a mean or hurtful way, it's their job either to state their needs clearly or to leave the situation with dignity. Invite them to role-play situations using these alternatives.

4. Teach students about using a "what/how" form to learn from their experiences and to identify what role their behavior played in a situation. Explain that they may want to fill out the form just for their own understanding, to learn from their mistakes, or as a basis for problem solving with others later.

5. Rather than protecting or rescuing a student from difficult situations, assist her in planning a course of action and determining how to accomplish her goal.

6. Hold regular class meetings so children learn social interest—to care about one another, to avoid hurting each other, and to focus on solutions to help the student who is assuming the victim role and/or the student who is a victim of disrespectful treatment from others.

Inspirational Story

A story from Delores Alexander, fifth-grade teacher, Waterloo, Ontario, Canada

Yesterday, I had the most incredible discussion during a parent/teacher/child conference with a mom, dad, and their two children. They are an integrated family that moved to our school late last year. We discussed my policy of using Positive Discipline in the classroom and the concept of "mistakes as wonderful opportunities to learn." The dad was very supportive. His input served as a wonderful model for the kids.

Then, the class meeting today was incredible. I discussed the Three R's of Recovery [see "Mistakes"], and it opened a can of worms I wasn't expecting. The discussion prompted a student to stand up and defend a newcomer to the class. We had been discussing inclusiveness and acceptance of others. The floodgates opened and the storm began. The problem was outlined, and the two people involved were stunned at the caring statements made by the class. One boy, the child of the parents in the first part of my story, announced that he was a friend to Sally and couldn't stand to see her hurt so badly. "After all, she's new to the school and shouldn't be left on her own. That's not fair." He then proceeded to announce that he no longer liked the first party who had started the meanness. The class then turned to him and announced that he was attacking the person and not the problem. Boy, was I humbled by this discussion. We had to ask the French teacher to give us some more time because we just couldn't leave the problem the way it was.

After a recess break, we continued the discussion asking for solutions. Many suggested that the two get together and discuss the problem. They were a little reluctant at first, both declaring that the other wouldn't do this. I offered a mediator if they wanted one. Finally, one of the girls boldly stated that she was prepared to solve the problem on an individual basis with the other girl, and they both agreed. One of the boys closed the class meeting by saying "If mistakes are wonderful opportunities to learn, we have really learned a lot in our class today." He continued by saying, "This discussion really started in religion class this morning when Mrs. A. said, 'God has no favorites and we should look at the situation with different eyes.'"

Wandering

Discussion

Some students seem to be in perpetual motion. Even when seated, they are moving—hands, fingers, legs, feet. They find many excuses to wander around and from the classroom—they need to sharpen pencils, go to the bathroom, get a drink of water, borrow paper from a friend, get something from a coat pocket, or retrieve yet another item that rolled across the floor after they dropped it.

Why do they wander? Could you sit at a school desk for hours at a time without moving? Remember the last day-long in-service program you sat through while your aching back screamed at you? The need to move around is normal. On the other hand, wandering can be a symptom of attention deficit disorder and an opportunity to get a child needed assistance. (Refer to "Attention Deficit Disorder [ADD] and Attention Deficit with Hyperactivity Disorder [ADHD].") But don't assume that every student who has difficulty keeping still suffers from ADD. Temperament is also a factor. (See chapter 6 of *Positive Discipline for Preschoolers* for a thorough discussion of temperament.[28])

Scientific investigation of the role of temperament began with the Berkeley Studies, a longitudinal study of two basic temperaments, active and passive. This study revealed that these two temperaments were lifelong characteristics; in other words, passive infants grew up to be passive

---

28. Jane Nelsen, Cheryl Erwin, and Roslyn Duffy, *Positive Discipline for Preschoolers* (Roseville, CA: Prima Publishing, 1999).

adults, while active infants grew up to be active adults.[29] Within the two categories are many degrees of activeness and passiveness. The wandering student may have a highly active temperament. Children are different; some need to move more than others, yet all are expected to sit for long periods of time as though they were all the same. What happened to respecting individual differences?

Of course, teachers should always consult the Mistaken Goal Chart (see pages 12–13) to see whether wandering behavior might indicate a need to belong. Is the wanderer in your classroom making a bid to gain undue attention, power, or revenge or to be left alone?

Does the child wander out of boredom with a curriculum that doesn't challenge her or that she finds irrelevant? A teacher may look at this problem as an opportunity for introspection and evaluation, and as a time to involve students in problem solving.

Suggestions

1. Plan for energizers every fifteen to twenty minutes: stand up and wiggle for two minutes, sing a short song that includes movement, or march around the room for one minute and then sit down. Older students (and teachers) enjoy standing in lines or a circle so everyone can rub the shoulders of the person in front of them. Change directions after thirty seconds.

2. A wandering student could serve as a reminder that people are unique and different energy levels and attention spans. Give the wanderer something constructive to do such as helping another student or choosing another student to help her.

3. Ignore wandering if it doesn't bother anyone and doesn't interfere with the student's work.

4. When you see a student wandering, ask the whole class, "What are we supposed to be doing now?" This often serves as a gentle reminder while addressing the whole class instead of embarrassing one child.

5. Ask the wanderer privately, "What did we decide about appropriate times for getting out of our seats?" (See the second item under "Planning Ahead.")

6. Notice how you feel about the wandering to see whether the behavior fits one of the four mistaken goals. Look at the Mistaken Goal Chart (see pages 12–13) for ideas on how to solve the problem.

Planning Ahead to Prevent Future Problems

1. During a class meeting, ask the students to discuss the reasons for wandering, what

---

29. J. Block, *Lives through Time* (Berkeley, CA: Bancroft, 1971).

problems this behavior causes, and how to solve those problems.

2. Involve the students in determining guidelines for appropriate times to move around the room, such as for three minutes after the bell rings, for three minutes after an assignment is given so they can get the necessary books and supplies, or anytime as long as the student has a good reason to wander, doesn't bother other people, and doesn't abuse the privilege.

3. During an individual conference, ask the wanderer to brainstorm with you for ways that she can satisfy her need to move as well as her need to sit down and do her work.

4. Try goal disclosure before working on solutions. An explanation of the process follows this list.

5. Confer with the student's parents and arrange for an evaluation to determine whether he requires a different or specialized program. This may mean tutoring for a child who has learning problems or medical intervention for a child who has attention deficit with hyperactivity disorder.

Goal Disclosure[30]

Students aren't aware of the goals behind their misbehavior. Goal disclosure is one way to help them become aware of the beliefs that are leading them to act in certain ways. Because the teacher's objectivity and friendliness are essential to the process, goal disclosure shouldn't be done at the time of conflict. Furthermore, it's best to talk to students privately.

First ask the student whether she knows why she is engaging in a certain behavior. Name the misbehavior specifically: "Mary, do you know why you keep wandering around the room when you are supposed to be in your seat?"

Students will usually say no, and it's true that they don't know at a conscious level. In this case, ask whether they're willing to have you guess. If your manner is matter-of-fact but friendly, the student will be intrigued. (If the student gives you a reason, say, "I have some other ideas. Would it be okay with you if I guess? You can tell me whether I'm right or wrong.")

Ask what psychiatrist Rudolf Dreikurs called the "could it be" questions, waiting for the student to respond to each:

1. "Could it be that the reason you wander around the room is to get my attention and keep me busy with you?" (The goal is attention.)

2. "Could it be that the reason you wander around the room is to show me that

---

30. Jane Nelsen, *Positive Discipline,* revised edition (New York: Ballantine, 1996), chapter 4.

you can do whatever you want?" (The goal is power.)

3. "Could it be that the reason you wander around the room is that you feel hurt and want to get even with me or someone else?" (The goal is revenge.)

4. "Could it be that you wander around the room because you don't feel you can succeed, so you don't want to try?" (The goal is assumed inadequacy, or to be left alone.)

Either of two responses will let you know when your guess is correct and the student has become aware of her goal. The first is a recognition reflex: the student smiles involuntarily. Sometimes the answer "no" accompanies this smile, but the reflex tells you that the student recognizes her purpose in behaving the way she does. The other response is a simple "yes." Even if you have a recognition reflex or an affirmative answer, continue to the last goal.

You can use goal disclosure to increase your understanding of a student's behavior and to show interest in the student, which is very encouraging. Once you know the goal, you have a basis for discussion and problem solving. If the goal is attention, explain to the student that everyone wants attention. Then redirect the student's efforts to constructive ways of seeking attention. Another option is to agree to give the stu-

dent attention for her mistaken goal behavior. Let her know that you will wink and smile to indicate that she has your attention. Make this a special conspiratorial arrangement between the two of you. This solution strikes many people as a reward for misbehavior. Actually, it is what Dreikurs called "spitting in the soup": Awareness makes it less appetizing.

If the goal is power, admit that you can't force her to behave differently. Then ask for her help in designing a plan of mutual respect and cooperation. Asking for help is important when you want to redirect both the student and yourself away from the power struggle and toward contributing individual power to a common purpose.

If the goal is revenge, express your interest in understanding how you or someone else hurt her. Caring enough to listen without judgment can be the most encouraging response to this goal. Don't rationalize, explain, or try to change her perceptions. It may help to paraphrase what she says to be certain that you both understand. When the student feels understood, she will be more willing to hear your point of view and to work on solutions.

If the goal is assumed inadequacy, tell her that you think you can understand how she feels because you feel discouraged sometimes, too. Express faith in her ability. Then work on a plan of small, achievable steps to ensure success.

Whining

Discussion

"Mrs. Lyyy-straaa, I don't like my lu-unch." Can't you just picture a small, scrunched-up face with mournful eyes pinned on you? The whining student believes that she belongs if others are constantly busy with her or aware of her. For some students, whining is the only way they know to get what they want. It is possible they have never been taught the skills for asking for what they want in respectful ways. For others, it's a phase they go through, and once they find better ways to belong, it disappears.

Suggestions

1. When whining begins, stop responding to the issue that the student is whining about. Say that you notice a change in her voice. Ask her to repeat what she just said in a different tone.

2. Ask the student to invent a signal for you to give him when you hear him begin to whine. Use it as a friendly reminder about what's happening.

3. Separate the deed from the doer. Let your student know that you really like him but that you don't like whining. Then decide what you will do and let him know: "When you whine, I won't respond. I will

be happy to answer or help you when your voice returns to its pleasant tone."

4. Use the emotional honesty formula: "I feel annoyed when I hear whining. I care about you and I wish you would care enough about yourself to use a pleasant tone of voice." Remember that stating what you wish doesn't mean a person will grant your wish; however, you are modeling that it is okay to feel what you feel and to want what you want without expecting anyone else to feel the same or to give you what you want.

Planning Ahead to Prevent Future Problems

1. If a student habitually whines, address his need to belong by scheduling special time with him and finding ways to involve him in the classroom. Offer him a job such as helping with the bulletin board, reading to a younger student, or sorting and stacking papers with you after school.

2. Take time to teach respectful ways of communicating wants and needs. Let students know that if they respect and honor themselves and their feelings, needs, or desires, it will be easier for them to communicate them in a respectful manner—and that others may not feel the same or give them what they want.

3. Having regular class meetings provides students with an arena in which they can

be heard as well as get feedback on how they present themselves.

4. Notice when a student who frequently whines uses a normal speaking tone: "I really appreciate your effort to speak clearly. Thank you."

5. The whining student may be a discouraged student who doesn't know how to tell you that her sense of belonging is threatened. Encourage her by pointing out times when she contributes to the classroom in positive ways.

6. Make note that whining is a method sometimes used when a person is unable to communicate a feeling or an idea clearly. Help a student become aware of this by giving her feedback in the moment: "I notice that you are choosing to whine and may not know how to ask clearly for what you want. How can I help you?"

Inspirational Story

It was September, and Mr. Garrison was getting to know his new class. As he handed out supplies, he heard Robert's voice rise to a high-pitched whine and was instantly annoyed. Taking a deep breath, Mr. Garrison said to Robert, "I will be happy to help you and answer your questions when you use your normal tone of voice." Robert changed his voice, and Mr. Garrison responded to his question. Twenty minutes later Robert's voice be-

came shrill again. Gritting his teeth, Mr. Garrison repeated his statement about using a normal voice. This pattern continued, and Mr. Garrison's annoyance level rose past the decibels of Robert's whine.

That night Mr. Garrison hauled out his text on *Positive Discipline*. Thumbing through it, he caught sight of the Mistaken Goal Chart. Right on the top line was his answer to handling Robert's whining. His own feeling of annoyance gave him the information that Robert's goal was to seek belonging and significance through undue attention. The suggested solutions in the final column that seemed to fit Mr. Garrison's needs best were to ignore the attention-getting behavior and to meet Robert's need for belonging more appropriately by involving him in the classroom.

The next day, though he was sure that Robert knew the "I won't respond until you talk in a normal voice" answer by heart, Mr. Garrison took a moment to explain it again in a private talk. This time he added that he wouldn't respond to a whining voice even with a reminder, because he now felt confident that Robert knew his expectation.

For the next few days, Mr. Garrison steadfastly ignored Robert's whining while pursuing a campaign to involve him in helping throughout the day. Mr. Garrison invited Robert to call the roll, to assist with passing out lunch boxes, and to hold up the flash cards for his group when the class was practicing math sums. By the second week of school, Robert was so caught up in the daily needs of the class that his need to whine had vanished. Mr. Garrison breathed a thankful sigh of relief and made a copy of the Mistaken Goal Chart to place on his desk. He had helped Robert change his belief that he needed to whine in order to be important and noticed.

The Zoo and other Field Trips

Discussion

Visits to the local zoo and other field trips should begin well before the class gathers in the parking lot. Planning ahead prevents many problems. The preparation may seem tedious or even unnecessary at times, but if the students work together on the details and arrangements, an atmosphere of cooperation and inclusion will be created. Remember that students have a strong sense of investment in the outcome of a project whenever they have contributed to making it happen. Involve parent volunteers, too. Students' and adults' participation from the start will increase everyone's enjoyment of the day.

Suggestions

1. During the field trip, use the Positive Discipline tools that you've found to be effective in your classroom; these may include offering choices, limiting yourself to one-word instructions, and asking for help. When students forget the guidelines for the trip, ask questions: "What was our agreement regarding this?" "What did we decide at our class meeting?"

2. If difficulties arise and you are feeling disappointed, embarrassed, or angry, share those feelings with your students without being vindictive or exaggerating the problem. Tell them, "I notice . . . ," or, "I feel upset about. . . ." Then ask who would be willing to put the problem on the class meeting agenda as soon as you get back to the classroom so the students can find solutions for the next field trip.

3. Avoid using field trips to reward or punish students. When a student misbehaves the week before a field trip, don't be tempted to tell him that he can't go on the trip as a consequence (or veiled punishment). Deal

with those problems as separate issues using the class meeting agenda, the Problem-Solving Wheel of Choice, positive time-out and follow-through, or any of the other Positive Discipline methods discussed through this book.

4. Be clear about the purpose of the field trip and your expectations for the students. Tell them what they should be looking for and what you would like them to learn, and let them know about any follow-up work you will assign.

5. Throughout the field trip, share your feelings of delight whenever students follow the plans they helped create.

Planning Ahead to Prevent Future Problems

1. Take time during class meetings to plan upcoming field trips. (You may even want your students' input on where to go for a field trip.) Study the agenda for the day of the trip, looking for parts that students can help plan. If, for example, a one-hour lunch break is scheduled, have the class brainstorm for ideas about how lunch should be handled: Will the students each share a lunch with a partner, bring their own lunches, or arrange a potluck? What will they do if they finish their lunches before other students? In higher grades, teachers may have students make most of the arrangements for field trips—they can make phone calls to schedule tours or find parent volunteers. During class meetings, the students can form teams to handle the different aspects of planning the trip. After researching its part, each team can report its findings to the rest of the class during another meeting.

2. Take time for training. Discuss and practice appropriate behavior, such as speaking quietly in museums.

3. As a class, identify potential problems that might occur during the field trip. Use role playing and brainstorming to find solutions together.

4. Have your students prepare a presentation for the parent volunteers in which the students share information about the day's agenda, problems that might arise, and corresponding solutions that they have selected.

5. Plan ahead to have enough parents involved. Make sure they are clear on the agenda for the day, guidelines you have for student behavior, and details such as returning directly to school. Ideally, there is a parent for every small group of students, so everyone gets the attention he or she needs.

Inspirational Stories

Planning Brings Cohesion

A south Texas high school had four teachers who worked as an academic team with students who had many at-risk factors, including poor performance in class, poor attendance, drug problems, undeveloped social skills, and inadequate self-control and self-discipline. A number of these students were in gangs.

The four teachers had been using permission to go on field trips as a reward for good behavior. But they soon noticed that the same students were going on every field trip. Being allowed to go didn't appear to be an effective incentive for good or improved behavior.

Then the teachers were introduced to the concepts of Positive Discipline in the classroom. They decided to use class meeting time to involve all 180 of their students in planning the next field trip. The students were told that they would all get to go as long as they brought their signed permission slips from home.

The students planned the entire field trip during their class meetings. A few parent volunteers were also involved in the planning. On the day of the field trip, the teachers were nervous about how the students would behave, particularly those who had been excluded in the past because of their misbehavior. To the teachers' amazement, all the students cooperated and contributed in positive ways to the experience. Even the lunch the students had planned to take place at a local park went off without a hitch.

The manager of the place they visited told the teachers that he had never seen a group of high school students behave so well

before. He said he planned to write a complimentary letter to the school's principal.

When the students and the teachers evaluated the field trip during their next class meeting, everyone gave it high marks. Many students went on to say that the time they had spent connecting with one another in a positive fashion made them want to do more as a team.

The teachers noted that tempers didn't flare up as easily among the students after this field trip. They believed that this change occurred because the students had worked together to plan a successful event and had been given an opportunity to see one another in a different light.

Planning Brings Safety

Kindergarten students at Maple School frequently went on field trips. They often had to cross very busy streets. Because the students were so small, the teachers feared that the driver of an oncoming car might fail to see a student alone at the back of the group and wanted to be sure that an adult was always the last person to cross the street. They decided that one teacher would lead the group while the second teacher would walk behind the group.

Before they set off on any field trips, the students practiced crossing streets as a group. For role plays, they laid out toys to represent either side of the street. One student pretended to be the traffic light and called out when it was time to walk. The students walked across the pretend street in pairs, each holding a partner's hand. This took several practice sessions, but mistakes were made in the safety of their classroom. When the time came to cross a real street, the students beamed with pride at how competent they felt. They consistently walked together safely on their field trips.

Class Meeting Solution

A tenth-grade class was going on a field trip to a nearby lake. One student wanted help because she didn't know how to swim and was fearful about falling in the water.

The class brainstormed for possible solutions and came up with the following suggestions:

1. Stay with a friend.

2. Bring safety equipment.

3. Don't go on the field trip.

The student was invited to select the solution that sounded best to her. She decided that she liked the idea of staying with a friend. She also felt safer just from having brought up her concern.

INDEX

A

Abuse, 63–66, 285

Accountability, 32, 286

Acknowledgment, 5

Activities

    "Do They Know You Care?," 140

    "It's a Jungle Out There," 159–160

ADD (Attention Deficit Disorder), 72–76

    focusing activities for, 75–76

    interrupting as, 178, 179, 181

    overview, 72

    preventing problems with, 74–75

    suggestions for, 73–74

    wandering as, 289, 291

ADHD (Attention Deficit with Hyperactivity Disorder). *See* ADD (Attention Deficit Disorder)

Adler, Alfred, 34

Adlerian psychology, 1

Affection

    displayed in public, 186–188

    touching students, 64, 191, 290

Agenda

    as class meeting tool, 86

    students' input on, 296, 297

Aggressiveness, 85, 181. *See also* Hurtful behavior; Violence

Agreements. *See* Limits

Alexander, Delores, 7, 288–289

Anger. *See also* Positive time-out

    dwelling on, 49

    managing, 17–19, 167, 168, 275

    tantrums, 272–273, 275

Animals

    cruelty to, 99, 100, 101

    death of, 107–108

Antibias curriculum, 118

Apologizing

    problem solving and, 45, 143

    Three R's of Recovery and, 42, 143

Appearance, sloppy, 251–254

Appreciations. *See also* Compliments

    cooperation and, 193, 236, 237

    during conferences, 60

    during training, 39

    as encouragement, 6–7

    respect and, 123

    sharing, 78, 88, 135, 236

    skill of, 57, 159

Arguments, 66–68, 268. *See also* Fighting; Positive time-out

Assertiveness

    aggressiveness vs., 85

    intimidation and, 181, 183

    teaching, 84–85, 167, 287–288

    for victims, 83, 287–288

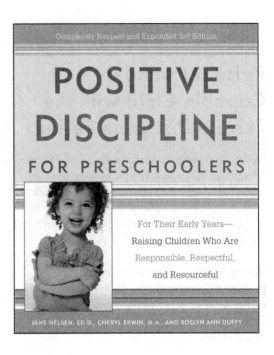

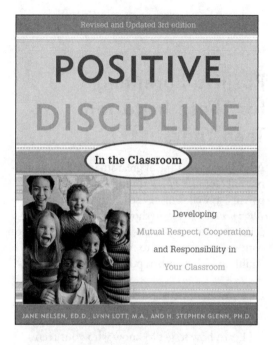

ABOUT THE AUTHORS

Jane Nelsen, Ed.D., is a popular lecturer and author or coauthor of the entire POSITIVE DISCIPLINE series and the author of *From Here to Serenity: Four Principles for Understanding Who You Really Are.* She has appeared on *Oprah!, Sally Jessy Raphael,* and *Twin Cities Live* and was the featured parent expert on the "National Parent Quiz" hosted by Ben Vereen. Jane is the mother of seven children and the grandmother of eighteen.

Linda Escobar, M.A., M.F.T., is an elementary school counselor in Santa Rosa, California. She also maintains a private practice as a marriage, family, and child counselor and facilitates workshops and classes for parents and teachers. Linda is a member of the California Association of Marriage and Family Therapists and the North American Society of Adlerian Psychology.

Kate Ortolano began her work as a parent educator in 1984 with the Family Education Center in Petaluma, California. She works with a multitude of families from Head Start programs to businesses. In addition to her work with families, Kate trains teachers and other educators in a workshop format with Positive Discipline Associates.

Roslyn Duffy is a counselor, author, and teacher. She cofounded the Learning Tree Montessori School in 1979, writes the international column "From a Parent's Perspective" for *Child Care Information Exchange* magazine, and produced the video *Class Meetings for Preschoolers.* She also developed the *Parent Report Card* with Elizabeth Crary and is a national and international speaker.

Deborah Owen-Sohocki, M.S., has 29 years of experience in education working at all grade levels with diverse student populations. As founder and president of the Alma Center, Inc., in Corpus Christi, Texas, she serves as a trainer and consultant to school districts, families, and communities nationally and internationally. Deborah and her husband John have a stepfamily of seven children.